英语案例教学论

A Coursebook on Case Method of Teaching

主　编　曹　明
副主编　梁　蕊　甘世安　强俊勇
参　编　刘云航

 南京大学出版社

图书在版编目(CIP)数据

英语案例教学论 / 曹明主编. —— 南京：南京大学出版社，2020.7
 ISBN 978-7-305-23318-0

Ⅰ. ①英… Ⅱ. ①曹… Ⅲ. ①英语课－教案(教育)－教学研究－中小学 Ⅳ. ①G633.412

中国版本图书馆 CIP 数据核字(2020)第 085579 号

出版发行	南京大学出版社
社　　址	南京市汉口路 22 号　　邮　编　210093
出 版 人	金鑫荣
书　　名	英语案例教学论
主　　编	曹　明
责任编辑	裴维维　　　　　编辑热线　025-83592123
照　　排	南京南琳图文制作有限公司
印　　刷	南京京新印刷有限公司
开　　本	787×1092　1/16　印张 14.25　字数 346 千
版　　次	2020 年 7 月第 1 版　2020 年 7 月第 1 次印刷
ISBN	978-7-305-23318-0
定　　价	39.80 元

网址：http://www.njupco.com
官方微博：http://weibo.com/njupco
官方微信号：njupress
销售咨询热线：(025) 83594756

* 版权所有，侵权必究
* 凡购买南大版图书，如有印装质量问题，请与所购
　图书销售部门联系调换

序

外国语言文学类教学质量国家标准中指出,"外语类专业可与其他相关专业结合形成复合型专业,以适应社会发展的需要"(教育部,2018)。2016年4月,教育部出台了《教育部关于加强师范生教育实践的意见》,指出要"构建全方位的教育实践内容体系""丰富创新教育实践的形式"等9条意见,为英语专业师范生实践教学创新指明了方向。曹明老师的这本《英语案例教学论》正是在此背景下编写而成的。

教材设计是教材开发的关键环节。按照应用技术型人才培养的特点,该教材对每一章的每一个任务都进行了精心的设计。每章由相应的几组任务组成,每组任务下设知识点和技能点,案例紧随其后,并以"亮考帮"作为讨论思考与评价的具体形式。这就巧妙地将"对分课堂"的设计理念与"做中学"的教学思想融为一体,展现了应用技术型大学课堂教学的特点。全书结构完整、清晰,易于学生学习。

教材理念体现教材的底色,也体现了编者对教学改革的力度与决心。对分课堂强调"先教后学",应用型课程注重"知识应用",均以知识内化为学习的核心过程。这本教材以学生为中心,关注学生的学习过程,很好地做到了促进学生的知识内化。更重要的是,该教材采用开放形式,匹配丰富的线上资源,可以随时更新。特别值得一提的是,该书的大部分案例来源于实习、见习基地一线场景,真实、生动,切合应用技术型大学教材的终极指向。

2014年我在复旦大学提出和首先实验了对分课堂新型教学法,经全国广大教师的实践检验,证明可用于各类学校和各个学科。大学英语课程听说读写译的对分教学都取得了良好的效果。2018年11月,曹明老师参加了我在西安举办的对分课堂专题培训,非常认可对分,表示与她原先的实践有很多相似之处,并很快将其更多地融入自己的教学当中,在交流中我对她有更深入的了解。曹老师在加拿大布鲁克大学获得"教、学与发展"专业的教育学硕士学位,是医学的本科,又是陕西师范大学基础心理学专业的心理学硕士,跟我都是心理学背景,我们在很多问题上有共同的看法。她从事英语教育多年,是英语教育界难得的跨学科人才。她有国内名校和海外的工作经历,知识丰厚,经验丰富,眼界宽广,对教育改革的前沿有着敏锐的洞察力,对实践教学的真谛有深刻的领悟。她对教学有高度的热爱和深入的钻研,教育理念先进,教学素养很高,是一位非常优秀的英语教师。在教师培养过程中,她积极主张在实践中学习,把各种实践教学的方法引入英语教育领域,特别是"工作任务课程化、教学任务工作化、工作过程系统化"的原则。同时,基于自己教学中的对分实践,她在这本教材中深度融入对分课堂理念,对对分课堂在英语教学中的发展做出了很大的贡献。我已经邀请她加入一个来自全国的优秀英语教师团队,参与我主编的《大学英语对分教程》新型教材的编写工作。

高质量的课堂和高质量的课程,需要有高质量的教材为支撑。该教材以实践为取向,以职前教师的成长为主线,注重教与学的全过程。编者以热情和智慧推动案例场景下理论与实践的结合,为增强创新教育实践、提升应用技术型大学的课程质量做出了可贵的探索,非常值得肯定。尽管这本教材还需要实践的检验,但我还是毫不犹豫地推荐给应用技术型大学相关专业的学生、教师以及从事英语教育的相关人员,因为我想它为打造应用技术型大学的优质课程,培养合格的中小学英语教师,贡献新的元素,提供新的思路。

张学新

2020 年 3 月于复旦大学

前 言

《英语案例教学论》是英语专业人才培养方案中教育方向课程的主要教材,通过案例搭建与职场的频繁联系,构建中小学英语教师培养的前沿阵地。英语专业学生通过使用本教材进行课程与教学论的学习,认识课程与教学的实质,掌握相关的教育教学知识,巩固所学的英语语言知识,提高判断、分析与解决问题的综合能力,以期成长为合格的中小学英语教师。

本教材的主要特色在于,将课程与教学论的理念与英语师范生的成长相结合,按照反思性实践的轨迹,通过案例呈现师范生成长过程中存在的问题,加以分析,以获得自我成长与发展。为体现"应用技术型"人才培养的特点,在各章中安排知识点和技能点,按"工作任务课程化、教学任务工作化、工作过程系统化"原则并结合对分课堂 PAD(Presentation—Assimilation—Discussion)的理念设计章节内容,使各个章节操作性强,便于教师引导学生进行教学,也便于学生在"做中学"。

采用中英文结合的方式编写也是本教材的另一特色。CBI(Content-Based Instruction)是目前英语专业与行业结合的热门术语,本教材秉承这一编写思路,以中英文穿插的形式进行编排,摒弃传统教材的过多考虑学科体系的逻辑联系等不利的方面,清晰地展现教学的目标与内容,易于被英语教育方向的学生理解和接受。

本教材的大部分案例来源于实习、见习基地,这些原生态的第一手资料,通过整理、提炼及前期的使用,对英语师范生的成长起到至关重要的作用,也充分体现了英语专业应用型课程的特点。知识点内容上,本教材参考大量国内外文献资料。值得关注的是,本教材采用线上线下相结合的方式进行编写,除了纸质版内容以外,还有电子版配套学习资源,随时更新、添加学科前沿知识。

本书主编具有国内外心理学和教育学双重背景,从事英语教育多年,教学上曾多次获得国家级奖项,编写团队成员包括一线教师及小学校长,均具有丰富的教学经验和编写实力。

　　本书分为八个章节:第一章关于案例教学;第二章教师成长;第三章英语学与教的理论;第四章走进学生;第五章英语课程及教材探析;第六章教学环境与班级管理;第七章课堂教学与组织管理;第八章课堂教学基本技能。本书每个任务的第一部分是知识点,包括概览和阅读材料两部分,概览主要介绍与任务相关的知识点的概念,体现学科的最新进展,以框架及段落的形式给出;阅读材料部分是给学生提供对所学概念进行深入挖掘与探索的机会,巩固理论知识,引发不同视角的思考。第二部分为技能点,通过案例分析,训练创新思维,提高认识、分析和解决问题的能力,并加深对理论的理解。第三部分是讨论思考与评价,主要以"亮考帮"的形式展现,帮助学生进行知识内化并进行自我评价与自我总结。

　　感谢对分课堂创始人、复旦大学张学新教授的细致耐心的传授与指导,感谢西安培华学院副校长刘越莲教授的悉心关怀、人文与国际教育学院梁蕊副院长及各部门的支持以及外语系领导及同事们的鼎力相助。本教材在编写过程中还受到西安市长安区黄良街道中心学校郝红老师和吴荣娜老师,以及西安市西咸新区沣西新城大王镇中心学校的支持和帮助,在此一并感谢! 最后,还要感谢我的家人在这本教材的编写过程中的默默奉献与支持! 由于本人水平有限,本书难免有不当或错误之处,敬请专家及读者批评指正。

曹　明
西安培华学院　人文与国际教育学院
2020 年 7 月

目 录

第一章　关于案例教学 ·· 1
  Task 1　Case Description ·· 2
  Task 2　Case Method and Teachers' Education ································ 5

第二章　教师成长 ·· 8
  Task 1　Reflective Practice ·· 9
  Task 2　Professional Portfolio ·· 16
  Task 3　Action Research ·· 25
  Task 4　Learning Community ·· 32

第三章　英语学与教的理论 ·· 41
  Task 1　Major Psychological Theories of Learning ························ 42
  Task 2　Theories of English Teaching Methodology ························ 61

第四章　走近学生 ·· 84
  Task 1　Understanding Primary School Students ···························· 85
  Task 2　Understanding Middle School Students ···························· 103

第五章　英语课程与教材探析 ·· 112
  Task 1　The National English Curriculum ···································· 113
  Task 2　Course Materials ·· 131
  Task 3　Instructional Design and Lesson Planning ························ 141

第六章　教学环境与班级管理 ·· 156
  Task 1　Learning Environment ·· 157
  Task 2　Class Management ·· 164

第七章　课堂教学与组织管理 ·· 174
  Task 1　English Classroom Teaching ·· 175
  Task 2　English Classroom Activities ·· 185

第八章　课堂教学基本技能 ·· 191
  Task 1　Lead-in and Questioning ·· 192
  Task 2　Classroom Discourse and Teaching Manners ···················· 202
  Task 3　Multimedia, Board Writing and Stick Figures Teaching ······ 206
  Task 4　Assessment and Assignment ·· 215

第一章 关于案例教学

主要内容

1. 案例的描述
   - 案例的概念
   - 案例的特征
   - 案例的类型
2. 案例教学法与教师教育
   - 案例教学法的概念
   - 案例教学法的意义
   - 案例教学法的过程
   - 教师教育中的案例教学

✓案例学习
✓专业参考
✓学术探讨

Case method has been used to teach preservice or newly recruited teachers since the 1990s. Due to its scientificity and practicability, it has been accepted to be an effective method adding to the wave of education reform in recent years. To make clear the meaning of case method and to make better use of this method, we should learn its concepts and understand how it assists the development of student teachers. The following tasks are designed for you to learn the description of a case and case method for teachers' development.

Task 1 Case Description

Like many students, you may have a mixture feeling to take this course because we will use a special method, a case method to study. But before we begin, let's make clear its concepts as follows.

1.1 Knowledge Points

Outline

In the first part, we offer you the concept and features of a case as well as the types of cases.

1.1.1 What is a case?

According to Zheng Jinzhou (2004), a case is a typical event that happens in the real situation including problems or difficult circumstances.

1.1.2 Features of a case

A case is an event with problems in difficult condition. It has to be typical to represent the real situation, or a statement of facts involving a question for discussion or decision. Of course, it has many features, such as authenticity, typicality, storytelling, purposiveness, and narrativity. Please pay attention to the following key words.

- Event
- With problems or difficult situation
- Typical
- Real event
- Features
- Authenticity
- Typicality
- Storytelling
- Purposiveness
- Narrativity

1.1.3 Types of cases

(1) Exemplar-oriented and reflection-oriented cases(实例取向和反思取向的案例)

实例取向的案例企图说明成功的实例,与解决问题或做决定无关;反思取向的案例则强调反思和建构的过程,鼓励学生批判思考及解决问题,而不只是未经判断,简单地接受。

(2) Topic-specific and participant-targeted cases(特定主题和特定学习对象的案例)

案例依据其使用的教学内容及学习对象,可分为特定主题的案例及特定学习对象的案例,比如我们这本书所涉及的案例就是针对英语教育学方向学生的案例。

(3) Narrative and non-narrative cases(书面叙述型和非书面叙述型的案例)

案例依据呈现方式来分,可以分为书面叙述型和非书面叙述型案例。如以书面文字呈现的案例为书面叙述型案例,以影像和声音呈现的案例为非书面叙述型案例,实际运用中也可同时制成书面叙述型和非书面叙述型。

(4) True cases, disguised cases and fictitious cases(真实、匿名和虚构的案例)

使用真实案例能够知道案例来源,可以利用他们对事实的了解分析案例;匿名案例是以真实案例为基础,为保护隐私将人名、机构名、时间等信息进行了改动;虚构案例是杜撰而来,但也尽量贴近真实情况。

Reading Materials

Using Case Studies in the ESL Classroom

The terminology surrounding "case studies" tends to be confusing, running the gamut from simply "case," to "case history," "case analysis," "case problem," and the familiar "case study."

As you know I am always on the lookout for original materials for use in my classes. I find that my students appreciate real world experiences in the classroom and case studies provide them with real life situations for discussion and evaluation. They are particularly useful for business English classes. Jolliffe writes, "through class discussions of the situations and people in the cases, students will hone their insights, perceptions, thought processes and interpersonal skills ..."

The following aspects should be paid attention to when we use cases.

Clarify objectives

- What do you learn from the discussion of the case?
- What do you know that applies to the case?
- What are the issues (central and peripheral) that may be raised in discussion?
- Can the case "carry" the discussion?

Plan and prepare
- Reading the case
- Raising questions
- Spending enough time for preparation
- Applying/extracting concepts
- Summarizing the ideas
- Evaluating the study results

Running a case study

For an English teacher to get started—select a short case study that covers the skills you want your students to practise. Read it several times and consider how it fits with your student-learning objectives for the class (you need to think about why you are teaching this case at this time).

Arrange the classroom so that students can talk face-to-face.

Prepare a set of questions for students to write out as homework before running the case in class.

For class, prepare another set of questions to move students through the stages of case analysis.

Who are the people in the case?

Where is the case study situated?

Why has the situation (problem) occured?

What possibilities for action are there?

How should the people in the case study proceed?

At the end, conduct a teacher-led summary and conclusion discussion, assessing what your students have achieved (Adapted from Hand, 2015).

1.2　Skills and Abilities

In order to train your thinking ability, and enhance you to understand more about case method, please think about the following questions:

(1) What is case method of teaching and learning? Please illustrate the features and types of case method.

(2) When we analyze a case, what kinds of questions do we often discuss?

Task 2 Case Method and Teachers' Education

Case method plays an important role in teachers' education. First, let's clarify the concept, significance and the process of case method, and then do further exploration.

2.1 Knowledge Points

Outline

In this part, we look at the concept, significance of the case method, the process of the case method, and its relation to teachers' education.

2.1.1 Concept of case method

Case method refers to a process of teaching and learning in which cases can be used as teaching materials. Teachers combine the materials with the topic of class to achieve teacher-student interaction by discussing, questioning, and answering. It is the teaching method that makes learners understand the relevant concept or theory in connection with the topic, and cultivates the higher-level teaching capacity.

2.1.2 Significance of case method

- Skills of analysis
- Skills of decision-making
- Skills of application
- Verbal expression skills
- Time management skills
- Personal communication skills
- Skills of creativity
- Written presentation skills

2.1.3 Process of case method: Preparing-discussion-reflection

Beginning: (1) Reading; (2) 5W-1H questions; (3) Appendix and other information; (4) About the titles; (5) Skimming and scanning; (6) Questions.

Further preparation: (1) Recognizing the problem; (2) Analyzing: Cause-effect; conditions & opportunities; (3) Alternatives; (4) Determining the criteria; (5) Analyzing and evaluating; (6) Forming the action and implementing.

Discussion in class:

(1) Discussion in group;

(2) 3—5 in one group;

(3) Making clearly the contents and procedures;

(4) Problem-solving: Pay attention to the discussion; listen effectively; note-taking; participate in solving special problems.

Reflection after class:

(1) After discussion, have a short summary immediately.

(2) Questions you may ask: Have I understand the whole materials of the case? What do I learn from it?

(3) Reflect yourself and other members.

2.1.4 Case method in teachers' education

案例在教师教育中起着越来越重要的作用，对英语教育方向的学生来说，利用案例，可以提前了解职场环境及工作中可能存在的问题，通过案例分析，提高认识问题、解决问题的能力，是为培养英语教育方向的学生从事教育、教学工作的专业能力的重要手段之一，能够克服教师专业性不足和经验匮乏的弊端，也体现了新时期教学改革和发展的要求。本书版权页的二维码中有延伸阅读资料，详细地讨论了案例教学在教师教育中的应用。

教师教育中的案例教学具有多种取向，并以案例为重心，以提高教师的专业性。

(1) 教师教育中案例教学的取向

一是理论取向，主张案例即理论。舒尔曼（Shulman，2007）认为案例的界定、分析和拓展都奠基于教育的专业理论之上，并将案例教学界定为教师专业化的重要组成部分。二是实践取向，突出教师教育中的教育实践能力。三是技术取向，突出教师将理论或科学原则应用于实际情景的技术、技巧。四是教师发展取向，主张教师在解决教育问题的同时推动个人发展。五是批判取向，把进步的社会观与激进的教育批判相结合。

(2) 案例教学的重心：案例而非教学

教师教育中的案例教学，更多地在于培养教师的专业性，以解决人们对于教师专业性欠缺的不满，其注重教育专业理论的应用，即"教师不在于拥有知识，而在于应用知识"。案例具有多重"再认识和多重表征的潜力"，并反映出案例的多样化应用。同时，学科中心论的教学取向，也要求案例教学是通过案例来统整教学而非相反。事实上，在满足教学目标方面，案例教学相对于讨论法和启发式教学并没有明显优势。由此可见，案例教学的重心与优势在于案例而非教学。

因此，教师教育中案例教学的核心在于深化教育教学理念，并通过以案例为中心的教学来提高教师的专业性。

2.2　Skills and Abilities

After studying the contents above, do you have any sense about case method? What enlightenments did you get from case method and teachers' education? How are you planning to study this course?

✦ 亮考帮

亮闪闪：请总结学习过程中，哪些是自己记忆深刻、受益最大、最欣赏的内容呢？请写出具体内容。

考考你：请把自己弄懂的但觉得别人可能存在困惑的地方，用问题的形式表述出来，挑战一下其他同学。

帮帮我：请把自己不懂、不会的地方或想要了解的内容，用问题的形式表述出来，并带到课堂上加以讨论。

✦ 参考文献

[1] Hand, L. Using Case Studies in the ESL Classroom[EB/OL]. (2017-03-02)[2020-03-06]. http://www.learnenglish.de/teachers/casestudies.html#sthash.gWuMk2gD.dpuf.
[2] 郭满库.英语案例教学论[M].杭州：浙江大学出版社，2012.
[3] 刘录护，扈中平.教师教育中的案例教学：理念、案例与研究批判[J].教师教育研究，2015(05)：79-80.
[4] 张民杰.案例教学法——理论与实务[M].北京：九州出版社，2006.
[5] 郑金洲."案例"ABC[J].教育文汇，2004(01)：40-43.

第二章　教师成长

主要内容

1. 反思性实践
2. 专业成长档案
3. 行动研究
4. 学习共同体

✓ 案例学习
✓ 专业参考
✓ 学术探讨

　　Tracking the route of teachers' growth, we can clearly catch the path—from student teachers to newly recruit teachers, and then senior teachers. Along with the path, this chapter introduces four important concepts. Reflective practice is the basic knowledge for teachers' development. You will learn it by understanding the concept of internship. Then, professional portfolio comes to your view. You are going to learn how to make your own professional portfolio, which is pretty interesting. After that, action research is the third concept you need to learn. It also brings you the method of mind map to help you broaden your eyes. Finally, you are going to study the last concept, learning community. It makes you further understand the path of teachers' development.

Task 1 Reflective Practice

Reflective practice is the central point within the four concepts we mentioned at the beginning of this chapter. So digging out the meanings will help you understand more about teachers' development.

1.1 Knowledge Points

Outline

There are many ways to make you realize your dream of being a teacher. Reflective practice has been recognized as one of the most effective ways to guide you there. For those who would like to achieve your goals, this part offers you the key concepts and the theoretical expositions.

Reflective practice involves thoughtfully considering one's own experiences in applying knowledge to practice while being coached by professionals in the discipline. Reflective teaching combines John Dewey's philosophy on the moral, situational aspects of teaching with Schon's process for a more contextual approach to the concept of reflective practice. Although there is no agreed definition about reflective practice, Farrell (2013) described it into four main types: reflection-in-action, reflection-on-action, reflection-for-action, and action research.

Reflection-in-action is concerned with thinking about what we are doing in the classroom while we are doing it; this thinking is supposed to reshape what we are doing at that moment.

Reflection-on-action deals with thinking back on what we have done in our class after it has happened. This includes reflecting on our reflection-in-action, or thinking about the way we think, but it is different from reflection-in-action because here the language teacher reflects on his/her class after it has happened.

Reflection-for-action is the designed outcome of both previous types of reflection, reflection-in-action and reflection-on-action, and is circular in nature as one feeds the other and so on, as one is difficult to consider without the other.

Action research comes under the umbrella of reflective practice because it is a form of self-reflection that has become popular in recent years in TESOL, because it is focused directly on problem-solving within the classroom. This term will be further discussed in Task 3.

Besides classroom teaching, internship is one of the key steps to practice. Let's drill the meanings bit by bit.

1.1.1 What is an internship?

In broad sense, an internship is an agreement between you and a company or organization for a fixed period of time, such as a semester or quarter. You agree to work for them and they agree to mentor and teach you; internships can offer valuable insight into a particular field or career. Most internships are unpaid but some offer a low wage; many internships are organized through colleges and high school programs. Many companies go on to hire their successful interns full time.

An educational internship is a form of practice for normal university/college students in an education organization. It is a main and indispensable teacher training procedure for normal education system carrying out the principle of connection between theory and practice, and implementing the goal of teacher training objectives. With educational internship, students can combine their knowledge with practice, cultivate their professional skills, and consolidate their specialty thinking before they become a real teacher.

1.1.2 Tasks that English student teachers need to do during educational internship

(1) To adapt to the environment

(2) To change the identity

(3) To be familiar with the class

(4) To listen to your mentor's class

(5) To have a collective lesson preparation

(6) To prepare your teaching plan

(7) To have a trial teaching

(8) To learn from your classmates

(9) To concentrate on your own class

(10) To do your reflection

1.1.3 How could one become an excellent English student teacher?

(1) Studying hard

(2) Observation

(3) Being energetic

(4) Being active

(5) On time

(6) Practice

(7) Keeping good relationship with your students and mentors

(8) Asking questions

(9) Being cooperative

(10) Reflection

There are seven Principles of Good Teaching Practice WebCT (Web Course Tools), which is from University of British Columbia in Canada. Good practice encourages interaction between students and faculty; Good practice encourages interaction and collaboration; Good practice uses active learning techniques; Good practice gives prompt feedback; Good practice emphasizes time on task; Good practice communicates high expectations; Good practice respects diversity—talents, experience, and ways of learning. To be an excellent student teacher, we need to be active and show our eager minds to study from the field. Internship will be the starting point of reflective practice.

1.2 Skills and Abilities

Reflective practice is the key method for teachers' development. After studying the concept, please think about whether you feel reflective practice is worth doing or not. To be a student teacher, do you often have a reflection? The following cases provide chances for you to rethink the questions.

Cases

Case One

愉快而又艰辛的实习工作结束了。在这一个月的实习期里我们顺利完成了从学生到教师的转换。实习期间,我在教案的准备和书写上、在课堂的管理上、在授课的掌握上,都有了很大的提高。一个月的时间令我感受颇多。现将实习情况总结如下:

一、听课。在实习的第一周我们开始去听课。在听课过程中,我发现听课的组员都在认真地做笔记。听了一节课,我们认认真真地记下了授课老师所讲的内容,并且认真地对老师讲课的各个环节进行了思考评价,写下了自己的收获和意见。虽然以前也有去听课的经历,但是都没有认认真真地去思考分析,现在才发现,原来一节课中我可以学到如此多的东西,无论是对教材的处理还是教学方法或是与学生的沟通等,都让我受益匪浅。每节课我都总结经验,并将其转化成自己的知识。

二、上课。相信每个新任教师的第一课都是很紧张的,我也不例外。在上课前,我不断地看教材及自己准备好的教案,生怕自己上课时会忘词,又不断地检查上课时要用的教学工具,反复地进行试讲。终于,我走上了讲台,开始了我的第一节课。通过书本上的图画对话引导学生进行思考讨论,希望通过这一方法能让学生对知识有更加深刻的理解。就这样,在愉快的气氛中顺利地结束了我的第一节课。

课后我马上找带课老师进行交流讨论。老师首先肯定了我,让我很高兴。同时,老师也给出了很多中肯的意见和建议,让我能马上调整讲课的思路以及修改教案,更加完善自己的教学。课后我会反思自己哪些地方做得好、哪些地方做得不好,并且一一记录下来,为以后上课做参考。

三、批改作业。从改作业中可以看出学生这节课的学习效果,也能知道学生的不足之处和容易犯错的地方。改完作业之后的评语也很重要,一句中肯的评语或是一句鼓动的话也会激励学生在下次完成作业时更加用心、更加认真。

通过这次实习,我不仅感受到了当一名教师的辛苦,还感受到了当教师的乐趣。在我和学生说我实习工作快结束时,学生们都叫我不要走,这对我是一种极大的肯定与安慰,也让我对教师工作有了新的认识。

做一名老师,特别是做一名好老师的确很难。教学工作复杂而又烦琐。首先,要管理好整个班集体,提高整体教学水平。然后,又要顾及班中的每一名学生,不能让任何一名学生掉队。这就要求教师不能只完成教学任务,还要多关心、多留意学生,经常与学生进行交流,给予他们帮助。做学生学习上的良师,生活当中的益友。

思考问题

1. 什么是教育实习?教育实习的意义是什么?
2. 该案例中,实习生是怎样安排自己实习的每一步以达到锻炼自己能力的目的?有哪些地方值得借鉴?

Case Two

一开始实习的时候,我还不熟悉班级,因此备课时,我是按照自己的节奏准备的,但上了几次课后,一点点总结出来了班级课堂情况,然后做出总结、反思,找出缺点,在下次上课时加以改正。记得有一节课讲到单词 uncle,aunt 时突然卡壳,我不知道该用什么方法引导学生对新单词加深印象,因为我的教案里只写到了教学新单词却没写如何带领学生复习掌握,加深印象。课后我也认识到了教案的重要性,也同时感受到课堂经验的重要性,因为有课堂经验的铺垫,所以再遇到这种情况时,就不会出现冷场或感到手足无措。

课前准备真的很重要,心态也真的很重要。有几节课我没有做好课前准备,所以上课时节奏有些乱,一堂课下来完全抓不到重点。有时候英语老师会站在后面听我的课,我就会不自觉地看向英语老师,担心自己哪里没有讲对,但英语老师不在时,我上课会比较放松,发挥就会好一些。但根本原因还是我自己心态不够好,不够有自信。但我明白这些东西只能通过自己调整和一次一次锻炼来改善。

当老师真的不是一件容易的事,一开始我认为只要上好自己的课就行了,但我还是太天真。当老师不只要备好课,还要在课堂上带好节奏,要关注学生上课的情况,要批改作业,从作业中了解到学生的知识薄弱点。单从备课这一点来说就特别麻烦,你需要考虑到方方面面,比如教材上的内容是否全面、是否讲得太深奥、有没有拓展知识、拓展知识的难易程度、讲课的进度、每节课的重点是什么等,实在太多太多,更不用说其他方面的了。

除了上述的那些,我在实习时还发现了一点,那就是老师自身的知识储备也要够细致够庞大,因为上课时你也不知道学生会问出什么问题。学生的学习积极性和课堂氛围是最能影响到老师的上课热情的。一个死气沉沉的班级和异常吵闹的班级,都会影响课堂教学的发挥。比如我实习期间带的这个班级,学习积极性不高,学生每次交上来的作业只有几本,效果也不好,这令我感到头疼。为此我也向其他英语老师请教过,他们说在群里跟学生家长反映是比较好的办法。但我实习的这个学校,不是所有的家长都能管好孩子的学习,所以这个办法起到的作用有限。

除去辛苦和无奈,也还是能收获欣慰和喜悦。每天走在校园里学生都会叫一声"老师好",那种感觉是其他行业从业者体会不到的。还有每次给学生讲完课,看着他们学到了知识的时候,内心也是极其自豪的。所以说任何事情都有两面性,有好处也有坏处,不能只往坏的方面看,也要朝好的方面看看。

思考问题

1. 该实习生在实习中遇到了哪些问题?如果你是这位实习生,应该怎样帮他/她解决这些问题?

2. 案例中,该实习生在实习中学到了哪些知识?有哪些体会?有哪些方面值得借鉴?

Case Three

首先,在英语教学方面,按照实习之初的计划,实习的前两周我们的主要任务是听课和评课,从实习的第三周开始正式上课。真实的英语教室与我们平日的模拟教室是完全不一样的。实习期间试讲时,面对的是自己的同学。但是,在真实的课堂中,学生的水平参差不齐,掌握知识的程度不同,接受新知识的速度也不一样,而老师要面对全体学生展开教学不能仅仅局限于几个人。比如当老师提出问题学生答不上的时候,老师该怎么办呢?站在讲台上吹胡子瞪眼睛是解决不了问题的。而这是我们在上课时经常碰到的情况。再加上自己此次是在三年级实习,一堂课的知识结构是十分紧凑的,只要一个环节出错或者中断,就会影响整个教学流程。

在遇到这种情况的时候,我会更加注意自己的引导方法并适当地简化自己的问题。

此外,不能要求每一位学生都能一学就会、一听就懂。对成绩相对较好的学生,就要求他们在课堂内消化这节课的重、难点;对成绩中等的学生,要求他们至少要接受70%的教学内容;对成绩较差的学生,要求他们接受40%的知识点;对完全不学的学生,对他们的要求就是能记住这节课里面的5个单词。

基础不是很好的孩子自信心就不足,又加上害羞、胆小、怕错了被人笑,所以教师一定要多鼓励他们,表扬他们,给予他们肯定,让他们逐渐突破自我、转变自我,从而相信自我。

作为老师,不仅要关注自己的教学,更要善于观察学生,多与学生聊天、接触,才能真正抓住学生的心。

其次,按照实习计划,每个实习生至少要体验为期一个星期的教室领导工作。为了能够有机会与学生们接触,我将七天的教室领导工作分散到每个星期,平均每周做两至三天的教室领导工作。我所在的实习教室是三年级班,刚开始面对这个班的时候,心里慌慌的,生怕这些学生不听自己的话。但是,这种想法在第一天做教室领导的时候就被否定掉了。在学生们的眼中,老师都是很"神圣的",只要我出现在教室里,大家都是规规矩矩的,丝毫没有违纪的现象。在本次的实习中,我还配合原任教室领导组织学生参加年级的广播体操比赛。另外,我还召开了一次主题为"生活中的点滴感动"的班会,对学生进行情感方面的教育。通过这一次实习教室领导工作,我初步掌握了如何去引导教育学生。

思考问题

1. 案例中,该实习生是如何将学生分类的?分析一下他/她分类的依据,以及认识班级中学习程度不同的学生的方法。
2. 你从该实习生的经历中学到了哪些东西?有哪些方面需要提高?

Case Four

早上7:50在某国际小学门口集合,由老师带进学校。我和另外一位同学分到二年级,这个班的班主任对小朋友们比较严格,而且这个班的班主任是英语老师,这有利于小学生对英语学习的重视。第一节是英语课。正式上课之前,先放音乐,小朋友站起来跳一段舞,活跃气氛,前面还有3个小朋友当领舞。在讲试卷的时候,以学生为主,小朋友们回答对问题时用掌声鼓励自己。教室有盆栽、气球、彩带装点,更有学习氛围。对不认真听讲的同学批评教育,但教育占大部分。教学中教师先教学习方法,再教学生自己记笔记、造句,然后分配任务叫学生做,学生答对了,进行表扬。

听了两节课后,我开始自己准备讲课,我发现想要上好一节课真的好难。我认真从书本、教案和网络上搜集资源,把自己的教学思路、教学理解融入进去,然后请带课老师给我指导。她从教学流畅连贯性、教学时间的把控、学生的配合程度等方面来给我做指导,这些方面是我没有考虑到的。我终于登上讲台给学生上了第一次课。这个班的学生还是比较配合的,我顺利地上完了第一节课。课后学生反馈我上课声音太小,以后一定改正。

随着时间的推移,通过听课和实践,我开始有了一些进步。这时指导老师给我多次机会,分不同层面锻炼和培养我的授课能力。在实习单位,我最大的感受是,讲台下坐着的不是自己的同学而是真正的学生。他们不会像自己的同学那种随意附和,快速地回答我提出的问题。他们在听不明白的时候会突然提问,或者干脆就趴在桌子上看书和睡觉。在上课的过程中,我也遇到了困难,如如何有效维持课堂秩序。这更让我懂得,作为一名教育工作者,就要想方设法实现和谐的教学气氛,在教学活动中建立良好的师生关系,而且教师要把自己当成活动中的一员、学生们的良师益友。

对于已经具备了一定程度自学能力、能够独立思考的学生,我的体会是要充分调动他们的主观能动性,将他们的学习兴趣调动起来,让他们在快乐中学习。我采用以学生为主、教师为辅的启发式教学,适当列出提纲,设置思考题,加以点拨,由"要我学"的教学方式转化成"我要学"的学习方式。实习结束了,自己亲身经历过了才知道其实上好课不是一件容易的事情。当老师没有以前自己想的那么简单。自己距离心中那个角色还有很长的路要走。

思考问题

1. 案例中,该实习生遇到的是低年级的学生,试分析他/她在管理低年级学生时有哪些体会?小学低年级同学的管理方法与高年级同学有哪些方面的不同?哪些方面可以共享?
2. 班级管理是一门学问,也是一门艺术,谈谈你对这一问题的认识。

亮考帮

亮闪闪:请总结学习过程中,哪些是自己记忆深刻、受益最大、最欣赏的内容呢?请写出具体内容。

考考你:请把自己弄懂的但觉得别人可能存在困惑的地方,用问题的形式表述出来,来挑战一下其他同学。

帮帮我:请把自己不懂、不会的地方或想要了解的内容,用问题的形式表述出来,并带到课堂上加以讨论。

参考文献

[1] Chickering, A., & Gamson, Z. Implementing the seven principles of good practice in undergraduate education:Technology as lever [J]. *Accounting Education News*,2001:9-10.
[2] Farrell, T. S. C. *Reflective Practice:Reawakening Your Passion for Teaching* [M]. Beijing:Forcign Language Teaching and Research Press,2013.
[3] Wiki User. What is an internship? (2018-12-17) [2019-05-18]. http://www.answers.com/Q/What_is_an_internship.

Task 2 Professional Portfolio

Professional portfolio has been used in North America since the 1980s. It was highly concerned by educators and practitioners for its powerful reflective nature. Until now, more and more educators accept this method and try to update the effectiveness, such as using e-portfolio to record student development. It also draws student teachers' attention because of its practice-oriented, individualized, easy-to-operate, and reflective nature. In the following parts, we will introduce this magic method and hope it will enhance your professional development in your teaching journey.

2.1 Knowledge Points

Outline

There are many tools to guide you to go reflective practice. Professional portfolio is one of the most effective methods. Let's study together.

2.1.1 Definition of professional portfolio

A portfolio is a collection of work that, when put together, demonstrates that achievement or learning has taken place. This collection of information and examples describe or give a profile of who you are as a professional. It is a collection, record or set of material or evidence that gives a picture of an individual's experience in an educational or developmental situation.

2.1.2 The way we compile a professional portfolio

The portfolio allows the adult learners to have ownership of their learning and development. For many the development of a portfolio is a method of bridging the theory-practice gap as reported to exist by Briggs (1972) and Reed and Proctor (1993). The production of a portfolio can facilitate the development of learning skills allowing the practitioner to learn from experience and clinical/teaching practice.

2.1.3 Portfolios in education field

Portfolios encourage beginning teachers to gather in one place significant artifacts representing their professional development; It can assemble materials that document their competencies; It includes a reflective component, for when the teacher decides which materials to include, he or she must reflect on which teaching practices worked well and why. The portfolios are modified at points throughout a teacher's career, as the teacher continues to apply learning to practice. A professional portfolio offers teacher interns an opportunity to explore attitudes, develop management skills, and reflect on the ethical implications of practice in classrooms with cultural compositions vastly different from their previous experiences. It also assemble materials that document their competencies. Besides, it causes teachers to step back and critically reflect not only on how they teach, but also on why they teach in a particular way.

2.1.4 How do I develop my own professional portfolio?

The process of making a professional portfolio has three phases:

(1) Reviewing: the process of looking at one's life experiences;

(2) Reflecting: sorting through what you have learned from these experiences;

(3) Recording: documenting insights gained from taking an honest look at oneself.

A well-known categorization divides portfolio content into (1) material from oneself, for instance a statement of teaching responsibilities, course syllabuses and self-evaluations; (2) material from others, such as feedback from peers or students, and (3) products of good teaching, such as evaluations by students and information about the effects of courses on student career choices.

A professional portfolio is a goal-driven, organized collection of materials that demonstrates a person's expansion of knowledge and skills over time. You need to develop the contents by writing, editing, and collecting relevant information. You may put these documents into a binder so that you could use it for your future career development. Here are contents of making a mini professional portfolio.

(1) Statement of originality and confidentiality

(2) Philosophy statement

(3) Goals

(4) Resume

(5) Work samples

(6) Academic plan of study

(7) Being individualized & creative

(8) Other achievement

(9) Letters of recommendation
(10) Evaluation from teachers and peers

Reading Materials

Reading Material One

Defining the Extremes of the Dimensions in Portfolio Use

Zeichner and Wray (2001) developed a conceptual framework for identifying different types of portfolio on the basis of portfolio practice and findings from the literature. The framework they developed was intended to help researchers to describe the approaches to teaching portfolios used in various settings. The framework consisted of the following dimensions: (1) the purposes of the portfolio; (2) who determines what goes into the portfolio and to what extent this is specified beforehand or left to the compiler of the portfolio; (3) the social interactions in the process of portfolio construction, and (4) what happens with portfolios once they have been completed.

Portfolio Purpose

The first dimension in Zeichner and Wray's conceptual framework is portfolio purpose. The purpose of a *learning portfolio* is to engage teachers in inquiry about their teaching and to document growth in teaching performance and teacher knowledge over time. A learning portfolio provides structure for the teachers' self-reflection as to which areas of their teaching performance are in need of improvement. This kind of portfolio is also called *a professional growth portfolio*. The *credential portfolio* is used to assess a prospective teacher's readiness to be given an initial teaching license, and a *showcase portfolio* presents the best work of a teacher. Credential and showcase portfolios are used to take decisions, for example, about certification or promotion. To sum up, two main portfolio purposes can be distinguished: a *formative* purpose, i.e., to stimulate learning and professional development, and a *summative* purpose, i.e., for promotion decisions (Edgerton, Hutchings, & Quinlan, 1991; Seldin, 1991). These two purposes can be seen as the extremes of the portfolio purpose dimension.

Portfolio Organization and Evidence

The second dimension concerns "*who determines what goes into the portfolio and to what extent this is specified beforehand or left to the compiler of the portfolio*". We have adapted this dimension to focus on the organization of the portfolio process and the type of evidence to be included in the portfolio and therefore, we call this dimension "portfolio organization and evidence". The extremes of this dimension are: *open-ended* versus *tightly organized* for organization and *non-standardized* versus *standardized* for evidence. If portfolios are open-ended, this means that there are no specific requirements for portfolio organization; it is all left to the portfolio compiler's choice. Not only portfolio organization, but also the type of evidence included in the portfolio can range from highly varied sources of evidence to a clearly specified set of teacher work (Wolf & Dietz, 1998). Most portfolio programs are likely to include a combination of prescribed and self-selected evidence (Barton & Collins, 1993). However, it is not only the degree of specification that is important, the key distinction is the one between materials that provide non-standardized versus standardized information (Peterson, 1995; 2001). Most portfolios consist of work samples, lesson plans and feedback from students and colleagues and these materials are often qualitative and non-standardized. The interpretation of this type of evidence requires a great deal of effort (Delandshere & Petrosky, 1998), whereas standardized content, such as uniform rating scales for peer-, student-, or self-evaluations, can be interpreted at a single glance.

Social Interactions in the Process of Portfolio Construction

The third dimension is that of *the nature and quality of social interactions in the process of portfolio construction*. As Edgerton et al. (1991) put it, portfolios can foster a culture of teaching and a new discourse about it. Because learning is a social process, portfolio construction should be so too. In the *process* of constructing a portfolio, teachers gain insight into their learning processes and learn about their professional development. Reflection and feedback are crucial in this process (Tillema & Smith, 2000). It has been argued that the value of teaching portfolios can be greatly enhanced by enabling teachers to interact with others on a regular basis when they are constructing their portfolios (Seldin, 1991; Wolf & Dietz, 1998). Examples of social interactions are meetings with peers or supervisors (Freidus, 1998). By helping portfolio composers to select materials and reflect on them, coaches and supervisors can provide important support for the cognitive and emotional components that play a role in portfolio construction. Peer coaching can be a very useful way of obtaining feedback and advice from colleagues. In interactions in relation to the portfolio construction process it is often the teachers' learning goals that are the focal point. By contrast, social interactions concerning the portfolio as a *product* focus on the selection of portfolio items for use in promotion decisions. In this case, portfolio composers discuss what constitutes good teaching and which items best represent their performance.

Portfolio Assessment

The fourth dimension is related to *what happens with portfolios once they have been completed*. We modified this dimension to focus on assessment. The extreme positions on this dimension are holistic and analytic assessment. Holistic assessment refers to the extreme that portfolio is assessed in a holistic way, according to teachers' learning goals. For analytical, the portfolio is assessed in an analytical way, according to precise criteria.

Holistic assessment is often combined with a learning dialogue, in which assessors give teachers feedback about areas that need improvement and involve them in a debate about what constitutes good teaching (Moss, Schutz, & Collins, 1998). Analytical portfolio assessment, on the other hand, uses more precise, uniform standards and standardized rating procedures. Portfolios for formative evaluation are often open-ended or loosely organized and contain mostly non-standardized materials. For formative purposes, social interactions around portfolio construction are focused on the process of portfolio construction and assessment is usually holistic. Portfolios for summative purposes, on the other hand, are often highly structured and contain evidence in the form of prescribed and standardized materials. Social interactions focus on the portfolio as a product and assessment is analytic and according to well-defined criteria. This means that the intended purposes of the portfolio influence how the portfolio process and content are organized, used and assessed.

(Tigelaar, et al., 2004)

Reading Material Two

Teaching Portfolios

Cultivates reflection and self assessment

The process of portfolio development requires the teacher to seek answers to the following issues: Who you are as a teacher, what you do, why you do it, where you have been, where you are now in your teaching, where you want to go, and how you plan to get there. In order to address these issues, teachers must become researchers of their own practice.

Provides self-renewal

Teachers are sometimes their own worst critics. Developing teaching portfolios can breathe new life into practice because teachers are forced to look at what they are doing as opposed to perceiving what they are doing, by collecting materials that give concrete evidence about their teaching.

Promotes collaboration

If teaching portfolios are used for assessment of practicing teachers, then this provides an opportunity for a teacher to enter into a collaborative relationship with a reviewer, mentor, or supervisor in order to obtain feedback on their work. It can lead to self-reflection for both parties, as both must mutually identify their goals for professional development.

Encourages ownership and empowerment

It encourages teachers to take more responsibility and ownership for their own professional development. Teachers can become more self-directed as they must identify their goals and plans for the future as opposed to allowing a supervisor or an administrator to outline their professional development.

A teaching portfolio is an album (much like a photo album) of many different aspects of a teacher's work. They tell the story of the teacher's efforts, skills, abilities, achievements, and contributions to students, colleagues, institutions, academic disciplines, and/or community. Teaching portfolios can provide teachers with opportunities for self-reflection and collaboration with colleagues. Teaching portfolios can also provide teachers with opportunities to plan their own professional development journey. The analogy of a traveler on a journey is applicable to preparing teaching portfolios. Just as travelers must decide their point of departure, the course they will take, and their destination, a professional teaching portfolio encourages teachers to think about their starting point, direction, and goals for the coming year(s).

A teaching portfolio might include lesson plans, anecdotal records, student projects, class newsletter, videotapes, annual evaluations, and letters of recommendation. A teaching portfolio is not a one-time snapshot of where the teacher is at present; rather, it is an evolving collection of carefully selected professional experiences, thoughts, and goals. This collection can be accompanied with the teacher's written (or oral) reflection and self-assessment of the collection itself and plans for the future.

(Farrell, 2013)

2.2　Skills and Abilities

Now is the time for you to make your own professional portfolio. You may study some cases listed below first, and then try to train yourself to be a designer, a writer, or an artist. It will be interesting to find your potential and to know your own development in teaching and learning.

Cases

⌈Case One⌋

我的哲理陈述

对教育的态度：教育是一个复杂、长期的过程并且伴随着隐藏性的劳动成果。

对教书的态度：其过程需要老师有耐心，并且运用多种教学方法找到最适合学生个人发展的教学方法以促进其能力培养和良好的课堂气氛。

对学生的态度：老师应有耐心，用不同方法对待不同性格的学生，因为个人发展有差异性。

对家长的态度:家长要明白自己对孩子发展的重要性,不能把孩子交给老师之后不加管理。我会与家长成为朋友,相互合作,帮助孩子成长。

对同事的态度:大家应相互学习,提高自我教育能力和沟通能力,因为我们有共同的目标,那就是让我们的学生变得更好。

思考问题

1. 在个人的专业成长档案中,该学生是如何描述自己对教育、教学、学生、学生家长以及同事的看法的?
2. 谈谈自己对教育教学的认识。

Case Two

我的教学哲理陈述

公众认为教师职业非常值得敬佩。教师有机会在自己的工作过程中接触和改变许多人的生活。关于我的教学哲学陈述有以下三点:

首先,我认为老师和学生互相了解至关重要。学生知道教师的专业背景、教师了解将要教授的内容,这有利于课堂活动的展开。

其次,我相信,老师应该被看作课堂的统治者。应该告诉学生在整个课程中教师的期望是什么,并解释课堂中正确的行为和规则。如果这些规则是在一开始就规定的,那么那些不遵守规则的人就要得到惩罚。

最后,我觉得应该给学生一些权利选择他们想要的学习方式。有些孩子在小组中学习得更好,有些孩子更喜欢参加活动,有些孩子喜欢从教科书中获得材料。我相信孩子们应该有机会选择他们想要完成课程的方式。

思考问题

1. 在个人的专业成长档案中,该学生是如何认识教师这个职业的?
2. 陈述中为什么认为"老师应该被看作课堂的统治者"? 你同意这种说法吗? 为什么?

Case Three

我的六年目标

短期目标(第一个两年):考取教师资格证、英语专业八级证并且保持高的平均分申请澳大利亚名校研究生,保持并取得高的平均分(超过90分)。

中期目标(第二个两年):我将在澳大利亚好好完成研究生学习,学习之余积累社会工作经验、找到我的另一半和考取驾驶资格证。

长期目标(第三个两年)：希望在澳大利亚工作两年挖掘自我，探索更多能丰富我生活的东西。在此期间，可能会结婚。

思考问题

1. 案例中该学生是如何规划自己专业发展的 6 年目标的？对你有什么启示和帮助？
2. 谈谈自己职业成长的短期(2 年内)、中期(5 年内)以及长期(10 年内)的规划。

Case Four

我未来的目标

短期目标(1 年)：考取英语专业八级证书、教师资格证书，参加公务员考试以及当地的招教考试。

中期目标(2 年)：在毕业之后，在当地培训机构找一份兼职老师的工作，考察当地市场，发展客户、了解当地客户需求，综合利用身边的资源，和朋友开一家属于自己的培训机构。

长期目标(大于 3 年)：稳定工作，夯实基础，通过自己的努力创造财富，考虑结婚。

思考问题

1. 案例中该学生是如何规划自己的短期、中期和长期专业发展目标的？对你有什么启示和帮助？
2. 该学生谈及未来结婚的事，你觉得是否应该在自己的专业成长案例中提及此事，为什么？

亮考帮

亮闪闪：请总结学习过程中哪些是自己记忆深刻、受益最大、最欣赏的内容呢？请写出具体内容。

考考你：请把自己弄懂的但觉得别人可能存在困惑的地方，用问题的形式表述出来，来挑战一下其他同学。

帮帮我：请把自己不懂、不会的地方或想要了解的内容，用问题的形式表述出来，并带到课堂上加以讨论。

参考文献

[1] Farrell, T. S. C. *Reflective Practice: Reawakening Your Passion for Teaching*[M]. Beijing: Foreign Language Teaching and Research Press, 2013.

[2] Harris, S., Dolan, G., & Fairbairn, G. Reflecting on the use of student portfolios[J]. *Nurse Education Today*, 2001(21),4: 278-286.

[3] Neades, B. L. Professional portfolios: all you need to know and were afraid to ask[J]. *Accident and Emergency Nursing*, 2003, 11: 49-55.

[4] Tigelaar, D. E. H., Dolmans, D. H. J. M., Wolfhagen, I. H. A. P. & van der Vleuten, C. P. M. Using a conceptual framework and the opinions of portfolio experts to develop a teaching portfolio prototype[J]. *Studies in Educational Evaluation*, 2004(30): 305-321.

Task 3　Action Research

Action research (AR) has become more and more popular in English teaching circle in recent years. To better understand its functions and how it works for teachers' development, we offer the following knowledge points, reading materials and cases for you to explore.

3.1　Knowledge Points

Outline

Since action research is closely related to the idea of reflective practice and encourages teachers to do research, as a student teacher, you should first understand what action research is and put it into practice.

3.1.1　Action research

Since action research is an effective method for our development, as a student teacher standing at the entry point, we also need to understand the concept of action research, cultivate, and practice in the way we are going on.

1. Concept

Action research is part of a broad movement that has been going on in education generally for some time. It is related to the ideas of "reflective practice" and "the teacher as researcher". Action research involves taking a self-reflective, critical, and systematic approach to exploring your own teaching contexts. We often see gaps between what is actually happening in our teaching situation and what we would ideally like to see happening. So first, we need to identify the problem or issue, then intervene in a deliberate way in the problematic situation in order to bring about changes and, even better, improvements in practice. The changes made in the teaching situation arise from solid information rather than from our hunches or assumptions about the way we think things are. After that, we observe whether it has a positive change or improvement. At the end, we reflect on, evaluate and describe the effects of action to make sense of what has happened and to understand the issue we have explored more clearly.

2. Steps in action research

According to Kemmis and Mctaggart (1988), who are major authors in this field, AR typically involves four broad phases in a cycle of research. The first cycle may become a continuing, or iterative, spiral of cycles which recur until the action researcher has achieved a satisfactory outcome and feels it is time to stop.

(1) Planning

In this phase you identify a problem or issue and develop a plan of action in order to bring about improvements in a specific area of the research context. This is a forward-looking phase where you consider: i) what kind of investigation is possible within the realities and constraints of your teaching situation; and ii) what potential improvements you think are possible.

(2) Action

The plan is a carefully considered one which involves some deliberate interventions into your teaching situation that you put into action over an agreed period of time. The interventions are "critically informed" as you question your assumptions about the current situation and plan new and alternative ways of doing things.

(3) Observation

This phase involves you in observing systematically the effects of the action and documenting the context, actions and opinions of those involved. It is a data collection phase where you use open-eyed and open-minded tools to collect information about what is happening.

(4) Reflection

At this point, you reflect on, evaluate and describe the effects of the action in order to make sense of what has happened and to understand the issue you have explored more clearly. You may decide to do further cycles of AR to improve the situation even more, or to share the story of your research with others as part of your ongoing professional development.

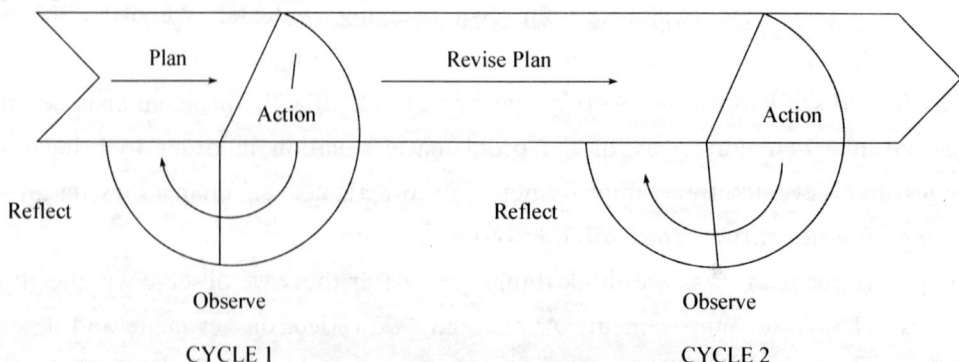

Fig. 2-1 Cyclical AR model based on Kemmis and McTaggart (1998)

3.1.2 Mind map

There are many ways to teach primary school and middle school students. Mind map is one of the effective methods to teach children, and also improve our own learning. To be a young teacher, we absolutely need to grasp this method to help solve our problems and make us further develop in a professional way. So we introduce it here.

A mind map is a graphical representation of topics, ideas, or concepts in a radial, non-linear manner. A mind map focuses on a central keyword or topic, with other items linked to and arranged around the central idea. Mind maps encourage a brainstorming style approaching to planning and organizational tasks.

1. Characteristics of a mind map

A mind map can consist of words, images and additional rich-media content (audio, video, digital files). The arrangement or order of ideas is based on the importance of the concepts, and can be classified into groups, enforcing the relationships of the topics and their overall involvement with the central topic. By including words, images and color schemes, a mind mapping diagram allows for greater creativity when brainstorming ideas and documenting information, or planning for a project. The arrangement of ideas and inclusion of contents enhances organization, memorization and presentation skills.

2. Uses of a mind map

Mind maps are used to visualize, organize, and classify ideas, making them perfect for study aids, organizing information, problem-solving, writing and making decisions. Mind maps have many applications in educational and other situations, including note-taking and writing to creating agendas and running meetings. Mind maps can be used for problem-solving, brainstorming, business plans, SWOT analysis, outlining documents, collaboration, creating presentations, and education sector.

3.2 Skills and Abilities

In previous part, we offered some concepts which are related to action research. We also introduced a concept of mind map. The following cases are examples of implementing these methods and skills. Please pay attention to analyze these cases and practice the skills of mind mapping as well.

Cases

Case One

As part of the introduction of a new syllabus, a teacher wishes to know whether the use of group work will improve students' ability to speak English.

She first consults the literature on this area of research. She then decides on the approach and methods to be used. The teacher's hypothesis is: group work will increase the development of both fluency and accuracy in oral tasks.

She assigns one group of students in a school to an experimental group, where all classroom tasks are conducted through group work for a period of two months. An equal number of students (the control group) are taught using the same tasks through a whole-class teacher fronted approach for the same period.

In order to ensure that the students in the experimental group are not at higher levels of language learning to begin with, the teacher first administers a test. She then assigns students to the groups on the basis of the test results. At the end of the two months, each of the groups is given a further identical test in order to, see whether the use of group work has resulted in higher results for the experimental group.

The results show that the students assigned to group work have performed at a higher level in relation to fluency, but that their performance on some aspects of grammatical accuracy is lower than the control group. The teacher publishes the findings of the study in a journal.

(Burn, 2011)

思考问题

1. After studying this case, would you like to summarize what action research is?
2. Share with your classmates what you have learned from this case.

Case Two

张老师是一位从教 13 年的小学英语教师，十多年的磨炼使她从一个刚刚走出大学校门的英语教育专业的女大学生，成长为一名独当一面的乡村中心学校的优秀英语教师。十多年的功夫，弹指一挥间，回想当年她刚刚走出校门的时候，怀抱理想，觉得自己是位英语教育的高才生，可以到工作单位施展拳脚，但事实与她的想法相距甚远。

2006 年，张老师来到这所乡村小学，一个月的工资也就几百块，还没有自己上学时父母给的伙食费高，学校的教学环境也不如自己想象的那样好，学生来自周边的乡村，没有很好的英语基础与学习环境，看到一起毕业的同学有些去了大公司，有些拿到高薪，也萌生过转行或转工作的想法。但是，自从她给学生上了第一堂课，就深深地被这些天真可爱的孩子们所吸引,每当给他们上英语课,看着这些小学生渴求知识的脸,她就设法说服自己留下。另外还有年长的教师及老校长对她的关怀与鼓励,使她最终想清楚了,自己最初的理想就是成为一名小学教师,自己的兴趣爱好、特长与所学都与学校有着不可分割的联系,于是她下定决心安心在这所乡村小学扎根。

十几年来,有很多事情令她难忘,有一次在五年级的英语课堂上,她要求学生朗读课文中学过的句子,有的同学觉得读起来比较困难,就想放弃,还有同学趁机做起了其他作业,张老师那节课上得很提不起精神,到底是自己的方法有问题,还是学生不上心呢?她课后反思了自己的教学方法,下课后找个别学生谈话,同时每天早读去教室领着大家读,并观察学生朗读的习惯,经过一周的摸索,她发现几个问题:首先,农村学生英语环境比较薄弱,父母督促有限,留守儿童更是如此,学生读的机会很少;其次,由于缺乏文化背景知识,不少学生不理解朗读的意义,也体会不到语言的美,时间长了就没有兴趣再朗读了。针对这些问题,她修改了自己的教学计划,首先联系学生家长,了解学生的学习情况,特别是英语学习的情况;其次针对学生们对异国文化不熟悉的问题,她带来自己大学同学在澳大利亚生活的照片,使同学们开阔眼界,调动了他们学习的好奇心与积极性;她坚持早读时间跟班进行英语早读,进行个别辅导。短短几星期过去了,同学们的英语朗读习惯发生了很大的变化,至少不太惧怕朗读了,当然更多的变化还是远期的,这使得张老师对自己的教学更加充满信心。

十多年来,她努力钻研教学方法,使自己能够发现学生学习中的问题,创设英语环境,激发学生学习英语的兴趣。发现有些内容比较枯燥时,她就立即自己动手制作教具,创设各种游戏活动,使学生们积极投入英语学习中;发现有些学生英语学习不太主动,就深入了解情况,走访家庭,给学生制定学习计划,使学生迎头赶上。功夫不负有心人,她所带的班级学生屡屡在全区英语竞赛中获奖,并且平均成绩也名列前茅。与此同时,自己的专业发展也不断提升,公开发表学术论文探讨如何提高农村小学英语课堂教学效率。为了提高自己的教学能力、管理能力以及全科教育的能力,张老师潜心钻研,学习绘画、手工制作等技术,将这些技能用于课堂教学中,同时还自学其他学科的知识,适应小学的教学要求。如今的张老师,已经是一位深受学生喜爱的、专业娴熟的全科教师,不仅英语课带得好,还涉猎其他诸如音乐、美术、自然科学等课程。当实习生步入该所学校实习时,她悉心照顾、耐心带教、现身说法,使很多实习生真正了解并爱上小学英语教育。

现在,张老师经常自豪地说:"我的很多同学都羡慕我是一名小学英语教师,尽管工作繁忙,但我仍然觉得很有价值。"

思考问题

1. 案例中,张老师是如何转变自己的思想,扎根乡村小学成为一名优秀的乡村小学英语教师的?试分析张老师的成长过程,对自己在职业生涯中确定目标有哪些启示?

2. 行动研究少不了从发现问题开始,张老师是如何根据她们学校学生的具体情况,发现问题,制定解决方案,实现目标的?

3. 反思性实践是教师成长的一个重要环节,和其他教师成长方式密不可分,该案例中反思性实践是否在张老师坚定职业目标上起到关键作用?作为一名普通的小学英语老师,张老师为什么觉得自己很有价值?

Case Three

小魏老师从师范大学毕业2年,已经积累了一些班级管理经验,她所带的班级是三年级二班,平时比较活跃,同学们上进心也比较强,但最近有些同学有些好动,坐不住,有其他老师反映课堂纪律不太好。作为班主任,也是英语老师,她决定寻找有效的办法,因此她开始细致观察学生,以下是观察记录:

1. 周一一早,小强穿着一身带蜘蛛人花纹的衣服,跟几个男生谈起蜘蛛人,并声称自己有特殊能量,可以爬高,其他同学羡慕不已。

2. 周三上午,小明与邻桌同学发生小矛盾,由于对方语言有些不文明,然后差点产生肢体冲突。

3. 周三下午,课外活动,几个女同学从花园边走过,发现花丛中有蜘蛛结的网,有个女生胆小,立马想走开,另外一个女同学试图用手抓蜘蛛,小魏老师及时赶到,叮嘱同学们不要触碰这些小动物。

经过一周的观察,小魏老师希望利用这些线索来促进同学们的学习,进行正向引导,她想到自己在大学里听的一次讲座,讲到mind map的方法,正逢讲到动物这一章节,她决定用mind map的方法,结合新的《义务教育英语课程标准》,来设计英语课堂教学,小魏老师是怎么做的呢?让我们一起来看看。

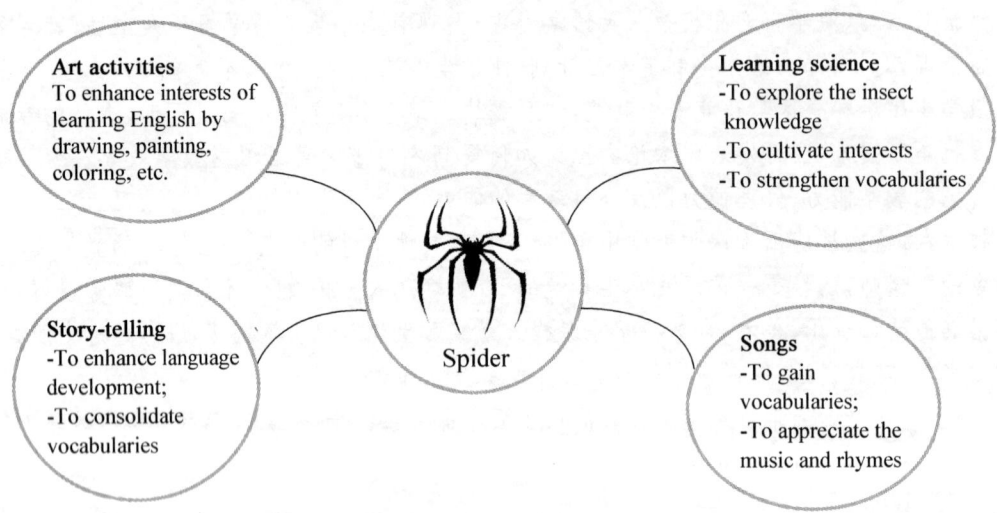

思考问题

1. 学习了以上用思维导图解决问题的案例,对你学习和解决问题有什么帮助吗?请谈谈你的想法。

2. 如果你今天的教学内容是教学生一些交通工具的英文说法与描述,如何用思维导图的方法设置一些活动来促进学生的学习呢?

参考文献

- Burns, A. *Doing Action Research in English Language Teaching: A Guide for Practitioners*[M]. Beijing: Foreign Language Teaching and Research Press, 2011.

Task 4 Learning Community

Learning community is the last concept you need to grasp in this chapter. It plays a key role in teachers' education in recent years. Nowadays, it has been widely used to improve, not only in-service but also pre-service teachers' teaching ability. We hope the materials and cases we offered will make you understand more about it.

4.1 Knowledge Points

Outline

The following part provides you the definition, the understanding, and the examples about the concept of "learning community". Enjoy your learning.

4.1.1 Learning community

"Learning community" is a general term we often called. In many situations, we also call it "Professional learning community" (PLC).

(1) Definition

A group of people share and critically interrogate their practice in an ongoing, reflective, collaborative, inclusive, learning-oriented, growth-promoting way (Mitchell & Sackney, 2000; Toole & Louis, 2002); operate as a collective enterprise (King & Newmann, 2001). Summarising the literature, Hord (1997: 1) blended process and anticipated outcomes in defining a "professional community of learners" (Astuto, et al., 1993) as one:

> ... in which the teachers in a school and its administrators continuously seek and share learning, and act on their learning. The goal of their actions is to enhance their effectiveness as professionals for the students' benefit; thus, this arrangement may also be termed communities of continuous inquiry and improvement.

The notion, therefore, draws attention to the potential that a range of people based inside and outside a school can mutually enhance each other's and pupils' learning as well as school development.

(2) Five key characteristics or features:
- Shared values and vision
- Collective responsibility
- Reflective professional inquiry
- Collaboration
- Group, as well as individual, learning is promoted

4.1.2 共同体和学习共同体

"共同体"一词首先是一个社会学概念,由德国社会学家和哲学家斐迪南·滕尼斯于1887年最早提出,而学界对"学习共同体"(learning community)的概念有诸多描述,但基本公认是杜威最早将此理念引入教育学领域,由美国教育家博耶尔(1995:56)正式提出并使用。我国学者钟启泉(1998:13-16)教授将"学习共同体"的概念引入国内,其内涵主要包括:(1)共同体的构建;(2)共同体的愿景;(3)共同体的具体目标;(4)达到目标所采用的方式;(5)评价与反思。近年来我国对学习共同体的研究主要集中在网络学习共同体、学习型社区、终身学习、教师学习共同体、教师专业发展共同体、虚拟学习共同体等方面。在建立课程学习共同体时,根据具体的课程可将学习共同体具体细化为:由教师与学生组成的,为达到提高英语语言输出能力以及具有合作、执行、创新、应变等品质的综合素质和发展潜力为愿景的,以行知为取向的,以互动、启发、探究、合作等为方法策略的,以个人进步成长为结果进行反思及相应评估的生态学习系统。

"学习共同体"是建构主义教学论中的一种教学隐喻,直接与建构主义中"学习是知识的社会协商"这一学习隐喻相对应。它强调知识的社会性特征,是一群有着共同关注点或者对共同话题感兴趣的人们组织起来的一个以知识建构与意义协商为内涵的学习团体,其实质是为"有相同或相近的价值取向和偏好的人提供一种特殊的学习环境"。

Reading Materials

Reading Material One

1. What are professional learning communities?

There is no universal definition of a professional learning community. PLC may have shades of interpretation in different contexts, but there appears to be broad international consensus that it suggests a group of people sharing and critically interrogating their practice in an ongoing, reflective, collaborative, inclusive, learning-oriented, growth-promoting way (Mitchell & Sackney, 2000; Toole & Louis, 2002); operating as a collective enterprise (King & Newmann, 2001). Summarising the literature, Hord (1997:1) blended process and anticipated outcomes in defining a "professional community of learners" (Astuto, Clark, Read, McGree, & Fernandez, 1993) as one:

... in which the teachers in a school and its administrators continuously seek and share learning, and act on their learning. The goal of their actions is to enhance their effectiveness as professionals for the students' benefit; thus, this arrangement may also be termed communities of continuous inquiry and improvement.

The notion, therefore, draws attention to the potential that a range of people based inside and outside a school can mutually enhance each other's and pupils' learning as well as school development.

2. Five key characteristics or features of PLC

• Shared values and vision. Having a shared vision and sense of purpose has been found to be centrally important (Andrews & Lewis, 2007). In particular, there is "an undeviating focus" on all students' learning (Hord, 2004) because individual autonomy is seen as potentially reducing teacher efficacy when teachers cannot count on colleagues to reinforce objectives (Louis et al., 1995; Newmann & Wehlage, 1995). Louis and colleagues (1995) suggest that a shared value base provides a framework for "shared, collective, ethical decision making".

• Collective responsibility. There is broad agreement in the literature that members of a PLC consistently take collective responsibility for student learning (King & Newmann, 2001; Kruse, Louis & Bryk, 1995; Leithwood & Louis, 1998). It is assumed that such collective responsibility helps to sustain commitment, puts peer pressure and accountability on those who do not do their fair share, and eases isolation (Newmann & Wehlage, 1995).

• Reflective professional inquiry. This includes: "reflective dialogue"(Louis et al., 1995), conversations about serious educational issues or problems involving the application of new knowledge in a sustained manner; "deprivatization of practice" (Louis et al., 1995), frequent examining of teachers' practice, through mutual observation and case analysis, joint planning and curriculum development (Newmann & Wehlage, 1995); seeking new knowledge (Hord, 2004); tacit knowledge constantly converted into shared knowledge through interaction (Fullan, 2001); and applying new ideas and information to problem-solving and solutions addressing pupils' needs (Hord, 1997).

• Collaboration. This concerns staff involvement in developmental activities with consequences for several people, going beyond superficial exchanges of help, support, or assistance (Louis et al., 1995), for example, joint review and feedback (Hord, 2004). The link between collaborative activity and achievement of shared purpose is highlighted (Newmann & Wehlage, 1995). Feelings of interdependence are central to such collaboration: a goal of better teaching practices would be considered unachievable without collaboration, linking collaborative activity and achievement of shared purpose. This does not deny the existence of micropolitics, but conflicts are managed more effectively in some PLCs, as Hargreaves (2003: 163) notes:

> Professional learning communities demand that teachers develop grown-up norms in a grown-up profession—where difference, debate and disagreement are viewed as the foundation stones of improvement.

• Group, as well as individual, learning is promoted. All teachers are learners with their colleagues (Louis et al., 1995). In Rosenholtz's (1989) "learning enriched schools", "professional self renewal" is "a communal rather than solitary happening". Collective learning is also evident, through collective knowledge creation (Louis, 1994), whereby the school learning community interacts, engages in serious dialogue and deliberates about information and data, interpreting it communally and distributing it among them.

Our own research broadly confirms these five characteristics, also identifying three others: mutual trust, respect and support among staff members; inclusive membership—the community extending beyond teachers and school leaders to support staff, and it being a school-wide community rather than consisting of smaller groups of staff; and openness, networks and partnerships—looking beyond the school for sources of learning and ideas (Bolam et al., 2005; Stoll et al., 2006).

(Adapted from Stoll et al., 2006)

4.2 Skills and Abilities

How are we going to put the concept of learning community into practice? The following cases make us understand more about it. Besides, we need to try to learn the methods they used in the cases to enhance our teaching and learning.

Cases

Case One

Big Idea #1: Ensuring that students learn

School mission statements that promise "learning for all" have become a cliché. But when a school staff takes that statement literally—when teachers view it as a pledge to ensure the success of each student rather than as politically correct hyperbole—profound changes begin to take place. The school staff finds itself asking: What school characteristics and practices have been most successful in helping all students achieve at high levels? How could we adopt those characteristics and practices in our own school?

What commitments would we have to make to one another to create such a school? What indicators could we monitor to assess our progress? When the staff has built shared knowledge and found common ground on these questions, the school has a solid foundation for moving forward with its improvement initiative.

As the school moves forward, every professional in the building must engage with colleagues in the ongoing exploration of three crucial questions that drive the work of those within a traditional learning community:

—What do we want each student to learn?

—How will we know when each student has learned it?

—How will we respond when a student experiences difficulty in learning?

The answer to the third question separates learning communities from traditional schools.

Here is a scenario that plays out daily in traditional schools. A teacher teaches a unit to the best of his or her ability, but at the conclusion of the unit some students have not mastered the essential outcomes. On the one hand, the teacher would like to take the time to help those students. On the other hand, the teacher feels compelled to move forward to "cover" the course content. If the teacher uses instructional time to assist students who have not learned, the progress of students who have mastered the content will suffer; if the teacher pushes on with new concepts, the struggling students will fall farther behind.

What typically happens in this situation? Almost invariably, the school leaves the solution to the discretion of individual teachers, who vary widely in the ways they respond. Some teachers conclude that the struggling students should transfer to a less rigorous course or should be considered for special education. Some lower their expectations by adopting less challenging standards for subgroups of students within their classrooms. Some look for ways to assist the students before and after school. Some allow struggling students to fail.

When a school begins to function as a professional learning community, however, teachers become aware of the incongruity between their commitment to ensure learning for all students and their lack of a coordinated strategy to respond when some students do not learn. The staff addresses this discrepancy by designing strategies to ensure that struggling students receive additional time and support, no matter who their teacher is. In addition to being systematic and schoolwide, the professional learning community's response to students who experience difficulty is:

—*Timely*. The school quickly identifies students who need additional time and support.

—*Based on intervention rather than remediation*. The plan provides students with help as soon as they experience difficulty rather than relying on summer school, retention, and remedial courses.

—*Directive*. Instead of inviting students to seek additional help, the systematic plan requires students to devote extra time and receive additional assistance until they have mastered the necessary concepts.

The systematic, timely, and directive intervention program operating at Adlai Stevenson High School in Lincolnshire, Illinois, provides an excellent example. Every three weeks, every student receives a progress report. Within the first month of school, new students discover that if they are not doing well in a class, they will receive a wide array of immediate interventions. First, the teacher, counselor, and faculty advisor each talk with the student individually to help resolve the problem. The school also notifies the student's parents about the concern. In addition, the school offers the struggling student a pass from study hall to a school tutoring center to get additional help in the course. An older student mentor, in conjunction with the struggling student's advisor, helps the student with homework during the student's daily advisory period.

Any student who continues to fall short of expectations at the end of six weeks despite these interventions is required, rather than invited, to attend tutoring sessions during the study hall period. Counselors begin to make weekly checks on the struggling student's progress. If tutoring fails to bring about improvement within the next six weeks, the student is assigned to a daily guided study hall with 10 or fewer students. The guided study hall supervisor communicates with classroom teachers to learn exactly what homework each student needs to complete and monitors the completion of that homework. Parents attend a meeting at the school at which the student, parents, counselor, and classroom teacher must sign a contract clarifying what each party will do to help the student meet the standards for the course.

Stevenson High School serves more than 4000 students. Yet this school has found a way to monitor each student's learning on a timely basis and to ensure that every student who experiences academic difficulty will receive extra time and support for learning.

Big Idea #2: A focus on results

Professional learning communities judge their effectiveness on the basis of results. Working together to improve student achievement becomes the routine work of everyone in the school. Every teacher team participates in an ongoing process of identifying the current level of student achievement, establishing a goal to improve the current level, working together to achieve that goal, and providing periodic evidence of progress. Such goals as "We will adopt the Junior Great Books program" or "We will create three new labs for our science course" give way to "We will increase the percentage of students who meet the state standard in language arts from 83 percent to 90 percent" or "We will reduce the failure rate in our course by 50 percent."

Schools and teachers typically suffer from the DRIP sydrome—Data Rich/Information Poor. The results-oriented professional learning community not only welcomes data but also turns data into useful and relevant information for staff. Teachers have never suffered from a lack of data. Even a teacher who works in isolation can easily establish the mean, mode, median, standard deviation, and percentage of students who demonstrated proficiency every time he or she administers a test. However, data will become a catalyst for an improved teacher practices only if the teacher has a basis of comparison.

When teacher teams develop common formative assessments throughout the school year, each teacher can identify how his or her students performed on each skill compared with other students. Individual teachers can call on their team colleagues to help them reflect on areas of concern. Each teacher has access to the ideas, materials, strategies, and talents of the entire team.

Freeport Intermediate School, located 50 miles south of Houston, Texas, attributes its success to an unrelenting focus on results. Teachers work in collaborative teams for 90 minutes daily to clarify the essential outcomes of their grade levels and courses and to align those outcomes with state standards. They develop consistent instructional calendars and administer the same brief assessment to all students at the same grade level at the conclusion of each instructional unit, roughly once a week.

Each quarter, the teams administer a common cumulative exam. Each spring, the teams develop and administer practice tests for the state exam. Each year, the teams pore over the results of the state test, which are broken down to show every teacher how his or her students performed on every skill and on every test item. The teachers share their results from all of these assessments with their colleagues, and they quickly learn when a teammate has been particularly effective in teaching a certain skill. Team members consciously look for successful practice and attempt to replicate it in their own practice; they also identify areas of the curriculum that need more attention.

Freeport Intermediate has been transformed from one of the lowest-performing schools in the state to a national model for academic achievement. Principal Clara Sale-Davis believes that the crucial first step in that transformation came when the staff began to honestly confront data on student achievement and to work together to improve results rather than make excuses for them.

Of course, this focus on continual improvement and results requires educators to change traditional practices and revise prevalent assumptions. Educators must begin to embrace data as a useful indicator of progress. They must stop disregarding or excusing unfavorable data and honestly confront the sometimes-brutal facts. They must stop using averages to analyze student performance and begin to focus on the success of each student.

Educators who focus on results must also stop limiting improvement goals to factors outside the classroom, such as student discipline and staff morale, and shift their attention to goals that focus on student learning. They must stop assessing their own effectiveness on the basis of how busy they are or how many new initiatives they have launched and begin instead to ask, "Have we made progress on the goals that are most important to us?" Educators must stop working in isolation and hoarding their ideas, materials, and strategies and begin to work together to meet the needs of all students.

思考问题

1. The case is from the local schools in the U. S. After reading the case, could you please share some key points with your classmates to show your understanding of PLC?

2. The case described the problems in Adlai Stevenson High School and the strategies the teachers adopted from PLC. What enlightenments have you learned? Please illustrate from the PLC's point of view.

3. The second part of "Big Idea" is about focusing on students' learning result. What kind of method did the teacher teams develop? How did they achieve the result?

Case Two

我国的中小学教研组制度设立于新中国成立之初,作为学校基本教学研究组织,与学校发展同步,颇具中国特色。在70多年的教育教学历程中为学校教学活动的正常运转、提升教育教学质量、教师发展以及教学改革做出了重要贡献,现阶段仍然发挥着她的作用。

我国中小学教研组制度存在以下实践优势:(1) 形成了比较完善的教师集体备课制度;(2) 有助于新任教师尽快提升教育教学能力;(3) 教研组活动成为教师专业发展的重要途径(单志艳,2014)。然而,随着社会的发展,教研组制度也面临挑战,比如在其组织结构设置上容易导致一言堂的现象,教研组负责人、高年资教师容易形成领导角色掌控整个教研活动;在集体讨论和备课过程中容易形成教师被动参与;重视教学而不重视科研等问题。这似乎与学习共同体的设计理念相悖,同时也不利于教师的创新理念的形成与教师职业的进一步发展。如何更好地发挥教研组的作用,使其承担起教师共同体的重担,惠及教师、学生、家长甚至所在社区,共同促进所在区域基础教育的发展,是值得考虑的问题。

有学者研究指出,首先,要建立平等、互助、合作的教师文化,实现教师自主合作,互相促进,平等对话的氛围,使教研活动真正凸显包容、互助的主题;其次,教研组活动可以是教师个性化的体现,根据各自所教授的不同学科、教学经验等制定共同体的目标,分享各自的教学成果,促进教学及研究的发展;最后,组织运作机制是另外需要考虑的问题,应该多反思现有教研组运行的弊端,改进组织管理形式,使其更加适应新时期教育教学改革的发展。

思考问题

1. 该案例列举了我国教研组制度的实践优势,你认为这是不是一种有中国特色的学习共同体?请列举教研组制度的一些特征并进行分析。

2. 从学习共同体的概念出发,你认为我国现有的中小学教研组制度有哪些不足之处?如何改进使之成为有中国特色的教师专业学习共同体?

✦ 亮考帮

亮闪闪:请总结学习过程中,哪些是自己记忆深刻、受益最大、最欣赏的内容呢?请写出具体内容。

考考你:请把自己弄懂的但觉得别人可能存在困惑的地方,用问题的形式表述出来,来挑战一下其他同学。

帮帮我:请把自己不懂、不会的地方或想要了解的内容,用问题的形式表述出来,并带到课堂上加以讨论。

✦ 参考文献

[1] DuFour, R. What is a "Professional Learning Community"? [J]. *Educational Leadership*, 2004 (05): 6-11.

[2] Stoll, L., Bolam, R., McMahon, A., Wallace, M., & Thomas, S. Professional learning communities: A review of the literature [J]. *Journal of Educational Change*, 2006(07), 4: 221-258.

[3] 曹明. 基于课堂学习共同体的"综合英语"课程个案研究[J]. 大学英语教学与研究, 2019, 4: 33-38.

[4] 单志艳. 走向中国特色教师专业学习共同体的教研组变革[J]. 教研研究, 2014(10): 86-90.

第三章　英语学与教的理论

主要内容

1. 学习的主要心理学理论
   - 行为主义理论
   - 人本主义理论
   - 认知学习理论
   - 建构主义理论
2. 英语教学法主要理论
   - 情景教学法
   - 交际教学法
   - 任务教学法
   - 全身教学法

✓ 案例学习
✓ 专业参考
✓ 学术探讨

In this section, we first look at how human beings study by exploring the major psychological theories of learning. We dissect the topic through Behaviorism, Cognitive Learning Theory, Humanism, and Constructivism. It is essential to understand the knowledge of psychology in order to be a qualified primary school or middle school English teacher. The second part of this section introduces practical and effective English teaching methods, including Total Physical Response (TPR), Situational Teaching Method (STM), Task-based Teaching Method and Communicative Teaching Method. Based on these we analyze English teaching strategies, and then provide a systematic guide.

Task 1 Major Psychological Theories of Learning

Since no one could be a good teacher without learning psychology and pedagogy, in order to know how students study, we offer you some portable knowledge of learning psychology.

1.1 Knowledge Points

> Outline

The following points are about the fundamental knowledge of behaviorism, cognitive learning theory, humanism and constructivism.

1.1.1 Behaviorism

Behaviourism focuses on observable behaviour as a means to study the human psyche. The primary tenet of behaviourism is that psychology should concern itself with the observable behaviour of people and animals, not with unobservable events that take place in their minds.

(1) Classical conditioning

The main influences of behaviourist psychology were Ivan Pavlov (1849—1936), who investigated classical conditioning though often disagreeing with behaviourism or behaviourists.

(2) Reinforcement

Edward Lee Thorndike (1874—1949), who introduced the concept of reinforcement and was the first to apply psychological principles to learning.

(3) John B. Watson (1878—1958), who rejected introspective methods and sought to restrict psychology to experimental methods.

(4) Operant conditioning

B. F. Skinner (1904—1990), who conducted research on operant conditioning.

1.1.2 Cognitive learning theory

Cognitive learning theory is based on the research of cognitive psychology. Cognitive psychology is the study of mental processes such as attention, memory, perception, language use, problem-solving, creativity, and thinking. Much of the work derived from cognitive psychology has been integrated into various other modern disciplines of psychological study including social psychology, personality psychology, abnormal psychology, developmental psychology, educational psychology, and economics.

1.1.3 Humanism

Humanistic approaches emphasize the importance of the inner world of the learner and place the individual's thoughts, feelings and emotions at the forefront of all human development. These are aspects of the learning process that are often unjustly neglected, yet they are vitally important if we are to understand human learning in its totality.

When we study humanistic approach, we inevitably would like to introduce two main figures Carl Rogers (1902—1987) and Abraham Maslow (1908—1970) into our view, and know some key terms, such as client-centred, and hierarchy of needs. During the 1950s and 1960s, Carl Rogers, for instance, introduced what he called person or client-centred therapy, which relies on clients' capacity for self-direction, empathy, and acceptance to promote clients' development. Maslow developed a hierarchy of motivation or hierarchy of needs culminating in self-actualization.

1.1.4 Constructivism

Constructivism is a perspective on learning focused on how students actively create (or "construct") knowledge out of experiences. Constructivist models of learning differ about how much a learner constructs knowledge independently, compared to how much he or she takes cues from people who may be more of an expert and who help the learner's efforts (Fosnot, 2005; Rockmore, 2005). For convenience, these are called psychological constructivism and social constructivism, even though both are in a sense explanations about thinking within individuals.

We should also know the famous figures like John Dewey (1938—1998); Jean Piaget and his key points of assimilation, accommodation, equilibration, and schema; Lev Vygotsky (1978) and his key points of zone of proximal development (ZPD) and his social cultural perspective.

Reading Materials

Reading Material One

Behaviourist Psychology

(1) Classical conditioning

Ivan Pavlov (1849—1936) is a Russian physiologist. In his research with the dogs, Pavlov began pairing a bell sound with the meat powder and found that even when the meat powder was not presented, a dog would eventually begin to salivate after hearing the bell. In this case, since the meat powder naturally results in salivation, these two variables are called the *unconditioned stimulus* (UCS) and the *unconditioned response* (UCR), respectively. In the experiment, the bell and salivation are *not* naturally occurring; the dog is conditioned to respond to the bell. Therefore, the bell is considered the *conditioned stimulus* (CS), and the salivation to the bell, the *conditioned response* (CR). (Figure 3 - 1)

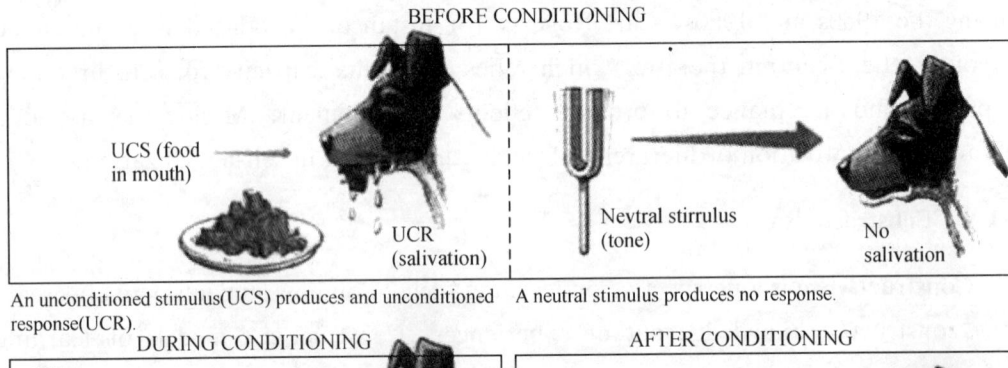
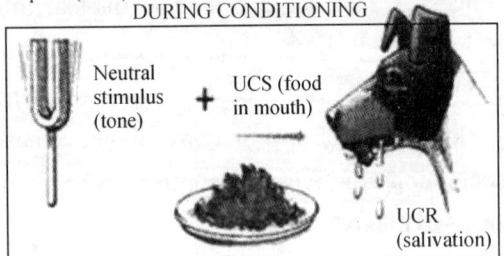
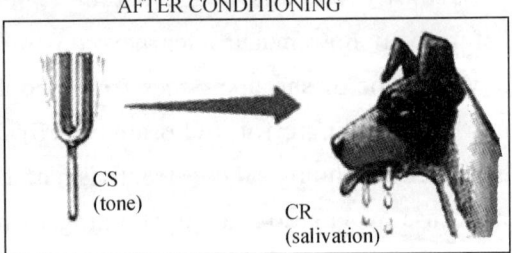

Figure 3 - 1   Classical conditioning

Many of our behaviours today are shaped by the pairing of stimuli. The smell of a cologne, the sound of a certain song, or the occurrence of a specific day of the year can trigger distinct memories, emotions, and associations. When we make these types of associations, we are experiencing classical conditioning.

(2) Reinforcement

It was Edward Lee Thorndike (1874—1949) who introduced the concept of reinforcement, means to strengthen, and is used in psychology to refer to any stimulus which strengthens or increases the probability of a specific response. For example, if you want your dog to sit on command, you may give him a treat every time he sits for you. The dog will eventually come to understand that sitting when told to will result in a treat. This treat is reinforcing the behaviour because the dog likes it and will result in him sitting when instructed to do so. There are four types of reinforcement: positive, negative, punishment, and extinction.

• **Positive reinforcement** involves adding something in order to increase a response. For example, adding a treat will increase the response of sitting; adding praise will increase the chances of your child cleaning his or her room. The most common types of positive reinforcement are praise and reward, and most of us have experienced this as both the giver and receiver.

• **Negative reinforcement** involves taking something negative away in order to increase a response. Imagine a teenager who is nagged by his parents to take out the garbage week after week. After complaining to his friends about the nagging, he finally one day performs the task and, to his amazement, the nagging stops. The elimination of this negative stimulus is reinforcing and will likely increase the chances that he will take out the garbage next week.

• **Punishment** refers to adding something aversive in order to decrease a behaviour. The most common example of this is disciplining (e. g., spanking) a child for misbehaving. The child begins to associate being punished with the negative behaviour. The child does not like the punishment and, therefore, to avoid it, he or she will stop behaving in that manner.

• **Extinction** involves removing something in order to decrease a behaviour. By having something taken away, a response is decreased.

Research has found positive reinforcement is the most powerful of any of these types of operant conditioning responses. Adding a positive to increase a response not only works better, but allows both parties to focus on the positive aspects of the situation. Punishment, when applied immediately following the negative behaviour, can be effective, but results in extinction when it is not applied consistently. Punishment can also invoke other negative responses such as anger and resentment.

Thorndike's (1898) work with cats and puzzle boxes illustrates the concept of conditioning. The puzzle boxes were approximately 50 cm long, 38 cm wide, and 30 cm tall (Figure 3-2). Thorndike's puzzle boxes were built so that the cat, placed inside the box, could escape only if it pressed a bar or pulled a lever, which caused the string attached to the door to lift the weight and open the door. Thorndike measured the time it took the cat to perform the required response (e. g., pulling the lever). Once it had learned the response he gave the cat a reward, usually food.

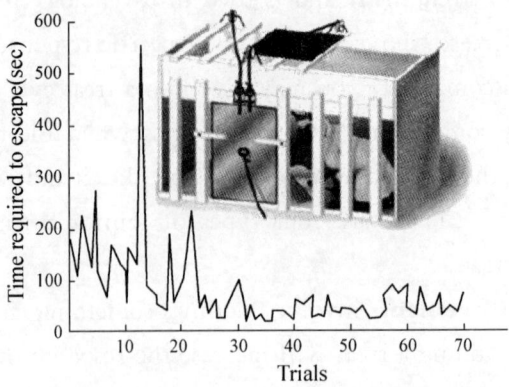

Figure 3 - 2　Thorndike's puzzle box

Thorndike found that once a cat accidentally stepped on the switch, it would then press the switch faster in each succeeding trial inside the puzzle box. By observing and recording how long it took a variety of animals to escape through several trials, Thorndike was able to graph the learning curve (graphed as an S-shape). He observed that most animals had difficulty escaping at first, then began to escape faster and faster with each successive puzzle box trial, and eventually leveled off in their escape times. The learning curve also suggested that different species learned in the same way but at different speeds. His finding was that cats, for instance, consistently showed gradual learning.

From his research with puzzle boxes, Thorndike was able to create his own theory of learning. It listed 16 points. The main points of learning includes:

Law of effect. If an association is followed by satisfaction, it will be strengthened, and if it is followed by annoyance, it will be weakened.

Law of use. The more often an association is used, the stronger it becomes.

Law of readiness. A quality in responses and connections that results in readiness to act.

...

(3) About John B. Watson and his research

John B. Watson promoted a change in psychology through his address, Psychology as the Behaviourist Views It (1913), delivered at Columbia University. Through his behaviourist approach, Watson research on animal behaviour, child rearing, and advertising while gaining notoriety for the controversial "Little Albert" experiment. Immortalized in introductory psychology textbooks, this experiment set out to show how the recently discovered principles of classical conditioning could be applied to condition fear of a white rat into Little Albert, an 11-month-old boy. Watson and Rayner (1920) first presented to the boy a white rat and observed that the boy was not afraid. Next they presented him with a white rat and then clanged an iron rod. Little Albert responded by crying. This second presentation was repeated several times. Finally, Watson and Rayner presented the white rat by itself and the boy showed fear. Later, in an attempt to see if the fear transferred to other objects, Watson presented Little Albert with a rabbit, a dog, and a fur coat. He cried at the sight of all of them. This study demonstrated how emotions could become conditioned responses.

(4) Operant conditioning

Operant conditioning is another type of learning that refers to how an organism operates on the environment or how it responds to what is presented to it in the environment.

While a researcher at Harvard, Skinner invented the operant conditioning chamber, popularly referred to as the **Skinner box** (Figure 3-3), used to measure responses of organisms (most often rats and pigeons) and their orderly interactions with the environment. The box had a lever and a food tray, and a hungry rat inside the box could get food delivered to the tray by pressing the lever. Skinner observed that when a rat was first put into the box, it would wander around, sniffing and exploring, and would usually press the bar by accident, at which point a food pellet would drop into the tray. After that happened, the rate of bar pressing would increase dramatically and remain high until the rat was no longer hungry.

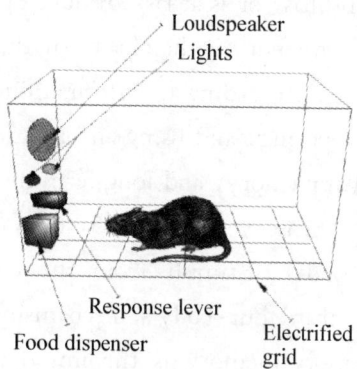

Figure 3-3 Skinner box

(Adapted from Stangor, 2014)

Here are some comparison to make clear of the concepts.

Table 3-1 Reinforcement, punishment and extinction
（强化、惩罚和消退）（李峰等，2017）

	条件	行为发生频率	例子
正强化	呈现愉快刺激	增加	如某种奖励、奖品等
负强化	撤销厌恶刺激	增加	如撤销处分等
惩罚	呈现厌恶刺激	减少	如谴责等
消退	无任何强化物	减少	如不予理睬等

Table 3-2 Difference between reinforcement and punishment
（强化和惩罚的区别）（李峰等，2017）

	行为被增强	行为被减弱
呈现刺激	正强化（呈现愉快刺激，如给予表扬）	呈现性惩罚或称施予性惩罚（呈现厌恶刺激，如关禁闭或者体罚）
消除刺激	负强化（消除厌恶刺激，如免做家务）	取消性惩罚或称剥夺性惩罚（消除愉快刺激，如禁吃KFC或者不给看电视）

Reading Material Two

Cognitive Views of Memory

Cognitive psychologists began exploring the cognitive processes involved with language in the 1870s when Carl Wernicke (1848—1905) proposed a model for the mental processing of language (1875/1995). Significant work has been done recently on understanding the timing of language acquisition and how it can be used to determine if a child has, or is at risk of developing, a learning disability.

Memory is the ability of the brain to store, retain, and subsequently recall information. According to information processing views, the human mind's activity of taking in, storing, and using information by using sensory memory, working memory, short-term memory, and long-term memory.

Sensory memory: System that holds sensory information very briefly (0.25—1 seconds). Stimuli from the environment (sights, sounds, smells, etc.) constantly bombard our body's mechanisms for seeing, hearing, tasting, smelling, and feeling. Sensory memory is the initial processing that transforms these incoming stimuli into information so we can make sense of them. Sensory memory is very large, and it can take in more information than we can possibly handle at once. But this vast amount of sensory information is fragile in duration. It lasts less than three seconds.

Working memory: The information that you are focusing on at a given moment. It is the "workbench" of the memory system, the interface where new information is held temporarily and combined with knowledge from long-term memory to solve problems or comprehend a lecture, for example. It "contains" what you are thinking about at the moment. For this reason, some psychologists consider the working memory to be synonymous with "consciousness". The capacity is very limited.

Short-term memory: Component of memory system that holds information for about 20 seconds. It is not exactly the same as working memory. Working memory includes both temporary storage and active processing—the workbench of memory—where active mental effort is applied to both new and old information. But short-term memory usually means just storage, the immediate memory for new information that can be held about 15 to 20 seconds.

Long-term memory: Permanent store of knowledge (several days, several years or even life long). The capacity of long-term memory appears to be, for all practical proposes, unlimited. Once stored, it can remain there permanently. Gaining access to information in long-term memory requires time and effort. Recently some psychologists have suggested that working memory is the part of long-term memory that works on currently activated information (Figure 3-4).

The difference between working memory and long-term memory just may be in how activated or inactive a particular memory is. This model sees memory as a set of nested systems with very short-term storage [phonological loop(语言回路), visuospatial sketchpad(视觉空间模板), other brief holding areas] nested in working memory. Which is just the active part of long-term memory that does the integrating old and new information.

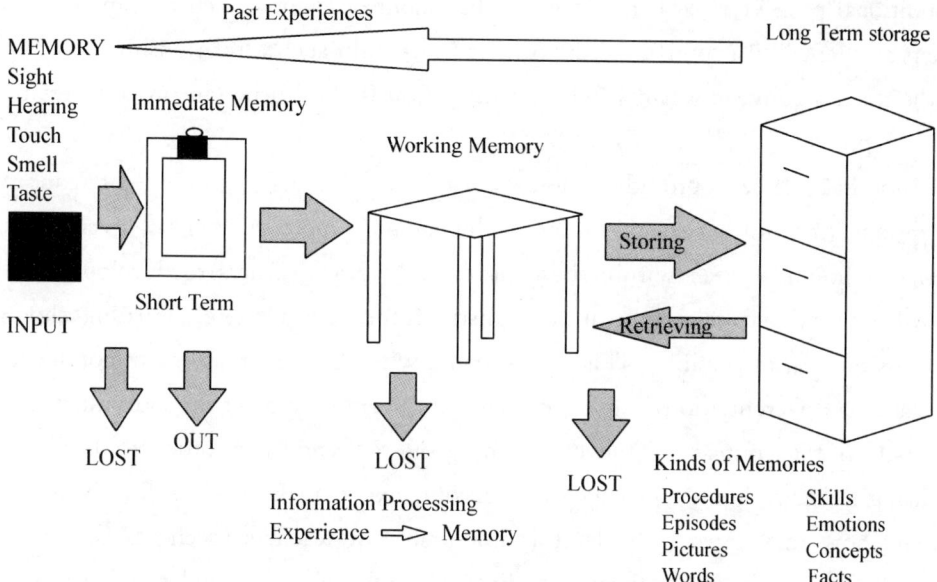

Figure 3-4 A model for processing data from environment

(Sternberg & Sternberg, 2012)

Reading Material Three

Humanistic psychology holds a hopeful, constructive view of human beings and of their substantial capacity to be self-determining. This wave of psychology is guided by a conviction that intentionality and ethical values are the key psychological forces determining human behaviour. Humanistic psychologists strive to enhance the human qualities of choice, creativity, the interaction of the body, mind, and spirit, and the capacity to become more aware, free, responsible, life-affirming, and trustworthy.

Rogers (1969) identified a number of key approaches to education. Beginning with the premise that human beings have a natural potential for learning, he suggested that significant learning will only take place when the subject matter is perceived to be of personal relevance to the learner and when it involves active participation by the learner, i.e. experiential learning. Learning which is self-initiated and which involves feelings as well as cognition is most likely to be lasting and pervasive.

Moreover, when there is a perceived threat to the learner's self-image, resistance to learning is likely to occur. Independence, creativity and self-reliance are most likely to flourish in learning situations where external criticism is kept to a minimum and where self-evaluation is encouraged. The most socially useful kind of learning to prepare learners to cope with the demands of the modern world is learning about the process of learning itself, a continuing openness to experience and a preparedness to become involved in the process of change.

Rogers suggests that this kind of learning best takes place in an atmosphere of unconditional positive regard. This can best be established when teachers come to see their learners as clients with specific needs to be met. Within such a relationship it is essential that the teacher conveys warm hand empathy towards the learner in order to establish a relationship of trust.

Hamachek (1977) provides some useful examples of the kind of educational implications that follow from taking a humanistic approach. First, every learning experience should be seen within the context of helping learners to develop a sense of personal identity and relating that to realistic future goals, i. e. learning should be personalised as far as possible. This is in keeping with the view that one important task to the teacher is differentiation, i. e. identifying and seeking to meet the individual learner's needs within the context of the classroom group. Second, in order to become self-actualising learners should be helped and encouraged to make choices for themselves in what and how they learn. Third, it is important for teachers to empathise with their learners by getting to know them as individuals and seeking to understand the ways in which they make sense of the world, rather than always seeking to impose their own view points.

Humanistic approaches have had a considerable influence on English language teaching (ELT) methodology. A number of different language teaching methodologies have arisen from taking a humanistic approach. The main ones being the silent way, suggest opaedia, and community language learning. These three methodologies have a number of things in common. First, they are based more firmly on psychology than on linguistic. Second, they all consider affective aspects of learning and language as important. Third, they are all concerned with treating the learner as a whole person, and with whole person involvement in the learning process. Fourth, they see the importance of a learning environment which minimises anxiety and enhances personal security.

However, rather than seeing what humanism has to offer to ELT as one or other of these "fringe" methods, we see the value of humanism in language learning as informing and enhancing the teacher's practices in a variety of ways, no matter what methodology the teacher is following.

To summarise the points made so far, humanism has a number of messages for the language teacher:

- creating a sense of belonging;

- making the subject relevant to the learner;
- involving the whole person;
- encouraging a knowledge of self;
- developing personal identity;
- encouraging self-esteem;
- involving the feelings and emotions;
- minimizing criticism;
- encouraging creativity;
- developing a knowledge of the process of learning;
- encouraging self-initiation;
- allowing for choice;
- encouraging self-evaluation.

(William, 2000)

Reading Material Four

Behaviorist models of learning may be helpful in understanding and influencing what students do, but teachers usually also want to know what students are *thinking*, and how to enrich what students are thinking. For this goal of teaching, some of the best help comes from constructivism, which is a perspective on learning focused on how students actively create (or "construct") knowledge out of experiences. There are two aspects as follows.

1. Psychological constructivism: the independent investigator

The main idea of psychological constructivism is that a person learns by mentally organizing and reorganizing new information or experiences. The organization happens partly by relating new experiences to prior knowledge that is already meaningful and well understood. Stated in this general form, individual constructivism is sometimes associated with a well-known educational philosopher of the early twentieth century, **John Dewey** (1938—1998). Although Dewey himself did not use the term constructivism in most of his writing, his point of view amounted to a type of constructivism, and he discussed in detail its implications for educators. He argued, for example, that if students indeed learn primarily by building their own knowledge, then teachers should adjust the curriculum to fit students' prior knowledge and interests as fully as possible. He also argued that a curriculum could only be justified if it related as fully as possible to the activities and responsibilities that students will probably have *later*, after leaving school. To many educators these days, his ideas may seem merely like good common sense, but they were indeed innovative and progressive at the beginning of the twentieth century.

A more recent example of psychological constructivism is the cognitive theory of

Jean Piaget (Piaget, 2001; Gruber & Vonechc, 1995). Piaget described learning as interplay between two mental activities that he called *assimilation* and *accommodation*. **Assimilation** is the interpretation of new information in terms of pre-existing concepts, information or ideas. A preschool child who already understands the concept of *bird*, for example, might initially label any flying object with this term—even butterflies or mosquitoes. Assimilation is therefore a bit like the idea of *generalization* in operant conditioning, or the idea of *transfer* described at the beginning of this chapter. In Piaget's viewpoint, though, what is being transferred to a new setting is not simply a behavior (Skinner's "operant" in operant conditioning), but a mental representation for an object or experience.

Assimilation operates jointly with **accommodation**, which is the revision or modification of pre-existing in terms of new information or experience. The preschooler who initially generalizes the concept of *bird* to include any flying object, for example, eventually revises the concept to include only particular kinds of flying, such as robins and sparrows, and not others, like mosquitoes or airplanes. For Piaget, assimilation and accommodation work together to enrich a child's thinking and to create what Piaget called **cognitive equilibrium**, which is a balance between reliance on prior information and openness to new information. At any given time, cognitive equilibrium consists of an ever-growing repertoire of mental representations for objects and experiences. Piaget called each mental representation a **schema** (all of them together—the plural—was called **schemata**). A schema was not merely a concept, but an elaborated mixture of vocabulary, actions, and experience related to the concept. A child's schema for *bird*, for example, includes not only the relevant verbal knowledge (like knowing how to define the word "bird"), but also the child's experiences with birds, pictures of birds, and conversations about birds. As assimilation and accommodation about birds and other flying objects operate together over time, the child does not just revise and add to his vocabulary (such as acquiring a new word, "butterfly"), but also adds and remembers relevant new experiences and actions. From these collective revisions and additions the child gradually constructs whole new schemata about birds, butterflies, and other flying objects. In more everyday (but also less precise) terms, Piaget might then say that "the child has learned more about birds".

Table 3-3 Piaget's stage of cognitive development (Woolfolk, 2014)

Stage	Approximate age	Characteristics
Sensorimotor	0—2 years	Learns through reflexes, senses, and movement-actions on the environment. Begins to imitate others and remember events. Shifts to symbolic thinking. Comes to understand that objects do not cease to exist when they are out of sight-object permanence. Moves from reflexive actions to intentional activity.

(to be continued)

Stage	Approximate age	Characteristics
Preoperational	Begins about the time the child starts talking, to about 7 yrs.	Develops language and begins to use symbols to represent objects. Has difficulty with past and future—thinks in the present. Can think through operations logically in one direction. Has difficulties understanding the point of view of another persons.
Concrete operational	Begins about first grade, to early adolescence, around 11 yrs.	Can think logically about concrete (hands-on) problems. Understands conservation and organizes things into categories and in series. Can reverse thinking to mentally "undo" actions. Understands past, present, and future.
Formal operational	Adolescence to adulthood	Can think hypothetically and deductively. Thinking becomes more scientific. Solves abstract problems in logical fashion. Can consider multiple perspectives and develops concerns about social issues, personal identity, and justice.

2. Social constructivism: assisted performance

Unlike Piaget's rather individually oriented version of constructivism, some psychologists and educators have explicitly focused on the relationships and interactions between a learner and more knowledgeable and experienced individuals. One early expression of this viewpoint came from the American psychologist **Jerome Bruner** (1960; 1966; 1996), who became convinced that students could usually learn more than had been traditionally expected as long as they were given appropriate guidance and resources. He called such support **instructional scaffolding**—literally meaning a temporary framework, like one used in constructing a building, that allows a much stronger structure to be built within it. In a comment that has been quoted widely (and sometimes disputed), he wrote: "We [constructivist educators] begin with the hypothesis that any subject can be taught effectively in some intellectually honest form to any child at any stage of development." (1960, p. 33). The reason for such a bold assertion was Bruner's belief in scaffolding—his belief in the importance of providing guidance in the right way and at the right time. When scaffolding is provided, students seem more competent and "intelligent," and they learn more.

Similar ideas were proposed independently by the Russian psychologist **Lev Vygotsky** (1978), whose writing focused on how a child's or novice's thinking is influenced by relationships with others who are more capable, knowledgeable, or expert than the learner. Vygotsky proposed that when a child (or any novice) is learning a new skill or solving a new problem, he or she can perform better if accompanied and helped by an expert than if performing alone—though still not as well as the expert. Someone who has played very little chess, for example, will probably compete against an opponent better if helped by an expert chess player than if competing alone against an opponent.

Vygotsky called the difference between solo performance and assisted performance the zone of proximal development (or ZPD for short)—meaning the place or area (figuratively speaking) of immediate change. From this perspective learning is like assisted performance (Tharp & Gallimore, 1991). Initially during learning, knowledge or skill is found mostly "in" the expert helper. If the expert is skilled and motivated to help, then the expert arranges experiences that allow the novice to practice crucial skills or to construct new knowledge. In this regard the expert is a bit like the coach of an athlete—offering help and suggesting ways of practicing, but never doing the actual athletic work himself or herself. Gradually, by providing continued experiences matched to the novice learner's emerging competencies, the expert-coach makes it possible for the novice or apprentice to appropriate (or make his or her own) the skills or knowledge that originally resided only with the expert. These relationships are diagrammed in the lower part of Exhibit 5.

(Adapted from Seifert, 2009)

Reading Material Five

学习理论与语言学习

一、行为主义与语言学习

在行为主义心理学看来,语言是人类行为的一个重要组成部分。在操作条件反射理论的基础上,行为主义心理学代表人物 Skinner 提出了著名的言语行为理论。在《言语行为》(1957)一书中,Skinner 指出,有效的语言行为是对刺激物做出的正确反应。当某一反应被强化时,它便保持下来,成为一种习惯。同样,语言学习也是一种习惯,是经过模仿、积极强化和不断重复而形成的。在语言学习过程中,外部影响是内因发生变化的主要因素,语言行为和语言习惯受外部语言刺激的影响而发生变化。

20世纪五六十年代的语言学习和语言教学深受行为主义学习理论的影响,反映在外语教学上就是使用听说法、视听法和采用以句型操练为主的教学模式,目的是让语言学习者对目的语进行大量的重复和操练,达到"刺激—反应"的效果,最终帮助他们形成语言习惯,塑造言语行为。反复操练一直被看作语言学习的一个重要的、有效的手段,尤其在外语学习初级阶段被广泛地应用。

迁移(transfer)、干扰(interference)和过度概括判断(overgeneralization)是影响外语学习的几个重要因素。迁移指将学会了的行为从一种情境转移至另一种情境。迁移包括正迁移(positive transfer)和负迁移(negative transfer,也叫干扰)。正迁移指在一种情境中学会了的东西有助于在另一种情境中进行学习,负迁移则指在一种情境中学的东西干扰在另一种情境中进行的学习。

行为主义学习理论认为,当母语习惯有助于习得第二语言习惯时,即当母语与目的语有相同的形式时,正迁移就发生了。当一个母语是英语的人学习法语的主—动—宾句型

"这只狗吃肉"时,英语句型(The dog eats the meat)可以直接迁移到法语句子上(Le chien mange la viande)。但如果我们将宾语"肉"改成代词"它"时,迁移就不可能发生。尽管英语句型依然不变(The dog eats it),但在法语句型中,要将宾语提至动词前(Le chien la mange)。当学习者生搬硬套母语的模式或规则而产生不符合目的语规则的用法时,负迁移或干扰就发生了。

干扰在第二语言学习过程中经常发生,要消除干扰,必须克服母语的影响、克服母语与第二语言之间的差异所带来的影响。受行为主义心理学影响,结构主义语言学家提出了著名的"对比分析假设"(The Contrasive Analysis Hypothesis),假设学习一门新的语言的主要困难来自第一语言的干扰,认为通过对母语和第二语言的语音、词汇和语法系统进行分析与比较,可以预测学习者在第二语言学习过程中可能遇到的难点和可能出现的错误,为课程设置、教材编写、有效地组织课堂教学提供理论依据,以便教师预先帮助学习者克服干扰,形成正确的语言习惯。然而,外语研究和外语教学实践证明,母语和第二语言项目并非一一对应,目前还没有一个成熟的、实用的语言学工具能让语言学家对母语和第二语言中的语言项目进行逐个对比。其次,"对比分析假设"并不能准确预测错误出现的地方,何时何地出现错误有一定的必然性,但很大程度上具有偶然性。再者,母语和第二语言项目之间的差异(difference)只是语言形式的不同,并不能代表心理学意义上的难度(difficulty)。

概括判断(generalization)是人类学习的一个重要策略,指所有学习共有的一个过程,包括通过对具体样例的观察形成一般规则或原理。例如,当学习者见到英语单词 book—books 和 dog—dogs,就可能会作出概括判断,英语的复数概念通过在可数名词词尾添加 s 形成。但过度概括判断是学习者将语言项目的语法规则的运用推到不应有的范围,通常的做法是将不规则的词或结构规则化。例如,用 mans 代替 man 的复数 men,用 goed,breaked 代替 go,break 的过去式 went,broke 等。过度概括判断是第二语言学习中常有的现象。

Skinner 的语言观和语言学习观对外语学习和教学产生了深远的影响,模仿、练习和强化等手段在外语学习和教学中得到了广泛的应用。然而,人们逐渐发现,Skinner 的言语行为理论无法解释人类习得语言的潜能、语言的发展、语言的抽象性、语义等问题,因此,对行为主义的学习理论产生了质疑,尤其是 Skinner 的言语行为理论受到来自美国著名语言学家 Chomsky 的批评。人们开始寻求其他的理论和途径来解释言语行为。

二、认知流派与语言学习

认知心理学流派取代了行为主义,对语言学习作出了新的解释。认知是心理过程的一部分,是信息加工过程中的最高阶段。认知活动最本质的特点是利用知识来指导人们当前的行为,它涉及信息的获取和表征并转换为知识、知识的记忆(存贮和提取)、运用知识进行推理等心理活动。认知流派认为,语言学习是人类认识世界的部分,因此,应将它放在整个人脑认识事物的框架中加以考察和分析。

以 Piaget 为代表的认知流派认为,认知发展是语言发展的基础,语言发展是认知发展的一个有机组成部分,语言能力是个体认知能力的一个方面,是主体与客体相互作用的产物。语言是伴随着认知发展而发展的,认知结构发展到一定阶段,才出现语言。语言发展受制于认知发展,例如,当一个儿童掌握了大小、比较的概念之后,才有可能说出以下句子:This car is bigger than that one。同时,语言的产生对认知能力的发展起很大的促进作用。一方面,有了语言,人们可以交流思想、信息;另一方面,语言能帮助人们更好地思考和认知新事物。可见,语言既是一种认知活动,又是以认知为基础的。

Piaget 认为儿童的认知发展经历了几个不同的阶段,这几个发展阶段分别是:感觉运动阶段、前运算阶段、具体运算阶段和形式运算阶段。每一个发展阶段均有一个独特的、基础的认知结构,所有儿童都遵循这样的发展顺序。语言在感觉运动阶段的最后几个月才出现,儿童将获得许多复合功能,如象征性游戏、初期绘画等。同时,语言功能也是一种符号功能,是儿童获得的许多符号功能中的一种特殊功能。前运算阶段的儿童处于自我中心语言阶段,缺乏倾听能力,没有信息和意念的交流,随后发展到能用语言进行社会交流。在具体运算阶段,儿童逐渐具有语言理解能力,能够理解、解决具体问题。在形式运算阶段,青少年的语言表达超越了具体事物。除了表达现实性以外,还具有表达可能性的语言能力。

Vygotsky 则认为儿童的语言发展在认知发展中起关键作用,语言的发展带动认知的发展。他相信,拥有高度语言发展的人,可以完成那些文盲所不能完成的复杂任务,这是因为人们在学习语言时,不仅在学习词语,同时还在学习与这些词语相连的思想。因此,语言是儿童用以认识与理解世界的一种中介工具,即一种思维工具。

语言作为儿童与他人进行社会交往的工具,具有交际功能。成年人以及同伴在儿童文化传递过程中起着重要作用。成年人通常进行解释,给予指导,提供反馈并引导交流。而同伴则在游戏与课堂情境中,通过对话来促进儿童之间的合作。儿童可以通过与更有能力的人一起进行有意义的活动来学习,通过活动进行对话,个体之间交流思想,并得以发展。

语言在儿童智力行为的形成中起着指导和调节的作用,语言的发展是在社会文化历史环境中实现的。Vygotsky 认为"自言自语式"的外在言语是个人言语内化的先兆,是内部言语的开端。个人言语是引导个体思维与行为的自我谈话,在自我调控的发展中起重要作用。随着儿童的成熟,这种喃喃自语逐渐发展为耳语、口唇动作、内部言语和思维,从而完成内化过程。具体的发展顺序为:外在社会言语→个体的外部言语→自我中心言语→内部言语。

认知心理学主张语言是受规则支配的创造性活动,语言学习是掌握规则、构建意义,而不是形成习惯。语言学习是一个认知过程,涉及词汇的提取、语法规则的选择等步骤,要求学习者对所学语言结构提出假设,做出判断,并根据新的语言输入证明假设的正确与否。语言学习是在对目的语不断进行预测,提出假设、验证、纠错过程中进行的。在学习的每一个阶段,学习者所掌握的是既不同于他的母语,又不同于目的语的中介语。在学习者取得进步之后,他的中介语就会距离目的语更近一步。在学习过程中,出现错误是难免的,错误往往解释了外语学习过程的本质,错误分析为有效地进行外语教学提供了一定的依据。

认知心理学强调有意义的学习,强调要在理解语言知识和规则的基础上操练外语,从而获得语言能力,主张在第二语言教学中发挥学习者的智力作用,通过有意识地学习语音、词汇、语法知识,理解、发现、掌握语言规则,并能从听、说、读、写等方面全面地、创造性地运用语言。

三、人本主义、建构主义与语言学习

以 Rogers 为代表的人本主义心理学家和教育学家提出学生中心论的教育思想,认为在教育过程中,教师一方面要突出情感的地位和作用,解决情感问题,统一学生的认知与情感,形成一种以情感作为教学活动的基本动力的新的教学模式。另一方面,现实世界千变万化,教师只有帮助学生掌握学习方法,学会学习,增强学习者主体意识和自主学习能力,促进学习者身心健康成长,学生在未来才有可能积极地适应不断变化的现实世界。简言之,人是教育的中心,也是教育的目的,教学必须服务于完整的人的发展,这是人本主义教育理论的核心。完整的人的发展主要包括认知、情感、态度和技能的和谐发展。

认知和情感是人的全面发展不可或缺的两个方面,在语言学习过程中二者也是相辅相成的。语言学习主要通过认知过程来实现,但解决情感问题有助于提高语言学习效果。消极情感如焦虑、害怕、羞涩等都影响学习潜力的正常发挥,积极情感如自尊、自信、动机等能创造有利于学习的心理状态。语言学家克拉申(Krashen,1982,引自 Ellis,1994)的"情感过滤"假说说明了语言学习者的动机、自信心以及焦虑程度等情感因素与语言学习的关系。克拉申指出:如果学习者动机水平高、自信心强、焦虑程度低,即他们的情感过滤程度低,那么他们的语言输入量就大,并且输入效果好。相反,缺乏动机、自信心弱、焦虑程度高的语言学习者的情感过滤程度高,语言输入量小,输入效果差。因此,在学生的情感活动管理方面教师应给予必要的情感支持,帮助学生建立自信心,调动积极情感因素,帮助学生克服消极情感因素的影响。

同时,外语学习过程也是新信息的摄入和组织过程,是知识的建构过程。学习者原有的知识对新知识的吸收会产生一定的影响,为了更有效地吸收新知识,学习者要对原有知识/认知结构进行重组。学习者选择、习得、建构和综合新的语言知识实际上就是一个运用学习策略的过程。这就要求教师在学生的认知活动过程中提供必要的认知支持。认知支持指教师在学生的认知活动管理方面提供适当的帮助,主要包括学习策略训练和拓展学习风格等。

建构主义是认知学习理论的一个重要分支,该理论认为个体在与周围环境相互作用的过程中逐步建构起关于外部世界的认识,从而使自身认知结构得以充实和发展。个体与环境相互作用涉及两个基本过程:同化与顺应。同化是指个体把外界刺激所提供的信息整合到自己原有的认知结构内的过程。顺应是认知结构因外部刺激的影响而发生变化。同化是认知结构数量的扩充,而顺应是认知结构性质的改变。

建构主义提倡的是教师指导下的、以学生为中心的学习。强调学生对知识的主动探索、主动发现和对所学知识意义的主动建构。由于学习是在一定的情境即社会文化背景下,借助其他人的帮助即通过人际间的协作活动而实现的意义建构过程,因此建构主义学习理论认为"情境""协作""会话"和"意义建构"是学习环境中的四大要素或四大属性。

建构主义学习理论认为在外语学习过程中,教师是语言学习的设计者、组织者和指导者;学习者是语言知识的建构者和实践者,学习者主动选择、同化、顺应输入的信息,使新输入的语言材料与已有的信息相互作用,重新建构,形成新的语言结构;学习方式是以合作—互

动为原理而形成的会话和讨论过程;教学过程应由学生的质疑、分析、综合、概括等一系列认知活动组成,目的在于帮助学生掌握外语学习的策略和方法,主动建构当前所学知识的意义。

(节选自张庆宗,2011)

1.2 Skills and Abilities

After studying the major psychological theories of learning, you should have the basics about how students learn. To gain the skills of analysis, develop your critical thinking, and strengthen your problem-solving ability, we arrange the following cases. Let's try to practice.

Cases

Case One

When my son Michael was old enough to talk, and being an eager but naive dad, I decided to bring Michael to my educational psychology class to demonstrate to my students "how children learn". In one task I poured water from a tall drinking glass to a wide glass pie plate, which according to Michael changed the "amount" of water—there was less now than it was in the pie plate. I told him that, on the contrary, the amount of water had stayed the same whether it was in the glass or the pie plate. He looked at me a bit strangely, but complied with my point of view—agreeing at first that, yes, the amount had stayed the same. But by the end of the class session he had reverted to his original position: there was less water, he said, when it was poured into the pie plate compared with being poured into the drinking glass. So much for demonstrating "learning"!

(Adapted from Seifert, 2009)

思考问题

1. Why did the author bring his son to his class? What did he do during the class time?

2. Does the case relate to Piaget theory? What enlightenment did you get from the case? Please explain it.

Case Two

人本主义的基本理念认为人人都有学习的潜能,只有当教师所创设的学习环境和所教授的内容能使学习者认识到与自己的生活密切相关,并能使学习者主动参与,学习才会真正发生。小王老师最近发现了一个特别的现象,就是自己执教的初中一年级学生鑫鑫在英语课上总是讲话,不能集中注意力学习,当老师提问到他时他总是表现出不在乎,还故意说笑、做鬼脸,弄得全班同学哄笑,造成课堂秩序混乱。小王老师虽然工作时间不长,但是在大学里学习了英语教学的诸多方法,还有班级管理的策略,但是他尝试不少方法好像都没有多大起色,小王老师陷入了沉思。

回想起自己在大学里老师讲授的各种理论知识和方法,再经过资料查找,"人本主义"的教学理念与方法映入眼帘,小王老师想起来了,在大学中对于"人本主义"的教学理念和方法有过诸多讨论,其中印象最深的是与学生建立信任的关系,对学生有足够的信任并正向评价学生的学习。带着这些想法,小王老师想,这些学生正处于青春期,是人生观价值观形成的关键时期,对人与人之间的关系非常敏感,而鑫鑫同学有些叛逆的表现,一定是教学中没有满足他的需求。于是小王老师对他进行了观察和了解,发现鑫鑫同学其他课程的学习还不错,且擅长绘画,于是她决定改变自己对待学生的方法。

第二周一上课,小王老师就给大家展示了一幅图画,图画中有与英语课文听力相关的教学内容,但是这幅图画并不完整,需要通过听力的描述补充缺失的画面。当小王老师讲明了上课的要求,就开始给大家放录音,小王老师发现,鑫鑫好像有点儿着急,想参加活动,但是又没有勇气。小王老师这时说,这幅画还差一点装饰,如果哪位同学可以装饰一下这幅画,让它变得更好看就更好了,这时鑫鑫举手了,他用不同的颜色勾勒出画的边框,将蓝天和白云加以修饰,整个画面顿时活了起来。小王老师有意表现出惊喜,并立即向全班展示这幅画,赢得了全班同学的掌声,这时,鑫鑫好像有些不好意思了,后半节课一直没有作声。下课后,小王老师收拾完教具回到办公室,发现鑫鑫同学已经站在办公室门口了,他不好意思地对老师说:"王老师,我刚才没有好好听您放录音,能否借我再听一下,下一节课上课还给您?"小王老师毫不犹豫地说:"没问题,不过老师想知道那幅画究竟还能怎样画?"鑫鑫笑笑,拿着碟片一溜烟地跑了。

第二天一大早,鑫鑫带着自己的作品来到办公室,给老师展示了自己听完录音后的画作。小王老师重新批改了他单独画出的画,并给他打了不低的分数。以后的英语课,鑫鑫好像变了,听课认真,想捕捉到老师上课的每个细节。小王老师发现了这个转变,并有意在绘画与英语之间创设相应的游戏或活动,鑫鑫每次都主动参加。小王老师还对他说希望与他合作,提前把本学期后续的听力和口语的训练任务画成作品展示出来,鑫鑫非常开心地领命,每单元都提前听录音,与老师一起画出简单的画作。在学期末,他的英语成绩有了很大的提高,更重要的是,他现在喜欢学习英语了。面对学生的这种转变,小王老师更加坚信,每个孩子都是有学习潜力的,建立信任,将他们纳入学习中来,接纳他们的特点,帮助他们展示自己,才是促进孩子成长的良方。

思考问题

1. 案例中小王老师遇到了什么问题?学生鑫鑫的学习状态期初是怎样的,后来经过了哪些转变?

2. 小王老师用了哪些方法使鑫鑫转变?是什么理论支撑了这些方法,请加以分析。

亮考帮

亮闪闪：请总结学习过程中，哪些是自己记忆深刻、受益最大、最欣赏的内容呢？请写出具体内容。

考考你：请把自己弄懂的但觉得别人可能存在困惑的地方，用问题的形式表述出来，来挑战一下其他同学。

帮帮我：请把自己不懂、不会的地方或想要了解的内容，用问题的形式表述出来，并带到课堂上加以讨论。

参考文献

[1] Memory. Clips for class[EB/OL]. (2016-05-31)[2018-05-12]. Retrieved from：https://clipsforclass.com/memory.html.

[2] Seifert, K., & Sutton, R. *Educational Psychology*[M]. Zurich：The Saylor Foundation, 2009.

[3] Stangor, C., & Walinga, J. *Introduction to Psychology*[M]. Victoria, B.C.：BCcampus, 2014.

[4] William, M., & Burden, R. L. *Psychology for Language Teachers*[M]. Beijing：Foreign Language Teaching and Research Press, 2000.

[5] Woolfolk, A. *Educational Psychology*[M]. Beijing：Pearson Education Asia Ltd., and Tsinghua University Press, 2014.

[6] 李峰,白雅娟. 教育心理学[M]. 北京：北京师范大学出版社,2017.

[7] 张庆宗. 外语学与教的心理学原理[M]. 北京：外语教学与研究出版社,2011.

Task 2　Theories of English Teaching Methodology

There are many English teaching methods in the current teaching field. The most popular ones include, Grammar-Translation Method, Direct Method, Audio-Lingual Method, Desuggestopedia, Content-based, Task-based Teaching Method, and Participatory Approaches. In this chapter, four typical methods will be introduced detailedly. They are Total Physical Response (TPR), Situational Teaching Method (STM), Task-based Teaching Method, and Communicative Language Teaching (CLT).

2.1　Total Physical Response

Total physical response (TPR) is a practical method to teach children, in which teachers believe in the importance of having their students enjoy their experience in learning, and make the students active to learn.

2.1.1　Knowledge points

Outline

1. **What is total physical response?**

Total physical response is a language teaching method built around the coordination of speech and action; it attempts to teach language through physical (motor) activities (Asher, 1966: 79 – 84). According to James Asher, a professor of psychology at San Jose State University, California, people can acquire a foreign language by acquisition of comprehensible input through reacting imperative drills and other activities in classes, which is just like babies learning their first language.

2. **Characteristics of successful language learners**

Dr. James J. Asher first described the TPR method in his book *Learning Another Language Through Actions*. He and other linguists observed the following characteristics about successful language learners:

> Good language learners achieve fluency faster when they are immersed in activities that involve them in situational language use.

Good language learners show comprehension by successfully accomplishing language-generated tasks.

Good language learners focus on overall sentence meaning rather than a sentence's grammatical parts.

Good language learners make faster progress when the language of instruction is consistent (though limited) on a daily basis.

Good language learners make faster progress when the content involves language that is clearly usable or valuable outside the classroom.

3. Three obvious features

(1) High-speed understanding of any target language

Some former experts claimed that talking and comprehension are located in different parts of the brain. TPR will input some new information into people's brain and then have reaction immediately.

(2) Long-term retention

This method claims to guarantee the long-term retention of English, since the use of physical actions while or after listening helps to gain sound and meaning most effectively. This study reveals that TPR is an effective method to promote long-term retention of the target language.

(3) Zero stress

It is common that people probably can do a good job in a stress-free atmosphere, so even are children when they are learning a new language. Fortunately, TPR makes it come true. Students may acquire words, phrases, even sentences through physical actions, playing games, and storytelling. All in all, they feel happy when they are learning English; therefore they will become centered roles in classes.

4. The specific teaching methods of TPR theory

TPR combined "memory trace" theory of psychology, which holds that the more often or the more intensively a memory connection is traced, the more likely association will be recalled.

Starting from developmental psychology, the process of child language acquisition is usually undertaken under the guidance of adults. The adult gives students some verbal and physical commands, and expects a child to imitate his or her actions. When students understand the commands, the adult gradually transforms these commands into a language code to learn the language. Theory of TPR claims to link language and behavior together and teach second language through body language.

(1) Activities

First, to change words into communication. At the beginning of English teaching, language input is provided in the form of dialogue. This dialogue is a reproduced living record of communication, which carries the English pronunciation, grammar, word meaning, language use and other information. These language contents should become impressive words with the help of the teacher or audios or videos so that students are fully aware of the new language.

Take the following dialogue as an example:

  Girl: Mum, this is my teacher, Miss Guo.
  Mum: How do you do?
  Teacher: How do you do?

When the teacher is presenting such a dialogue, he or she should vividly perform the scene of two people's first meeting instead of explaining the situation. Therefore, when the girl introduces Miss Guo, she must first look at her mother and then turn to the teacher with gestures.

(2) Drawing

Children are more interested in drawing than writing on the blackboard. Therefore, when the teacher presents new knowledge or new content, he or she can draw on a board to help students create a visual impression of the new knowledge. Appropriate drawing can mobilize the students to participate in and to help them better remember the content. When teaching colors, for example, the teacher should encourage children to bring color pens into the classroom. That is, when the teacher teaches "red", he or she should ask students to use red pen to paint. To use this method, the teacher can strengthen children's memory of knowledge.

(3) Games

Playing games in class can help students master the difficult words. Take the game of "passing down" as an example. When teaching some words about "fruits" or "vegetables", the teacher can use this game to help students to remember.

5. Disadvantages

The TPR method applies to the nature of children and matches the principle of happy-learning, which enables children to learn easily, to learn fast and finally to feel the happiness of English study. But its disadvantages are as follow:

This method just suits for the first period of language learning, especially beginners. Because most of its contents are gestures, through which children may not get further knowledge, and it has to be carried out with some other approaches.

The TPR method contains of lots of game activities, role-playing and group competitions. But children will easily get excited when they are happy so it will be hard to accomplish the expected results even if they have good control of class, in another place, it becomes an annoyance to some shy students. Students are not generally given the opportunity to express their own thoughts in a creative way. The teacher may find that it is limited in terms of language scope. Certain target languages may not be suited to this method.

Reading Materials

Reading Material One

TPR 教学法在幼少儿 ESL 教学中的应用

一、TPR 的理论基础

TPR 全称为 Total Physical Response,是一套由美国圣何塞州立大学荣休心理学教授 James J. Asher 开发、辅助二语学习的教学理论。运用这一理论,在教学过程中,学生主要通过聆听和肢体上的回应来学习。据 Pallen(1988)介绍,TPR 教学法主要有以下形式:第一,学生通过接受指令来学习词汇;第二,学生通过动作来展示他们对词汇的理解;第三,学生直到完全准备好才以说的方式运用词汇。整个过程中,老师鼓励学生有一段"沉默期"。TPR 课堂的基本教学步骤如下:

(1) 教师给出指令并动作演示,学生听和观察。
(2) 教师给出指令并动作演示,学生模仿动作。
(3) 教师给出指令但不做动作,学生演示动作。
(4) 教师给出指令但不做动作,学生动作演示并说出指令。
(5) 学生给出指令,教师或其他学生动作演示。

在以上步骤中,不同于中国传统的"read after me"教学模式,不断重复的是动作而不是语言,使之更加符合孩子的心理和生理特点。以此方式,首先学生能够建立目标语言和动作之间的联系,并主动理解目标语言;其次,学生能在无意识无压力的情况下记住目标语言;而且学生,特别是幼少儿的注意力容易集中在老师夸张的面部表情和肢体动作上。当学生做动作时,右脑的运作有利于他们的记忆。

二、TPR 教学的可行性

对于 TPR 的研究国内外已经长达 30 多年之久。TPR 教学法的主旨是模拟婴儿学习母语的过程对二语学习者教学。运用 TPR 的关键在于在说之前给予学生足够的时间听和准备。大量的实验表明了 TPR 的优势,如今它已被成功应用于各类二语学习课堂。

1. Whisman 小学项目

Jackson 和她的同事 1979 年在加州山景城的 Whisman 小学开始了一个长达三年的研究项目。研究对象是有英语语言缺陷的小学生。他们被分成两个组:实验组的学生采用 TPR 教学法一对一或者分小组强化他们的理解和表达能力;控制组用传统的教学方法。三年后,他们发现实验组的学生比控制组有以下优势:

(1) 词汇领先一年半。
(2) 多理解 80% 的内容。

(3) 综合表达能力强 130%。(Asher, 2003, pp.2-17)

2. Mary Hamilton 的实验室研究

Mary Hamilton 的实验表明通过动作反馈指令的孩子比坐着观察示范动作的孩子有更好的记忆力。实验组的孩子会听到一些俄语的指令，然后经过训练以动作表现该指令。过一段时间，被要求一对一以动作对那些指令做出反应。控制组的孩子同样听到一些指令，不同的是他们被要求观察相应的动作，一段时间以后，以书写英文（母语）单词的形式对俄语指令做出反应，结果显示前者答对的数量远高于后者。(Asher, 2003)

3. 安纳波利斯语言学校

学校的创始人 Adrienne Cruz 是美国一个经验丰富的西班牙语教师。他厌倦了传统的语言教学模式，于是自己创办了一个以 TPR 教学的学校。她用"charm"(魔力)这个词来形容 TPR 教学法。她告诉记者"TPR 的效果简直立竿见影"。事实上，学生们也给予 TPR 高的评价。她的一个学生 Carl Tenner 说："它是一个与众不同的教学方法。"到 2008 年为止，她已成功开设五个班级，并且准备聘请老师从而开设更多的班级甚至更多的语种。

三、TPR 教育在中国实行的意义

在中国，幼少儿英语教育从 20 世纪初开始流行。随着全球化的发展，人们普遍认识到英语的重要性，越来越多的人开始学习英语。许多语言学家表示 3—6 岁是语言学习的黄金期，因此许多家长都希望孩子在这一阶段学好英语。他们愿意选择双语幼儿园，或是送孩子上语言学校，让孩子接受专业的语言培训。这时，对于孩子的教学方法就显得尤为重要。正如凌玉玲(1999)所说，在英语课堂上，学生的兴趣和参与是教与学成功的关键。很明显，传统要求学生反复跟读的"read-after-me"模式不能够满足教师、孩子和家长的需求。所有的语言教师都希望能够找到一种能够激发孩子的兴趣、减轻孩子的压力、减少孩子学习过程中挫败感的教学方法。TPR 正是这样一种教学法。

(节选自《都市家教·上半月》2014 年第 04 期)

2.1.2 Skills and abilities

The application of TPR can motivate students' learning interest. Some cases are listed below.

Cases

⌈**Case One**⌋

The Pointing Game

A small group of students use a collection of pictures (such as those one might find in a mail order catalog) to instruct concepts that have been taught. Ask students to point to various specific body parts, colors, clothing items, etc.

Children will be willing to present their comprehension through a physical action long before they are willing to give a linguistic response. Moreover, the use of real objects in the classroom and the use of picture flashcards allow the teacher and children to respond to language long before they can respond linguistically.

This method also can improve students' capability of response and develop their left brain. Certainly, the most important thing is to enhance those words teachers command repeatedly.

思考问题

How does the Pointing Game act? Please practice in groups.

Case Two

Identifying Emotions

After students have acquired simple commands such as "cry" or "laugh," pictures can be placed across the front of the room that clearly demonstrate such emotional reactions. Students can be asked to take the picture of a person displaying a specific reaction. Later, this same procedure can be extended to other kinds of descriptions of emotions. Later this same procedure can be extended to other kinds of descriptions of emotions, perhaps more subtle ones (someone who is sad, someone who is angry).

This game is like a role play some times, being difficult to understand emotional words which are too abstract; teacher will use this action game to give the students hand to grasp these untouched words. When students act trainers' orders, they may comprehend what feelings are like.

思考问题

How does the Identifying Emotions act? Please practice in groups.

Case Three

Following Recipes

At much later stages, making birthday cakes, baking cookies, or preparing dishes can provide a TPR experience, and it can also involve students in the cultures of other countries and those within the United States.

First of all, display all the ingredients for any given recipe and introduce each item one by one.

And then, show each student with a written recipe. An extra large version to which you and the students can refer can be placed at the front of the room. While you or a student reads the recipe, other students can measure, mix the ingredients, and so on. As a follow-up, students can bring in favorite recipes to share. These can be put together to form a class recipe book to which others can be added.

> 思考问题
>
> 1. How does the Following Recipes act? Please practice in groups.
> 2. What are the pros and cons of TPR?

✦ 亮考帮

亮闪闪：请总结学习过程中，哪些是自己记忆深刻、受益最大、最欣赏的内容呢？请写出具体内容。

考考你：请把自己弄懂的但觉得别人可能存在困惑的地方，用问题的形式表述出来，来挑战一下其他同学。

帮帮我：请把自己不懂、不会的地方或想要了解的内容，用问题的形式表述出来，并带到课堂上加以讨论。

✦ 参考文献

[1] Asher, J. J. The Learning Strategy of the Total Physical Response: A Review[J]. *The Modern Language Journal*, 1966.

[2] Asher, J. J. The Total Physical Response Approach to Second Language Learning[J]. *The Modern Language Journal*, 1969.

[3] Jack, C. R. & Rodgers, T. S. *Approaches and Methods in Language Teaching*[M]. Cambridge: Cambridge University Press, 2001.

[4] Paula, C. Total Physical Response: An Instructional Strategy for Second-Language Learners Who Are Visually Impaired[J]. *Journal of Visual Impairment & Blindness*, 1999, 93(5).

2.2 Situational Teaching Method

Situational teaching method is a very useful way to bring students to a relaxing environment to learn. You may create realistic situation to stimulate students' emotional experience. The detail is as follows.

2.2.1 Knowledge points

Outline

1. What is situational teaching method?

As we all know, situational teaching method can activate students' study motivation and create relaxing classroom climate. It's an effective and practical method to teach a language. It is originally called oral approach, which is developed by British applied linguists from the 1930's to 1960's(束定芳、庄智象,1996).

It can make full use of language, material objects and music to create a realistic situation to stimulate learners' emotional experience and inspire their positive emotion and refine the character and form the perfect personality, which may help students gain the spirit of innovation, cooperation and practice and cultivate students' aesthetic activity through a feeling of beauty, appreciating beauty and creating beauty.

2. Objectives

The objective of situational language teaching method is to teach a command of the four basic skills of language.

Accuracy in both pronunciation and grammar is regarded as crucial, and errors are to be avoided at all costs.

Automatic control of basic structures and sentence patterns is fundamental to reading and writing skills, and this is achieved through speech work.

3. Teacher's and learner's role

In the presentation stage of the lesson, the teacher serves as a model, setting up situations in which the need for the target structure is created and then modeling the new structure for students to repeat.

Then the teacher is required to be a skillful manipulator, using questions and other cues to elicit correct sentences from the learners. Lessons are hence teacher directed, and the teacher sets the pace.

During the practice phase of the lesson, students are given more of an opportunity to use the language in less controlled situations, and the teacher is on the lookout for grammatical and structural errors.

In the initial stages of learning, the learner is required simply to listen and repeat what the teacher says and to respond to questions and commands. The learner has no control over the content of learning and is often regarded as likely to succumb to undesirable behaviors unless skillfully manipulated by the teacher.

4. Advantages and disadvantages

The creation of situation can accelerate the link between English and things. It helps to understand the language they are learning. The dialogue teaching, which should pay more attention to the overall structure, makes the classroom lively and also makes the language expressed accurately and naturally. While the disadvantage is neglecting appropriate analysis of single structure in the language.

Reading Materials

Reading Material One

浅谈情景教学法在小学英语教学中的运用

小学阶段是英语学习的基础阶段,也是英语学习的关键时期,对培养学生的英语学习兴趣和英语语言交际能力有着重要的作用。那么,小学英语教师如何在新课程标准下运用情景教学法,激发学生的英语学习兴趣,促进教育事业的不断完善和发展呢?

一、情景教学法的内涵

小学英语新课程标准要求教师指导学生自己去通过感知、体验、实践、参与和合作等方式,实现任务的目标,感受成功的喜悦。语言学家克鲁姆说过:"成功的外语课堂教学应该是创造更多的情境,让学生有机会用自己学到的语言材料。"在小学英语教学中运用情境教学,既能活跃课堂气氛,激发学生的学习兴趣,锻炼学生的语言能力,又能培养学生的思维能力和空间想象能力,使学生仿佛置身于英语世界,在轻松、愉悦的学习环境中积极地学习,加深语言信息的输入和输出,产生语言内化,做到学以致用。

二、小学英语情景教学的基本原则

1. 真实性原则。有学者认为,真实性是学习者在使用文本的过程中对文本的恰当反应,是文本与学习者之间的关系。从现行的教材来看,文本中的内容不足以体现真实的语言交际内容,所以作为教师的我们,要适当地融入情景教学法,为学生创设一个更加真实的学习环境,让学生体会到英语交际与实际生活是息息相关的,不能脱离实际去孤立地学习英语。真实性原则就是要求英语教师引导学生在实际应用中习得知识点,进而熟练地掌握本堂课所学的单词和句子的运用。

2. 主动性原则。教学的本质属性决定了学生是教学活动的主体,学生是否投入学习成为教学成败的关键因素。我们知道"真正的学习"通常不是常规教学的结果,相反,它往往来自于个体的体验和思考,通过个体的自我发现和自我发展而产生。英语教师在教学过程中,创设一个趣味性的教学情景,能调动学生学习英语的主动性,诱发学生思维,激起学生主动学习的兴趣。学生在"探究—满足—乐趣—产生动机"这一过程中,逐渐产生学习英语的主动性。

3. 创造性原则。对于创造性的理解,一般认为它是指个体产生新奇独特的、有社会价值的产品的能力或特性,故也称为创造力。在小学英语教学过程中,教师要坚持创造性原则,培养学生的创造性思维。众所周知,培养学生创造性思维能力已是一个全球性的问题,"为创造性而教"已经成为学校主要目标之一。学生发展的着眼点是学生创造性的发展,是对学生创新精神的培养。情景教学法从表象入手,注重学生思维的拓展,能够不断培养学生的创造性思维品质。

三、小学英语情景教学法的实施策略

情景教学法能够有效调动学生的学习积极性,从而提高课堂学习效率。那么,如何在小学英语教学中,进行有效的情景教学呢?可以从以下几个方面尝试:

1. 生活展现情景,轻松学习。教师细心观察生活中的一些细节,从生活中选取某一典型场景,巧妙地与本课知识要点联系起来,把学生或者带入社会,或者带入大自然,或者带入一个日常的生活空间,让学生体验到更加真实的情景,同时让学生感受到英语交际与实际生活是相互关联的,不是孤立存在的。课堂之外也要创设情景,这样有助于学生对英语学习保持持久的学习兴趣,进而培养学生的学习主动性,以及综合英语能力。

2. 游戏创设情景,抓住重点。小学生的心理特征决定了他们在这个年龄段所具有的特性:活泼好动,有意注意的时间较短,只对自己喜欢的事物感兴趣等。教育家夸美纽斯认为:"最好的学习动机莫过于学生对所学材料本身具有内在的兴趣。"小学英语教师要根据学生的心理特点,对教材进行挖掘,结合课本内容设计出有趣的情景游戏,使学生兴趣浓厚地来学习英语。

3. 表演体会情景,加深记忆。英语学习过程中对话与交流是学习的重点之一,进行角色扮演不仅可以增加学习兴趣,还可以使学生完全参与到课堂活动中来,高度集中精神,再利用一些道具与舞台效果,会使学生在愉快的体验中提高自己的口语表达能力,语言运用能力以及人际交往能力。综上所述,课堂是我们教师的主阵地,教的目的是为了帮助学生更好地去学。随着新课程改革的不断深入,教师要明确教学的根本目的,要基于学生的发展进行教学。在探索小学英语情景教学的道路上,还需要我们全体英语老师孜孜不倦地探索和实践。

(节选自《甘肃教育》2018年第03期)

2.2.2 Skills and abilities

The application of situational teaching method can make the complex language materials easier to understand and some cases are listed below.

Case

The text "A Night the Earth Didn't Sleep" is an example of how to use multimedia before reading, in reading and after reading to create situations in high school English reading teaching. First of all, this text can be divided into three sessions, which mainly talks about precursor before the Tangshan earthquake, phenomenon and destruction when it occurred and rescue after the earthquake. Before reading the text, the teacher plays a video with floods, tsunamis, typhoons, and other natural disasters on the earth. Then the earthquake appears on the screen, at the same time the teacher add some questions in it, for example, "What's happening when an earthquake begins? Please describe what you see in the video."

After watching the video, the teacher gives the students some hints such as hills, the ground, houses and buildings, trees and electric lines. It is helpful to students' applications of English. Next, use pictures on the screen to show the animals' action before the earthquake occurs. Let students think and ask some of them to describe these natural phenomena such as barking dogs, flying chickens and so on. After the description, the teacher raises some questions, "If you see such strange events, how do you feel and what would you do?" Based on their own knowledge, the students may talk about their feelings and experiences, this can achieve the application of language. To train students' divergent and expansive thinking, "What did the people in Tangshan think of the strange events?"

The second paragraph talks about what happened during the Tangshan earthquake. The teacher takes advantages of charts and pictures on the screen to prompt students to find details to make a brief conclusion of the damages of buildings and death tolls. It may help students to get information of the text. Later, the flash animation appears on the screen with a man crying and the earth crying. The painful experience causes students to think, "Why did the people and the earth cry? If the earthquake happened in modern society, would so many people die and so many buildings be destroyed?"

The third paragraph mainly talks about the rescue of the Tangshan earthquake. After showing pictures of the rescue work with the help of soldiers, doctors and paramedics, the teacher presents a photo and asks them, "If you are one member of them, what will you give?" It will help students to cultivate their own emotional attitudes and values. Later, a picture of the earth with a big smile flowing on the screen tells the students, "As long as love is given by each and every one of us it will make the world more harmonious and beautiful," allowing students to better understand the last sentence of the text, "Slowly, the city began to breathe again."

思考问题

结合实际教学,情景教学还有哪些案例?

亮考帮

亮闪闪:请总结学习过程中,哪些是自己记忆深刻、受益最大、最欣赏的内容呢?请写出具体内容。

考考你:请把自己弄懂的但觉得别人可能存在困惑的地方,用问题的形式表述出来,来挑战一下其他同学。

帮帮我:请把自己不懂、不会的地方或想要了解的内容,用问题的形式表述出来,并带到课堂上加以讨论。

参考文献

[1] Hadley, A. O. *Teaching Language in Context* [M]. Beijing: Foreign Language Teaching and Research Press, 2003.
[2] Harmer, J. *The Practice of English Language Teaching* [M]. Beijing: Foreign Language Teaching and Research Press, 1991.
[3] Harmer, J. *How to Teach English* [M]. Beijing: Foreign Language Teaching and Research Press, 2000.
[4] Nunan, D. *Second Language Teaching and Learning* [M]. Beijing: Foreign Language Teaching and Research Press, 2001.
[5] 黄远振.新课程英语教与学[M].福州:福建教育出版社,2003.
[6] 束定芳,庄智象.现代外语教学——理论、实践与方法[M].上海:上海外语教育出版社,1996.
[7] 王蔷.英语教学法教程[M].2版.北京:高等教育出版社,2006.
[8] 傅道春.教育学——情景与原理[M].北京:教育科学出版社,1999.
[9] 扈中平,李方.现代教育学[M].北京:高等教育出版社,2005.

2.3 Task-based Approach

Task-based approach is a very popular method in current educational reform, which aims to provide learners with a natural context for language use. Here are the keys.

2.3.1 Knowledge points

Outline

1. What is task-based approach?

"TBA is a kind of teaching or learning approach that takes specific learning or teaching tasks as the motivation, which takes the task completion presentation and task implementation as showing the effect of teaching and learning." It is a method of teaching with specific task for learning motivation, with the process of task finishing for the learning process.

Simply speaking, task-based approach means learning for doing and learning by doing. It stands on students, which means the students are the main body of teaching. Teachers design various kinds of teaching activities viewed from students to teach students forming the ability of language using in the process of completing all kinds of tasks. It makes task actualization and implementation of the goal in class teaching, thus cultivating students' ability of English using. In other words, it takes specific tasks as its carrier and takes the completion of tasks as motivation thereby integrating knowledge and skill. Students finish tasks by using target language and they can also develop their target language in the course of doing things.

2. Six steps of task-based approach

Task-based approach puts the fulfillment of the task at the center of the language learning session. Learners use target language and skills to achieve a successful outcome by interacting, negotiating and cooperating while the teacher acts as helper and promoter and so forth to facilitate the process. During the process of carrying out the designed communicative tasks, it integrates form-focused instruction with meaning-focused instruction. Meanwhile, task-based approach offers the learners all opportunities to process language that is being learned or recycled more naturally. In contrast, the task-based approach can better balance the meaning and forms, fluency and accuracy, which is more advanced than any other communicative approaches before.

In general, the implementation of task-based approach in English teaching follows the following stages.

(1) Pre-task

Pre-task is a kind of preparatory work. The teacher introduces some topics and gives the students clear instructions on what they will have to do at the task stage and might help the students to recall some language that may be useful for the task. The pre-task stage can also often include playing a recording of people doing the task. This gives the students a clear model of what will be expected of them. The students can take notes and spend time preparing for the task.

For example:

Task 1: Today we are going to deal with the topic "mobile phone". Before having this lesson, I have prepared several questions for you all. Please thinking about the following questions:

First, how many of you have a mobile phone?

Second, do you like the mobile phone?

Third, how often do you use the mobile phone? And for what purposes?

I'll give you five minutes to think about it.

This is the leading-in part for activating students' concern and interest on the topic.

(2) Task

The students complete a task in pairs or small groups by using the language resources that they have as the teacher monitors and offers encouragement. After the above pre-task, ask students to think about the following question.

For example:

> Task 2: Let's stop thinking and looking at the topic in the text "Mobile Phones Concern You". Before you read the text, what will you think about the topic when you see it in your first time. Try to predict the content of the text and think about the topic. After that, read the context and think it again.

(3) Planning

Students prepare a short oral or written report to tell the whole class what they have discussed during their task. And think about what they are going to say in their groups. Meanwhile the teacher is available for the students to ask for advice to clear up any language question they may have.

For example:

> Task 3: Discuss in groups: In what ways do mobile phones influence us in daily life? Sort out the above problems and divide the whole class into 4—5 groups. Discuss with your teammates, write down the ways in which mobile phones concern us, and recommend a person as a representative to do a report to the class. The more items the group writes down, the higher marks the group will get.

(4) Report

The teacher asks some groups to present their reports to the class, or to exchange written reports. Ask one representative of each group to report their results. The teacher acts as a chairperson, giving the students some comments or feedback on the content of the presentation. At this stage the teacher may also play a recording of others doing the same task for the students to compare.

For example:

> Task 4: Each group recommends one person as a representative to report the discussion result to the whole class. Compare the items each group provides. Then make a comparison between the items you mention and those mentioned in the text.

(5) Analysis

The teacher then highlights relevant parts from the text of the recording for the students to analyze. The teacher may ask students to notice interesting features within this text, and can also highlight the language that the students used during the report phase for analysis.

For example:

Task 5: Nowadays, mobile phone instruction is getting other writing tasks after class. For example: Can you live without a mobile phone? The mobile phone becomes more and more popular in China. Mobile phones play a very important role in our daily life. What do you think of it? Compare the advantages and disadvantages of mobile phones.

(6) Practice

Finally, the teacher selects language areas to practice based upon the needs of the students and what emerged from the task and report phases. The students then do practice activities to increase their confidence and make a note of useful language.

Learning by doing motivates students to fulfill their potential. Learners master the language by using it in the classroom, although they still have to learn grammar and memorize vocabulary. The communicative task is a piece of classroom work which involves learners in producing, interacting, comprehending or manipulating in the target language while their attention is focused on mobilizing their grammatical knowledge in order to convey meaning rather than to manipulate form.

3. The objectives

The task-based approach aims at providing opportunities for the learners to experiment with and explore both spoken and written language through learning activities which are designed to engage learners in the authentic, practical and functional use of language for meaningful purposes.

4. Advantages and disadvantages

The advantages are:

Firstly, "goal" is the first factor taking account of tasks. The second factor is "input", which refers to the verbal and non-verbal data such as a dialogue, a reading passage, a picture or a chart, etc.

While it takes more time to finish a task, it is time-wasting, and also classroom discipline controlling is a challenge to the teacher.

Reading Materials

Reading Material One

任务型教学法在初中英语教学中的应用研究

1. 当前阶段我国初中英语教学所存在的问题分析

在进行本文的研究之前笔者进行了大量的走访调研,对当前阶段初中英语教学中所存在的问题进行了分析与研究。根据笔者的调查研究,当前阶段初中英语教学中所存在的主要问题有以下几点内容。

1.1 学生对英语学习的积极性不高

当前阶段在初中英语教学当中,应试教育还是教育的主要形式,教师教学的主要目的在于提高学生的英语考试成绩,尤其是需要提高学生的中考英语考试成绩。在这样一个基本前提之下,英语教学的基本模式相对较为单一,大部分教师在授课的过程当中,都是采用传统的填鸭式教学模式进行初中英语的教学,即教师在课堂当中不断地为学生灌输相关的英语知识,而学生只能被动接受知识,在这个过程当中,学生的主体地位得不到充分的发挥,也只能通过记忆、背诵等机械的学习方式进行初中英语的学习,这就必然导致学生对于英语的学习积极性不高。

1.2 教学设计内容过于单一

一般情况下一个初中班级的学生至少三四十人,不同的学生在认知能力以及心理状态方面都存在着较大的差异,同时每个学生的英语基础也存在着较大的差异,客观上的差异性是必然存在的。而大部分的教师在进行教学设计时针对的是所有学生,这就必然导致教学的内容对于部分学生来说深度明显不够,而有些学生则跟不上。

1.3 评价机制不够合理

当前阶段初中英语教学在中考的指挥棒下基本都是通过学生的考试成绩对学生进行评价的,这种评价方式在很大程度上具有一定的不合理性,无法从总体上反映出学生的英语实际水平与英语综合能力。同时这种评价机制也忽略了学生的能力与素质的培养。英语的听、说、读、写都是基本的语言能力,但是由于英语口语不在中考的测评范围之内,因此,大部分英语教师也不会过多关注学生的英语口语水平。

2. 任务型教学法在初中英语教学中的实际应用分析

笔者对现阶段初中英语教学中所存在的问题进行了分析,在此基础之上笔者查阅了相关文献,并结合自己的实际工作经验,认为任务型教学法可以被有效地运用于初中英语教学当中,基于此种情况,在下文中笔者将论述具体的应用策略。

2.1 通过学习任务提高学生的英语学习积极性

由于传统的教学模式使得学生对于英语学习的积极性不高,学生无法有效融入教学的实际过程当中去,而将任务型教学法应用于初中英语教学,要求学生在教学的过程当中自主完成相关任务,教师仅仅是给予必要的引导,在这个过程当中学生必须要自己进行学习,真正融入教学当中去,从而提高英语学习的积极性。

2.2 设置合理的教学任务

初中英语教师必须要认识到学生在客观上是存在一定的差异性的,因此,在教学的实际过程当中,必须要设置合理的任务。任务的设置必须要与学生的实际能力与心理特征相吻合,循序渐进地提高学生的英语能力,只有通过这种方式才能不断提高学生的学习水平,并使得学生获得可持续性的发展。

2.3 改革评价机制

传统的评价机制过于强调学生的考试成绩,具有一定的片面性,因此必须要建立一种全新的多维度与多元主体的评价模式。学生的评价应该分为三个维度进行,即考试成绩、课堂表现、课后学习。考试成绩由教师进行评价,课堂表现则由教师与学生进行评价,而课后学习则由自己与家长共同评价,通过这种多元化的评价机制有效地对学生进行综合性评价。

(节选自《中学生英语·教师版》2017 年第 09 期)

2.3.2 Skills and abilities

The application of task-based approach helps to make the teaching process clearer and more logical.

Case

把任务型语言教学法运用到中学英语课堂,关键在于教师对任务的设计。下面以牛津英语 7B Unit 4 Finding your way 中"Integrated skills"一课为例阐述中学课堂中任务型语言教学法的应用。

本课的教学重点是让学生掌握用英语指明方向并正确指路。我在本课的设计中从 B 部分"Speak up"入手,让学生在掌握基础的指示性用语之后,开展"treasure hunt"的活动,并通过设置三把钥匙(包括方向之钥、顺序之钥和路线之钥),以完整的情境和主线串联 A 部分三块内容,完成三个不同的任务以达到教学目标。

挑战记忆性任务(Memory challenge task)

教师让学生在规定的时间内读一篇文章,然后总结并叙述文章的主要内容;或让学生叙述某个情节,或者学生根据文章的主要内容相互提问三至五个问题。这一类任务在阅读部分的课堂的使用频率十分高,在本课"Speak up"的环节中,设计学生通过听和通读对话,在直观的地图的帮助下复述出对话中从 Daniel 家到 English Corner 的路径。

对比性任务(Comparison task)

对比不同的材料、图片或叙述并从中找出它们之间的异同点,使学生举一反三。本课中,任务一即让学生通过完成任务获得"方向之钥"。学生不仅需要完成听选,还要根据所听内容选出相应图片,并针对此句内容进行挖空填词,重点突出方向指示的词组和单词,而后完成对同组另一幅图片的英文描述。如第一组图片当中,一听;二选(图 b);三填空:_____ the bridge and _____ _____. (Cross the bridge and turn right.);四仿写

（图a）：_____ the bridge and _____ _____ （Cross the bridge and turn left.）

排序性任务（Jumbles task）

排序性任务提高学生对文章的整体把握能力和逻辑条理性。本课中，任务二即让学生通过完成任务获得"顺序之钥"。学生听课文录音排序之前给出tips，并通读各条instructions，圈画出指示方向的词或短语，以便降低听力的难度。学生根据听力内容完成对instructions的排序，最终确定宝藏所在的位置。

预测任务（Prediction task）

在学生完成了任务二后，让学生根据所给的instructions，在宝藏地图上预测和联想宝藏所在的具体位置。学生提问，教师回答。"Is it under the big tree/next to the bridge? No or Yes?"确认位置后，让学生通过小组合作的方式，在所给宝藏地图上找出其所认为最为快捷的路径。以此，提高学生参与的积极性并培养学生发散思维的能力。

解决问题性任务（Problem-solving task）

解决问题性任务是要求学生根据自己的知识和推理能力，用英语解决现实生活中可能会遇到的问题。教师给学生设置的任务是开放式的，学生以小组为单位完成任务。以本课知识运用生成为例，设计了与学生现实生活联系紧密的情境，让其通过小组合作，帮助Google Map公司设计从"海悦花园"到"园区青少年活动中心"的路线，并进行语音指路的练习。

创造性任务（Creative task）

创造性任务是由两人小组或多人小组合作完成的。它包括列表、安排顺序与分类、对比和解决问题等类型的任务；此类任务一般要求学生在课外完成。本课的课外作业为：两人小组合作，设计一条从两人先碰头再一同去上学的路径，并录音上交。希望学生能用英语正确为他人指路，获得学习乐趣。

> **思考问题**
> 1. 教师如何将任务教学法应用在实际教学中？
> 2. 任务教学法的实例有哪些？

✦亮考帮

亮闪闪：请总结学习过程中，哪些是自己记忆深刻、受益最大、最欣赏的内容呢？请写出具体内容。

考考你：请把自己弄懂的但觉得别人可能存在困惑的地方，用问题的形式表述出来，来挑战一下其他同学。

帮帮我：请把自己不懂、不会的地方或想要了解的内容，用问题的形式表述出来，并带到课堂上加以讨论。

参考文献

[1] 程晓堂. 任务型语言教学[M]. 北京：高等教育出版社，2004.
[2] 龚亚夫，罗少茜. 任务型语言教学[M]. 北京：人民教育出版社，2003.
[3] 廖晓青. 任务型教学的理论基础和课堂实践[J]. 中小学外语教学，2001.

2.4　Communicative Language Teaching

Communicative language teaching （CLT） is a useful method for language learning，which aims to apply the theoretical perspective of the Communicative Approach by making communicative competence.

2.4.1　Knowledge points

Outline

1. What is CLT?

Communicative language teaching is an approach to the teaching of second and foreign languages that emphasizes interaction as both the means and the ultimate goal of learning a language. It is also referred to as "communicative approach to the teaching of foreign languages" or simply the "communicative approach".

2. Classroom procedures

Sano，et al. （1984） argues that communicative language teaching should meet the local needs and the methodology of foreign language teaching should vary significantly according to the environments in which teachers find themselves working.

（1） Warm-up

This offers learners interesting language activities to relax them and to let them use English creatively. Establishing a non-threatening environment is given prime importance here.

（2） Introduction of new contents

This is usually carried out through conversation between the teacher and learners concerning objects or incidents familiar to them.

（3） Practice

This is generally carried out either by stimulating learners' intellectual curiosity or by appealing to their emotional value judgments. Self-expression，activities，though sometimes quite limited in scope，are incorporated even at the earliest stage. Care is also taken to make learning and production "deep".

(4) Communicative practice

This requires not only mastery of the target item, but also creative use of the knowledge of language so far acquired. It can be totally oral, but quite often involves some writing.

3. Advantages of CLT

(1) Communication—according to ability

Firstly, the label implies a focus on communication and some might argue that this method can't be employed genuinely with low levels as there is no authentic communication, due to a limited vocabulary and restricted range of functions. Initially, many of a learner's utterances are very formulaic. As an aside, consider just what percentage of our own English expressions are unique, and how often we rely on a set phrase; just because it is delivered unselfconsciously and with natural intonation does not make it original. The aim is that the length and complexity of exchanges, and confident delivery, will grow with the student's language ability.

With the emphasis on communication, there is also the implication that spoken exchanges should be authentic and meaningful; detractors claim that the artificial nature of classroom-based (i. e. teacher-created) interactions makes CLT an oxymoron. Nevertheless, a proficient teacher will provide a context so that class interactions are realistic and meaningful but with the support needed to assist students to generate the target language. Teachers need to consider that producing language is a skill and when learning a skill, teachers practise in improvised settings. For example, before a nurse gives a real injection, they have punctured many a piece of fruit to hone their technique.

(2) Accuracy as well as fluency

This focus on accuracy versus fluency is one of the issues not often considered in a discussion of CLT. The teacher decides to pay attention to one or other end of this band, depending on the type of lesson, or the stage of a particular lesson, and accuracy is their choice if they want to deal with students getting things right, take an opportunity for correction, or gauge the success of their teaching. For example, freer speaking involves more choice, therefore more ambiguity, and less teacher intervention. While CLT implies the lessons are more student-centered, this does not mean they are unstructured. The teacher does have a very important role in the process, and that is setting up activities so that communication actually happens. There is a lot of preparation; accuracy practice is the bridge to a fluency activity. By implication, CLT involves equipping students with vocabulary, structures and functions, as well as strategies, to enable them to interact successfully.

(3) Promoting learning

This returns us to the consideration of who we are teaching, and why. Are our students aiming to learn or acquire English? Do they need to know lexical items and linguistic rules as a means of passing an exam, or do they want to be able to interact in English? For those inclined to maintain the dichotomy between learning and acquisition, and who argue that our primary focus is learners, CLT still has relevance. It is timely to review an early definition of CLT. According to Richards and Rodgers, CLT is basically about promoting learning.

Reading Material

一、交际教学法实施的必要性

近年来，在初中英语课程的教学活动中，英语意识以及交际能力的培养，一直都是学校和教育工作者努力实现的目标。语言和交际是密不可分的整体，语言帮助交际有效实现，交际能力在某些方面也影响着语言的发展。所以，在英语教学的过程中，教师运用交际教学法进行教学是非常有必要的：一方面交际教学法可以让学生们在掌握英语基础知识的时候，对英语有着更深层次的了解；另一方面交际教学法也可以为学生交际能力的培养打好基础，增强语言的敏感性和预见性。教师运用交际教学法所要实现的终极目标，就是让学生们拥有熟练的社会交际能力，在不同的场合能够把自己所掌握的语言应用自如，这同时也是我国初中英语课程改革所要实现的目标。

二、交际教学法在真实情景中的运用

传统的初中英语教学模式是教师对于课文逐字逐句讲解，而初中生被动接受教师传授的知识。虽然这种传统的教学模式可以为初中生在英语基础知识方面打下良好的基础，但是初中生的交际能力却没有得到应有的锻炼，更提不上综合素质的发展。由于初中是接触英语这门课程的初级阶段，如果从一开始就让学生们在脑海里对英语留下枯燥、乏味的印象，对于今后更高年级的英语课程的教学活动的开展将是非常不利的。初中英语教师必须要改善这个问题，在真实的情景中引用交际教学法便是解决这个问题的必要手段。

三、交际教学方法要以学生为核心

初中生所处的应该是一个承上启下的年龄段，学生们的特点就是活泼好动，善于表现自己。在英语课的教学过程中，教师可以利用交际教学法给学生们提供交流表演的机会，并让学生们亲自选择课文，自行编排表演，这种做法非常有利于学生英语方面的创作能力、理解能力以及交际能力的培养和提高。表演形式可以让学生进行任意选择，英语歌舞表演、英语音乐剧表演等都可以被搬到英语课堂上。这种以学生为核心的交际教学方法，非常有利于学生想象能力的发挥，对学生创新能力以及交际能力的培养也是非常有帮助的。

四、交际教学方法可以利用多媒体技术实现

多媒体技术是丰富课堂教学内容的重要手段之一，把交际教学法与多媒体技术有机

融合,对于初中英语教学目标的实现是非常有帮助的。多媒体技术包括幻灯片、照片、动画特效以及影片等,它们对于交际教学法所依赖的情景的还原是非常真实的。在学生受到视觉以及听觉双重感染的情况下,交际教学法的使用将取得更为有效的成果。

(节选自《中学课程辅导·教学研究》2013年第27期)

2.4.2　Skills and abilities

The application of CLT helps to make the classroom atmosphere active and relaxable. Some cases are listed below.

Cases

Case One

在人教版八年级《英语》下册Unit 5　If you go to the party, you will have a great time 的学习过程中,教师便可以以学生为核心进行交际教学法的实践。由于八年级是初中英语学习的关键年级,大部分英语课的课时都贡献给了较为枯燥单一的基础教学知识的讲解。在这种情况下,为了尽可能发掘同学们学习的积极性,教师可以利用 the party 的学习机会,把课堂变成一个真正的大 party。教师要求每一位学生都要为课堂 party 准备一个小的表演,并在表演之前对自己的节目进行报幕。在这个过程中,be going to 以及 will 句型都可以被应用以及复习到。以学生为核心的交际教学法的使用,不仅可以让学生们在繁重的课业压力下得到些许的放松,对于他们创新以及交际能力的提高也可以起到积极的推动作用。

Case Two

在人教版七年级《英语》下册Unit 3　This is my sister 的学习过程中,教师便可以在真实情景的创建下使用交际教学法,以提高学生基础知识的吸收率和交际能力。教师可以为学生创造一个介绍自己朋友的环节,在这个环节中每一个学生都要把自己和 sister/brother 的照片带到课上来,向每一位同学展示和介绍自己的 sister/brother。在介绍自己的 sister/brother 的时候,初中生们对于 Her/His name is, He/She is, He/She likes 等句型可以做到很好的利用和复习。接下来教师可以设立一个采访的情境,在座的每一位学生都可以对讲台上的学生进行提问,在提问的过程中,例如 What is, Who is 等问答句型也都可以被复习和利用到。虽然只是一个非常简单的情境,但是交际教学法在它的帮助下得到了很好的运用,对于学生主动学习能力的引导以及学生学习兴趣的激发有很大的推动作用。

Case Three

在人教版九年级《英语》Unit 13　Rainy days makes me sad 的学习过程中,教师可以利用幻灯片的放映实现交际教学法的使用。本篇课文主要学习了 excited，surprised，upset，bored 等几种表示心情的英文单词以及 how things affect us 等问答句型，因此交际教学法要针对这些知识点进行使用。教师可以为同学们准备不同人物在不同情景下的表情图片的幻灯片，每一张幻灯片都要自带一个音频提问的文件，当文件播放的时候教师指定学生回答问题，以实现学生与多媒体之间的人机交流。每当学生回答正确的时候，计算机都要发出鼓励的掌声。利用多媒体技术实现的交际教学法对于初中生学习兴趣的培养以及交际能力的提高可见一斑。

> **思考问题**
> 1. 教师在实际教学中如何使用交际教学法？
> 2. 交际教学法的实例有哪些？

✧ 亮考帮

亮闪闪：请总结学习过程中，哪些是自己记忆深刻、受益最大、最欣赏的内容呢？请写出具体内容。

考考你：请把自己弄懂的但觉得别人可能存在困惑的地方，用问题的形式表述出来，来挑战一下其他同学。

帮帮我：请把自己不懂、不会的地方或想要了解的内容，用问题的形式表述出来，并带到课堂上加以讨论。

✧ 参考文献

[1] Larsen-Freeman, D. *Techniques and Principles in Language Teaching* [M]. Second Edition. Oxford: Oxford University Press, 2000.
[2] 史宝辉.交际式语言教学二十五年[J].外语教学与研究,1997,(3).
[3] 徐强.交际法英语教学和考试评估[M].上海：上海外语教育出版社,2000.
[4] 张萍,张燕丽.交际教学法的折中取向[J].教育理论与实践,2000,(3).

第四章　走近学生

主要内容

1. 了解小学生
   - 小学生学习的特点
   - 学习是怎样发生的
2. 了解中学生
   - 中学生的特点——学习策略

✓ 案例学习
✓ 专业参考
✓ 学术探讨

　　If you think more about your school years, you may find that a lot of memories are related to not just academic knowledge but the feelings of friendships, loves and fears. In order to learn, you must be cognitively, emotionally, and behaviorally engaged in productive class activities or just sit still to listen to your teachers. Almost all the time, you seek for the interests of the learning contents. These are probably the most typical characteristics of our primary school and middle school students. Based on these characteristics, this chapter continues to discuss how our pupils and teenagers learn, and at the same time how they develop their bodies, cognition, emotion, personal relationship and so on. We also include a little bit of our brains' construction for you to further understand human being development. By the time you have completed this chapter, we hope that you will be more confident to face your students and help them learn effectively.

Task 1 Understanding Primary School Students

The primary school years is a precious period of one's life. Many people may think that primary school students are easy to teach because they know little. But these people may forget the characteristics of students of this age and the way they learn. We should not use the academic way to teach them. In this section, we offer some knowledge of how to teach primary school students.

1.1 Knowledge Points

Outline

Sensory input and the definition of development are the keys you must know before you go to the deep of this section.

1.1.1 Sensory input

Children need to have all five senses stimulated. Your activities should strive to go well beyond the visual and auditory methods that we usually feel are sufficient for a classroom. What are they?

- Sight
- Hearing
- Smell
- Taste
- Touch

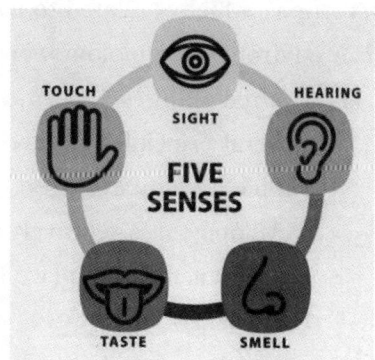

So, when they learn something, authentic, meaningful language is the key for them. Besides, we should create a context for them to understand. A whole language approach is essential. There are different views about when the best age for learning a foreign language is. The introduction of a foreign language to young learners is developing very rapidly all over the world. According to Tokuhama-Espinosa (2008), the first window to learn language is from birth to 9 months, the second window is from 4 to 8 years old, and the third window is from 9 years old to adulthood. However, for whether there is a "critical period", research has so far showed controversial results.

1.1.2 How does learning happen?

To understand how learning happens, we should know how development happens first. The following contents are about development.

1. A definition of development

The term development refers to certain changes that occur in human beings (or animals) between conception and death. It is not applied to all changes, but rather to those that appear in orderly ways and remain for a reasonably long period of time. A temporary change caused by a brief illness is not considered a part of development.

2. Development in different aspects

- Physical development: It deals with changes in the body.
- Personal development: The term is generally used for changes in an individual's personality.
- Social development: It refers to changes in the way an individual relates to others.
- Cognitive development: It refers to changes in thinking, reasoning, and decision making.

3. Many changes

- Maturation: It refers to changes that occur naturally and spontaneously and that are, to a large extent, genetically programmed. Malnutrition or severe illness can affect it.
- Other changes: They are brought about through learning, as individuals interact with their environment. We often have this concern: maturation and interaction, which is related to nature versus nurture. For example, there are heredity versus environment, biology versus culture, maturation versus learning, and innate versus acquired abilities.

4. General principles of development

- People develop at different rates
- Development is relatively orderly
- Development takes place gradually

5. For teachers

For teachers, we should not only know the strategies of teaching, but also development of children so that to use appropriate methods to help students' learning (See the details in Reading Material One).

Reading Materials

Reading Material One

The Brain and Cognitive Development

When talking about how learning happens, we should know something about our brain's development. And then, we will have some tips for teachers and some enlightenment for learning mother tongue and a foreign language.

(1) Some facts of our brain

The following pictures and words simply introduce the development of our brain and how the learning happens based on the current research of our brain. Our brain has different areas and each area is responsible for different functions. Language areas, the famous Wernicke's area(韦尼克氏区) is located in Temporal Lobe.

We should know the fact that people develop at different rates; development is relatively orderly; development takes place gradually. Our brain also has features as follows.

• Cerebral cortex(大脑皮层): The outer 1/8-inch-thick covering is the cerebral cortex—the largest area of the brain. It is a thin sheet of neurons, but it is almost 3 square feet in area for adults. It accounts for about 85% of the brain's weight in adulthood and contains the greatest number of neurons.

• Lateralization(偏侧优势): It is the specialization of the two hemispheres of the brain.

• Plasticity(可塑性): The brain's tendency to remain somewhat adaptable or flexible. (Figure 4-1)

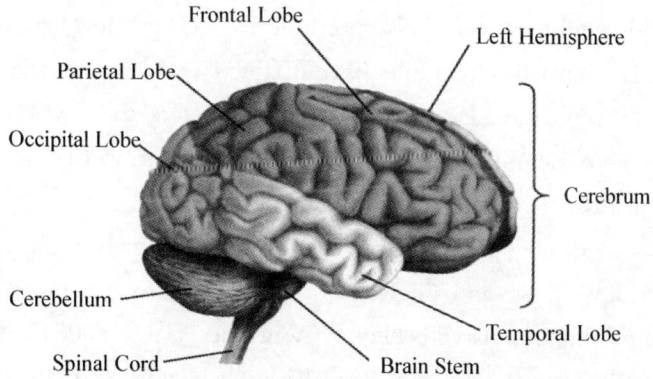

Figure 4-1 Functional areas of our brain

Neuron cells send out long arm- and branch-like fibers called axons(轴索) and dendrites(树突) to connect with other neuron cells. Neurons communicate using both electrical and chemical signals. (Figure 4-2)

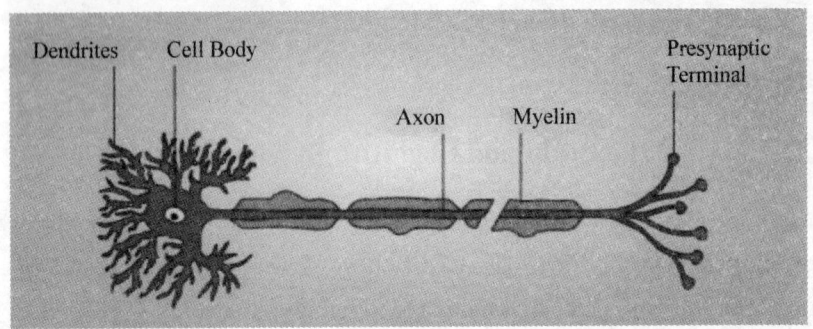

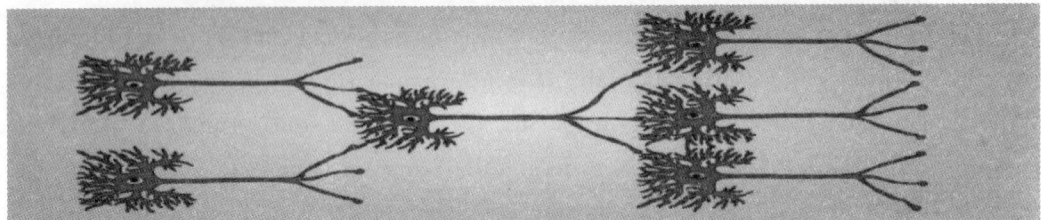

Figure 4-2 Neuron cells

Axons transmit information out to muscles, glands, or other neurons; dendrites receive information and transmit it to the neuron cells themselves. Synapses(突触) are tiny spaces between neuron cells. A newborn baby's brain weighs about one pound, barely one third of the weight of an adult brain. This infant brain has billions of neurons. At birth, each of the child's 100 to 200 billion neurons has about 2,500 synapses. By ages 2 to 3, each neuron has around 15,000 synapses, and it has many more synapses than they will have as adults.

There are two kinds of over production and pruning process: Experience-expectant (经验预期效应) and Experience-dependent(经验依赖效应). Experience-expectant means overproduction and pruning which are responsible for general development in large areas of the brain and may explain why adults have difficulty with pronunciations that are not part of their native language. Experience-dependent refers to new synapses which are formed in response to neural activity in very localized areas of the brain when the individual is not successful in processing information.

During adolescence, changes in the brain increase individuals' abilities to control their behavior in both low-stress and high-stress situations, to be more purposeful and organized, and to inhibit impulsive behavior (Wigfield et al., 2006). But these abilities are not fully developed until the early 20s. Risky behaviors and controlling impulsive behavior are two keys in the pace of development.

(2) Lessons for teachers: general principles

1) There are multiple ways to teach and to learn a skill, depending on the student.

2) Many cognitive functions are differentiated. Thus learners are likely to have

preferred modes of processing as well as varying capabilities in these modes. Using a range of modalities for instruction and activities that draw on different senses may support learning.

3) The brain is relatively plastic, so enriched, active environments and flexible instructional strategies are likely to support cognitive development in young children and learning in adults.

4) Some learning disorders may have a neurological basis. Neurological testing may assist.

5) The brain can change, but it takes time, so teachers must be consistent, patient, and compassionate in teaching and reteaching in different ways.

6) Learning from real life problems and concrete experiences helps students construct knowledge and also gives them multiple pathways for learning and retrieving information.

7) The brain seeks meaningful patterns and connections with existing networks, so teachers should tie new information to what students already understand and help them form new connections.

8) It takes a long time to build and consolidate knowledge. Numerous visits in different contexts over time (not all at once) help to form strong multiple connections.

9) Large, general concepts should be emphasized over small specific facts so students can build enduring, useful knowledge categories and associations that are not constantly changing.

10) Stories should be used in teaching. Stories engage many areas of the brain-memories, experiences, feelings, and beliefs. Stories also are organized and have a sequence—beginning, middle, end—so they are easier to remember than unrelated or unorganized information.

(3) Differences between learning mother tongue and a foreign language

For acquisition, we refer more about mother tongue, but learning is in a sense of a foreign language (Notes: a foreign language can also be acquired. Whatever we use, acquisition or learning, we refer that language gets after children were born. It does not focus on whether it is acquired before or after they are born or related genetically). Since children has stronger plasticity, stronger imitation, and stronger mechanical memory, we should concern these principles.

- Situation matching(情境匹配)
- Extended principle(扩充性原则)
- Principle of communication(交际性原则)
- Principle of activity and enjoyment(活动性、趣味性原则)
- Visual-audiolingual and read-write combination(视听说与读写结合)
- Speak in English in class(在教室中说英语)
- Repetition principle(重复原则)

Scholars believe that learning never takes place in a vacuum. For Piaget, a child develops by exploring individually his or her environment. For Vygotsky, learning from birth is the result of social interactions. It always occurs within a particular context. For Robert Sternberg, what may be deemed intelligent at one time and place will by no means necessarily be the case at another.

This is equally true of non-intellectual influences within the environment and their effects upon emotional development. It is clear that national and cultural differences have a profound influence upon the development of a language and the way in which it is used. A country's educational stem will affect the learning environment.

(Adapted from Woolfolk, 2014)

Reading Material Two

小学生身心发展特点与一般规律

一、小学生身心发展的特点

（一）小学生身体发展的特点

小学生的年龄般为6—7岁至11—12岁。童年期的小学生的身体发育处于相对平稳阶段。小学生身高平均每年增长4—5厘米，体重平均每年增加2—3千克，胸围平均每年增宽2—3厘米。从发育时间上来看，女生身体发育的高峰期均比男生早1—2年。

1. 骨骼

小学生的骨骼骨化（骨化指形成或转化成骨）尚未形成。没有完成骨化的骨骼有软组织、椎骨盆区和四肢的骨骼等骨骼组织。这些地方含水分多，含钙盐成分少，骨骼硬度小、韧性大，有弹性易变形。因此，家长和教师要特别注意孩子坐立行和读书写字的正确姿势的培养训练，帮助小学生养成良好的习惯，防止驼背的产生。

2. 肌肉

小学生的肌肉发育呈现"两早"的特点：（1）大肌肉群的发育早于小肌肉群；（2）肌肉长度的增加早于肌肉横断面的增大。因此，在小学阶段，尤其是体育教学过程，力量型和动作幅度较大的动作应该避免，此外，对于精确性要求较高的动作不能提出过高的要求。

3. 神经系统

小学生的神经系统，特别是大脑结构发育还未完全。儿童到了6—7岁时，脑重约1 280克，已接近成人脑重的90%，以后增长缓慢，9岁时约1 350克，到了12岁约1 400克，基本和成人一致。儿童大脑的兴奋过程与抑制过程逐渐趋向平衡，觉醒时间延长，睡眠时间缩短。儿童平均每天需要的睡眠时间：7岁为11小时，10岁为10小时，12岁为9—10小时。第二信号系统活动日益发展起来，小学儿童由于语言的发展，第二信号系统初步占主要地位，其发展主要是在教学活动中以及在与成人交际的过程中发展起来的。

4. 心脏和呼吸系统

小学生的心肺功能逐渐增强,血管发展的速度大于心脏的发展速度,血液的循环量加大,新陈代谢加快,孩子的肺活量大小随着年龄增长而显著增加,且体育锻炼的情况也直接关系到肺活量的大小,家长应该鼓励孩子多参加体育锻炼活动。小学生的心脏容积小于成人,脉搏频率远超过成年人,且心脏每搏输出量比成人小,心脏搏动频率为每分钟80—90次,因此要注意不让孩子参加过分剧烈的运动和繁重的体力劳动,以防损害心脏。

(二)小学生心理发展的特点

1. 认知发展的特点

(1)感知觉的发展特点

在小学生入学之初,小学生的感知觉已充分发展,具体表现在:听觉和视觉十分敏锐,能准确地辨别事物的颜色形状;味觉、嗅觉和触觉也较为发达,感知觉的发展为个体进行学习提供了保障。在儿童期,小学生的感知觉发展迅速,其感知觉的准确性和系统性都不断提高。

(2)注意的发展特点

小学生注意力的发展主要表现在注意的自觉性和注意品质的完善程度上。

① 有意注意逐渐发展,无意注意仍起作用

低年级的小学生,无意注意仍起很大作用,他们兴奋抑制的产生比较迅速,第二信号系统的抑制作用较弱,容易受外界新鲜、突变和运动的事物所吸引,从而容易分散注意力。随着教师向学生提出各种要求,特别是学习任务的增多,学习活动仅靠无意注意是无法完成的,所以就迫使小学生由无意注意向有意注意发展,就整个小学阶段而言,无意注意仍起着重要的作用。

② 注意的范围依然有限

由于小学生知识经验少,他们的注意范围要比成人小,尤其是小学低年级学生,其注意更具有狭隘性。低年级小学生还不善于注意事物的内部联系,因而注意的范围受到限制。例如,一年级小学生总是一个字一个字地阅读课文,注意的范围很小,到了高年级,才能把字和字连成句子阅读,并逐渐注意到句与句之间的联系。

要扩大小学生注意的范围,教师应做到:一是引导学生对教材的理解;二是充分运用直观教具;三是有条理地组织学习材料;四是知觉对象离学生近一些。

③ 注意的集中性和稳定性较差

小学生的注意稳定性较差,表现在集中于某一事物或活动上的时间较短。一般说来,7—10岁儿童可连续集中注意力约20分钟;10—12岁儿童约25分钟;12岁以上约30分钟。低年级儿童对一些具体的、活动的事物以及操作性的工作,容易集中和稳定注意力,对于一些抽象的公式、定义以及单调刻板的对象,注意就容易分散,随着年龄的增长,到了小学中高年级,对抽象事物的注意才会相应提高。另外,低年级小学生自制力还比较差,容易离开教师所讲的内容,将注意转移到偶然看到或听到的事物上去。小学生注意的稳定性与集中性,与其年龄、兴趣、健康、情绪及对课业的理解程度有关。

④ 注意的分配和转移能力较弱

小学生不善于分配自己的注意力,在听课时,眼耳、手脑的配合往往不够,表现为注意分配能力不强,听讲和记笔记不能同时进行。这主要是因为他们对要注意的事物不熟悉,如果儿童写字更加熟练,那他就能把注意力集中到听讲上,他也能边听边记了。注意的转移和大脑皮层神经过程的可塑性、灵活性有关,低年级小学生注意转移性较差,由一种活动立即转移到另外一种活动上的能力欠佳,往往是一种活动进行了很长时间,注意还停留在先前的那种活动上。随着年龄增长,小学生注意的分配和转移也将逐渐发展起来。

(3) 记忆的发展特点

① 有意记忆逐渐增强

小学低年级学生无意记忆常占优势,在许多情况下都是靠无意记忆获得知识的,他们常常凭借兴趣记住一些事物,对不感兴趣而要求记住的东西,记忆的效率较低,但随着年级的增加,学生不能只学习一些自己感兴趣的内容,而必须学习一些不感兴趣的内容,在这样的条件下,有意记忆逐渐发展起来。

② 意义记忆迅速发展

小学生在记忆的目的性上,比学前儿童有较高的自觉性,但小学低年级儿童还不完全具有意义记忆的能力,因为他们还缺乏知识经验,难以找出材料的内部联系,他们的语言虽有发展,但还不能用自己的话复述所记忆的材料内容,他们对意义记忆的方法还很生疏,不善于进行分类和对比。随着年级的增高,知识经验的积累,理解能力的增强,儿童对所学知识有了一定程度的理解,能够从知识本身去寻找联系,进行意义记忆。小学生年级越高,意义记忆所占的比例越大,机械记忆所占的比例越小。随着年龄增长,小学生的记忆方法便由机械记忆向意义记忆过渡。

(4) 想象力的发展特点

① 有意想象增强

小学低年级学生的想象仍以无意想象为主,随着知识经验的积累、表象的增多,到了中高年级,有意想象的成分大大增强,能够初步控制自己的想象。

② 想象更富于现实性

学前儿童的想象常与现实不符合,有时会出现"想入非非"的现象。小学低年级儿童的想象较接近于现实,但因缺乏空间透视能力,在事物的比例关系上仍把握不好,到了中高年级,想象更接近现实。

③ 想象的创造成分日益增多

小学低年级学生的再造想象成分占很大比例,创造和加工的成分不多。随着经验的逐渐丰富,认知能力的不断提高,大脑中的表象越来越多,想象的创造成分也随之增加,想象的内容也更细致、丰富,并且能在词的水平上进行生动和形象的联想,初步具有了创造想象的能力。

(5) 思维的发展特点

① 由具体形象思维向抽象逻辑思维

小学一、二年级的学生,其思维主要带有直观具体性和外部片面性的特点,对学习材料的分析,主要限于直观行动方面,依赖于实物或图形等,因此所揭示事物的特征往往是外部属性,对对象和情境的判断往往是片面的,推理则依靠由知觉得到的直观形象,结论也非基于逻辑论证,而是将判断与感知到的知识直接对比;三、四年级是小学生思维发展的质变时期,大多数儿童能借助分析和综合将以前积累起来的概念加以概括;不仅判断的数量在增加,而且判断中的直观因素被压缩到最少量,对客体的关系也能根据本质进行或多或少的说明。

② 思维的基本过程日趋完善

小学低年级儿童只能在直接感知的条件下进行分析综合,难以摆脱具体事物,在头脑中进行分析与综合,在进行比较时,常表现出困难,不善于分清本质与非本质特点。随着知识的积累,小学中高年级儿童已能在表象和概念的基础上进行抽象分析与综合,比较能力也随之提高,开始由正确区分具体事物的异同逐步发展到区分抽象事物的异同,从区分个别部分的异同逐步发展到区分许多部分的关系的异同,从直接感知条件下进行比较发展到运用语言在头脑中引起表象条件下进行比较。

2. 情绪情感发展的特点

(1) 小学生情绪情感的丰富性不断扩展

对于小学生来说,学习成了他们的主导活动,完成各项学习任务成为小学生最主要的需要,这些与学习活动和学校生活相关的事物内容构成了小学生情绪的主要内容。如完成老师布置的作业就会产生积极的情绪体验,反之就会产生消极的情绪体验。此外,儿童在班集体的地位以及与同伴之间、老师之间的关系、老师对学生的评价等,都会引起小学生负面的情绪体验。

小学生的社会性情也在不断发展。通过集体活动,儿童的集体观念得到增强,产生了集体荣誉感;同伴交往的增加、同伴交往的深入,使儿童产生了友谊感。此外,小学生的各种高级情感的不断发展也在丰富小学生的情感世界。

(2) 情绪情感的稳定性逐渐增强

随着儿童进入小学,在集体生活和独立学习生活的影响下,儿童控制情绪的能力逐渐提高。虽然与成年人相比,小学生的情绪仍然具有很大的冲动性,还不善于掩饰控制自己的情绪,但他们的情绪已开始逐渐内化,小学高年级学生已逐渐能意识到自己的情绪表现以及随之可能产生的后果,情绪的稳定性和平衡性日益增强,冲动性和易变性逐渐消失。

(3) 情绪的深刻性不断增加

小学生的情绪与学前儿童相比,不但在内容上丰富多彩了,而且其情绪体验也更加深刻了。随着儿童年龄的增长,儿童的归因能力不断得到提高,情绪体验逐步深刻,愤怒的情绪开始逐渐减少,并更加现实化。

3. 学习动机发展的特点

(1) 社会性动机日益明显

随着小学生心理不断成熟以及与外界交往的不断增多,他们的社会性动机在整个学习动机系统中的作用日益明显。

(2) 直接的近景性动机向间接的远景性动机转变

直接的近景性动机是由眼前的看得见的利益所驱动,与近期目标相联系;间接的远景性动机与长远目标相联系。低年级小学生的学习动机多受直接因素的影响。

(3) 外在动机向内在动机发展

低年级学生的学习动力主要来自外界的教师或父母的要求,以及由表扬、物质奖励等外在目标而产生的诱发力,在这个时期可以说他们是目光短浅的学习者。随着年龄的增长和经验的积累,学生对学习的需求、求知欲提高了,学习的动力主要来自内在的驱动力,学习的内在动机在学习过程中的比重不断加大,表现出来由外在的动机向内在的动机发展的趋势。

(4) 认识兴趣发展

小学生认识兴趣的发展主要表现在:直接兴趣向间接兴趣发展;笼统、短暂的兴趣向广泛而有中心且稳定的兴趣发展,兴趣发展水平由低水平向高水平发展。

4. 个性与社会性的发展

(1) 自我意识的发展

自我意识是指个体对自己的认识和态度,包括自我认识、自我体验、自我监控三种成分。自我意识的形成与发展经历了三个阶段:

第一阶段是生理自我:生理自我是自我意识的原始形态,在儿童3岁左右基本成熟,表现为儿童将自己和自己的动作、动作和动作的对象区分开来等。

第二阶段是社会自我:3岁后,自我意识的发展进入社会自我阶段。

第三阶段是心理自我:心理自我是在青春期开始发展和形成的。

在小学时期,儿童的自我意识正处于客观化时期,是获得社会自我的时期。在这一阶段,个体受社会文化影响,是角色意识建立的最重要时期。角色意识的建立,标志着儿童的社会自我观念趋于形成。

(2) 社会性认知的发展

所谓社会性认知,是指对自己和他人的观点、情绪、思想、动机的认知,以及对社会关系和对集体组织间关系的认知,与认知能力发展相适应。

① 社会性认知发展的趋势

第一,从表面到内部,即从外部特征的注意到更深刻品质特征的注意。

第二,从简单到复杂,从问题的某个方面到多方面、多维度地看待问题;从呆板到灵活的思维。

第三,从对个人及即时事件的关心到关心他人利益和长远利益;从具体思维到抽象思维。

第四,从弥散性的、间断性的想法到系统的、有组织的、综合性的思想。

② 社会性交往的发展

小学儿童的交往对象主要是父母、教师和同伴。父母和儿童的关系变化主要体现在:交往的时间和内容发生变化;日常教养问题类型发生变化;父母的控制模式发生了变化。

小学生同伴交往的发展特点为:与同伴交往的时间更多,交往形式更复杂;儿童在同伴交往中传递信息的技能增强；儿童更善于利用各种信息来决定自己对他人所采取的行动；儿童更善于协调与其他儿童的活动；儿童开始形成同伴团体。

师生关系方面，随着儿童年龄的增长，儿童的交往观念、交往行为、建立关系的特点都在发生变化。对三至六年级小学生师生关系特点的研究发现：小学生的师生关系具有亲密性、反应性和冲突性三个方面的特点。在不同年级，师生关系在这三个方面有不同的表现，五年级学生表现出高亲密、高反应和高冲突的特点，而六年级学生则表现出低亲密、低反应、低冲突的特点。

二、小学生学习的特点与规律

（一）童年期儿童的学习特征

1. 小学儿童的学习动机

小学儿童的学习动机可分为四类：一是为了得到好分数，不落人后，或为了得到表扬和奖励而学习；二是为履行组织交给自己的任务，或为集体争光而学习；三是为了个人前途而学习；四是为祖国的前途、人民的利益而学习。

调查结果表明，整个小学阶段，主导的学习动机是第一和第二类。低年级以第一种学习动机居多。这表明小学儿童一般还不善于把学习与社会需要联系起来，其学习动机往往是直接与学习活动联系在一起的。

对学习动机变化形式的研究也发现，儿童的年级越低，学习动机越具体，儿童的学习动机更多地与学习活动本身直接联系，与学习兴趣发生联系或为学习兴趣所左右。

2. 小学儿童的学习兴趣

（1）由直接兴趣逐渐向间接兴趣转化

在低年级，由于知识的贫乏，活动的目的性差，因而，他们的兴趣往往容易受当前具体生动的形象所吸引和诱惑，表现为直接兴趣。到了中高年级，他们的认识水平提高了，对于事物的兴趣就不完全是由于事物本身而引起的，而是由于他们的某些目的需要所激起的。这样，间接兴趣便得到了发展。

（2）兴趣广度逐步扩大，但缺乏中心兴趣

小学生入学后受到教育教学的影响，学习活动的兴趣范围逐步扩大，从课内的学习兴趣扩大到课外的学习兴趣，从阅读童话故事的兴趣扩大到阅读文艺作品的兴趣，从对玩弄小玩具的兴趣扩大到对科技活动的兴趣等。小学生的兴趣范围扩大了，但还未形成中心兴趣。教师应注意培养他们的中心兴趣，指导他们围绕中心兴趣扩大兴趣范围，增长知识，开阔眼界。

（3）逐渐由不稳定向稳定发展

小学低年级学生的兴趣还不够稳定，既可以很快产生，也可以很快消失。比如，他们可能一会儿喜欢写字，一会儿又喜欢计算。到了中高年级，小学生兴趣的稳定性稍微好一些，保持的时间也稍微长一些。

3. 小学儿童的学习态度

在小学的学习活动中，儿童初步形成了一定的学习态度。

（1）对教师的态度

低年级儿童对教师怀有特殊的尊敬和依恋之情，由于自己尚不理解学习的社会意义，因而教师对待儿童的态度是影响儿童学习态度的主要因素。中年级儿童逐渐对教师产生选择性的、怀疑的态度,只有那些思想作风好、教学好,对儿童有耐心、公正的教师,才能赢得儿童的信任。

(2) 对集体的态度

初入学儿童还没有班集体意识,同学之间彼此很少互相关心。在教师的组织和教学的影响下,儿童开始互相关心,互相交往,互相帮助,并在此基础上开始形成班集体意识。从中年级开始,儿童开始具有了比较有组织的自觉的班集体生活,开始把自己看成集体中的一员。重视班集体的舆论和评价作用,进一步提高自己对学习、对集体的责任感,从而不断提高学习质量和行为品质。

(3) 对作业的态度

初入学儿童还未把作业看成学习的重要组成部分,还不能经常以负责的态度来对待作业。在教师正确的教育下,儿童逐步形成对作业的自觉负责的态度,表现在:能按一定时间来准备功课、完成作业,主动安排学习时间,并排除外在诱因的干扰;能按一定顺序来完成作业;能集中、细心地完成作业。

(4) 对评分的态度

从小学开始,儿童开始认识到评分的意义并对其心理发展产生重要影响。在正确教育影响下,低年级儿童逐渐了解分数的客观意义,并树立对分数的正确态度,从中年级起,儿童开始了解到学习是一种社会义务,因而把优良的分数看作高质量地完成这一社会义务的客观表现。

(节选自《国家教师资格考试专用教材——小学》,2012)

Reading Material Three

外语学习者的生理因素——年龄

年龄在母语和外语学习过程中都是一个十分重要的生理因素。从母语习得研究来看,学习者如果超过了一定的年龄,即使有语言环境也很难顺利地习得一种语言,对"狼孩"以及其他脱离人类正常生存环境至一定年龄而未能习得人类语言的研究证明了这一点。Lenneberg(1967)发现,小孩左脑的损伤对语言功能一般不会产生什么影响,但成年人左脑损伤则往往意味着语言功能的丧失。Lenneberg认为语言是大脑发育的产物,语言能力的发展受到人的生理基础的制约。继而,Lenneberg提出了颇有影响的自然语言习得关键期假设(Critical Period Hypothesis),认为习得语言的关键期是2岁至发育期。在关键期内,大脑具有可塑性(plasticity),语言习得能够自然而轻松地进行。这时语言的理解和产生涉及大脑的两个半球,整个大脑都参与语言学习,所以吸收语言信息就快些,习得就容易些。青春期到来之后,人们大脑机能发生了单侧化(laterlization),即某些功能偏向左半球或右半球,语言功能主要集中在左半球,右半球的语言功能逐渐减弱。同时,大脑已经发育成熟,左脑负责语言处理的神经协调机制的自动化能力就会减弱,神经系统不再具有可塑性,这样学习语言就比较费力且成效不显著。

从目前的研究情况来看,对关键期终止的具体年龄尚未达成一致的看法。关键期假说虽然是解释母语习得现象,但被许多心理学家和语言学家应用于解释外语学习,并发现关键期对外语习得有着明显的影响。综观目前的研究结果,年龄因素对外语习得的影响可概括如下:

(1) 学习外语的起始年龄并不在很大程度上影响习得的顺序;任何年龄开始学习一门外语都有可能获得成功。

(2) 学习外语的起始年龄比较明显地影响习得的速度和效率。在单位时间内,少年比儿童和成年人在习得语法和词汇时表现更为出色。

(3) 学习时间的长短影响外语习得的成功程度。学习时间的长短与整体交际能力的获得之间关系极为密切,起始年龄对语言达到的精确程度起着决定性作用,尤其在语音方面。当学习外语的起始年龄超过了关键期,说外语时会不可避免地带有本族语的口音。

(节选自张庆宗,2011)

1.2 Skills and Abilities

After learning some theories, we have gained the knowledge about primary school students' development. Now it is the time to analyze some cases to enhance your abilities of critical thinking and problem-solving.

Cases

⌈**Case One**⌋

Our Master

Tuesday

My new teacher pleases me also, since this morning. While we were coming in and when he was already seated at his post, some one of his scholars of last year every now and then peeped in at the door to salute him, they would present themselves and greet him: "Good morning, Signor Teacher!" "Good morning, Signor Perbonil!" Some entered, touched his hand, and ran away. It was evident that they liked him, and would have liked to return to him. He responded, "Good morning," and shook the hands which were extended to him, but he looked at no one; at every greeting his smile remained serious, with that perpendicular wrinkle on his brow, with his face turned towards the window, and staring at the roof of the house opposite; and instead of being cheered by these greetings, he seemed to suffer from them.

Then he surveyed us attentively, one after the other. While he was dictating, he descended and walked among the benches, and, catching sight of a boy whose face was all red with light pimples, he stopped dictating, took the lad's face between his hands and examined it; then he asked him what the matter was with him, and laid his hand on his forehead, to feel if it was hot.

Meanwhile, a boy behind him got up on the bench, and began to play the marionette. The teacher turned round suddenly: the boy resumed his seat at one dash, and remained there, with head hanging, in expectation of being punished. The master placed one hand on his head and said to him:

"Don't do so again." Nothing more.

Then he returned to his table and finished the dictation. When he had finished dictating, he looked at us a moment in silence; then he said, very, very slowly, with his big but kind voice:

"Listen. We have a year to pass together; let us see that we pass it well. Study and be good. I have no family, you are my family. Last year I had still a mother; she is dead. I am let alone. I have no one but you in all the world; I have no other affection, no other thought than you: you must be my sons I wish you well, and you must like me too. I do not wish to be obliged to punish anyone. Show me that you are boys of heart, our school shall be a family, and you shall be my consolation and my pride I do not ask you to give me a promise on your word of honor; I am sure that in your hearts you have already answered me 'yes', and I thank you."

At that moment the beadle entered to announce the close of school. We all left our seats very, very quietly. The boy who had stood up on the bench approached the master, and said to him, in a trembling voice:

"Forgive me, Signor Master."

The master kissed him on the brow, and said, "Go, my son."

(Adapted from *An Italian Schoolboy's Journal*)

思考问题

1. 该案例写于一百多年前的意大利,是一位小学生的日记,案例中的小作者是怎样描写自己的老师的？透露出怎样的视角？

2. 品读这一日记对你认识小学生有怎样的启发？

「Case Two」

难忘的小学生活

如果,我们是花朵,母校就是美丽的花园;如果我们是鱼儿,母校就是美丽的花园;如果,我们是鱼儿,母校就是辽阔的海洋;如果我们是雄鹰,母校就是高远的蓝天。

多么美丽的季节,处处流光溢彩,芳香四溢,而我们就要与母校互道珍重。

六年里令我最难忘的就是秦老师。秦老师那双炯炯有神的眼睛总感觉代替了能说会道的嘴巴。记得秦老师对我们上的第一节课,就对我们说:"我的眼睛能看见你们所有人在干什么,我知道,你们可能不信,那我就给你们实验一下。"我们看见老师在看肖雨晴,可老师却说:"辛智博在不停地把他的笔摆弄来摆弄去的,肖雨晴在抠手指。"从这一刻开始,我就打心底里崇拜老师。

老师,您的爱如丝丝春雨能使沙漠冒新绿,您的爱如三月的春风,呵护着幼小的心灵,您的爱如温暖的河流,轻托我生命的小舟。

母校的四季最迷人。蓝蓝的天似乎哪儿都一样,只是校园的天更蓝更美。

春天,校园里万物复苏,鸟语花香。花园里的淡黄色的菊花,粉嫩粉嫩的杏花,碧绿的三叶草,玫红色的玫瑰,百花齐放,姹紫嫣红。坐在花园的石头凳上,闻着沁人心脾的花香,听着鸟儿的歌唱,看着蝴蝶优雅的舞姿,感到非常惬意。

夏天,男生们穿着短袖,在操场上你追我赶,女生们坐在教室围成一圈折纸扇子。玩热了,就去水管那儿洗把脸。

秋天是个美丽的季节,树的叶子黄了飘落下来,好像一个个叶子仙子在空中翩翩起舞,一下课同学们就去捡落叶,比谁捡的最漂亮。

冬天,天地被盖上了一层白色的毯子,同学们在操场上堆雪人、打雪仗,有的男生恶作剧,看见树下有人经过,就把树抱住摇一摇,下面的人一下子就变成了"雪人",玩得可开心了!

记得上三年级时,上课老师对我们说:"同学们,等一下要进行防火演练,同学们听见警报声就往外跑,听见了吗?"我们齐刷刷地点点头。不过一会,我们就听到了警报,一起往外跑。忽然,脚下一滑,我从台阶上摔了下来,站不起来了,同学们将我扶起,眼神里流露出关心。

六年了,六年的时光,仿佛只是一瞬间。怎么舍得,亲如父母的老师;怎么舍得,美丽可爱的校园;怎么舍得,情同手足的同学。至今还没有忘记,在小学里与同学们朝夕相处的时光,课堂上的争论,球场上的疯狂,班会中的歌唱。这一切多么值得回想。母校,送走了一批又一批的栋梁,迎来了一批又一批的幼苗。母校啊!感谢您的给予和付出!我们快要走了,但是,我相信今天我们因您而骄傲,明天,您一定会以我们而自豪。再见,我亲爱的母校!

(强俊勇提供)

思考问题

1. 这是一位小学生在即将毕业时写的一篇作文,文中充满了对学校的留恋与感激,如果你是他/她的老师,你有怎样的感受?作为教师,是否觉得自己肩上的担子更重了?

2. 这位小作者的感情非常细腻,内心世界也非常丰富,试分析他的心理特征。

「Case Three」

给老师的一封信

敬爱的老师：

  您知道吗？虽然每位老师在我心目中都有着重要的地位，但您是我心目中最重要的老师。快毕业了，请您听一听我的心里话吧！

  每次上课，一见您走进教室我就充满欣喜。当我们回答问题时，您的眼神透出对我们的信任，在这样的信任中，我绷紧的心渐渐放松了，那眼神鼓励我思考。当我回答对时您的眼神如鲜花绽放，更让我有成就感。当我答错时，您也微笑着让我坐下，眼神如潺潺的流水，微笑如同淡淡的波纹，冲淡了我的失落感。

  下课后您就像我们的朋友。我们一起聊天，聊得火热，时间似乎停止了。娱乐、学习、班级新闻都聊，和您也没了辈分，我甚至道出了自己的秘密。您的讲授总像磁铁般吸引着我，让我永远喜欢上您的课。

  快毕业了，我就要离开这里，我永远都不会忘记您，我的恩师，我会在以后求学的每一个日子里为您祈祷，愿您身体健康，幸福一生。

  此致

    敬礼！

您的学生：×××
2019年4月27日
（强俊勇提供）

思考问题

1. 这封信中描写了对老师怎样的情感？对你认识小学生有什么帮助吗？
2. 作为老师在教授知识的同时，应该怎样促进小学生的情感发展？

「Case Four」

回忆我的小学生活

  我时常怀着深深的感激之情，思念着我的启蒙老师们，是他们，在我幼稚的心里播下希望的种子。教导我们：要爱祖国，要勤勉，要做一个正直诚实的人。

  还记得我刚入学的时候，我的一年级班主任是吕老师，每天我们来到学校时，她都会笑着说："早上好！"上课时吕老师总能让汉字和拼音这两位陌生的朋友和我们相识。

  我还记得四年前的一节语文课上，我突然感到一阵恶心，把一些污秽吐到了自己的衣服上和桌子上。这时班主任老师飞快地向我走了过来急忙用卫生纸帮我擦掉了身上的污秽，还叫同学用沙子清理了桌子和地上的污秽。过了好久我才感到自己哭了。许多同学也都围了过来，有的端着热水，有的拿着卫生纸，每一个人眼睛里都流露出焦虑的眼神，忽然之间我感到了同学之间的友情和老师的关爱。

最让我记忆深刻的是上五年级时我们班的新班主任秦老师。开学第一天上第一节课,老师先自我介绍了之后,又给我们上了一堂特殊的课。但是第二节课刚上课时全班人都还在说话,就连那些全班同学认为学习好的同学也都在说话。老师一进教室很生气,我们突然安静了下来,安静得连一根针掉在地上都能听见。随后秦老师给我们讲了一个遵守纪律的故事,同学们听了很受感动……在秦老师的努力下我们班的纪律可以说是全校数一数二的。为什么这样说呢?因为每周的纪律流动红旗都挂在我们班。在老师的帮助下,我们不光纪律进步了,学习也有了很大的进步。

往事桩桩件件,历历在目,那是我们记忆仓库里一颗流光溢彩的珍珠啊!

现在我们只能在母校里待两个月,两个月后,我们将告别多彩的童年,告别鲜艳的红领巾,告别亲爱的母校,告别像父母一样的老师,告别情同手足的同学们。

再见,敬爱的母校,在您的怀抱里,我们从无知变得懂事,从幼稚变得成熟,从胆小变得勇敢。再见,敬爱的老师。再见,亲爱的同学。请记住我们在一起的每一天,让友情地久天长!

小学生活如此难忘,我永远不会忘记的。

(强俊勇提供)

> **思考问题**
>
> 1. 案例中这位小作者描述了自己在小学时的一桩桩难忘的往事,其中老师起到了相当重要的作用,通过这篇作文,你觉得小学老师除了讲授知识以外,还要做哪些工作?这些工作有意义吗?为什么?
>
> 2. 作为小学老师,你觉得应该怎样认识自己的工作,促进小学生的全面发展?

✦ 亮考帮

亮闪闪:请总结学习过程中,哪些是自己记忆深刻、受益最大、最欣赏的内容呢?请写出具体内容。

考考你:请把自己弄懂的但觉得别人可能存在困惑的地方,用问题的形式表述出来,来挑战一下其他同学。

帮帮我:请把自己不懂、不会的地方或想要了解的内容,用问题的形式表述出来,并带到课堂上加以讨论。

参考文献

[1] Amicis, E. D. *An Italian Schoolboy's Journal*[M].北京:中国国际广播出版社,2014.
[2] Science. National Geographic:Brain[EB/OL].(2013-01-01)[2020-06-17]. Retrieved from https://www.nationalgeographic.com/science/.
[3] Tokuhama-Espinosa, T. *Living Languages:Multilingualism Across the Lifespan*[M]. Westport, CT:Praeger,2008.
[4] Woolfolk, A. *Educational Psychology*[M]. Beijing:Tsinghua University Press,2014.
[5] 毕淑敏.谁是你的重要他人[M].北京:中国物资出版社,2009.
[6] 国家教师资格考试专用教材,教育教学知识与能力——小学[M].北京:世界图书出版公司,2012.
[7] 张庆宗.外语学与教的心理学原理[M].北京:外语教学与研究出版社,2011.

Task 2 Understanding Middle School Students

People often believe that middle school students are the most difficult group of people because they are in the special period in our life span. But this period is the most important time for human beings' development. This section offers you some knowledge about it.

2.1 Knowledge Points

Outline

To understand more about middle school students, we offer you characteristics of adolescence, and strategies for learning.

2.1.1 About teens

They are an age of transition, confusion, self-consciousness, growing, and changing bodies and minds. Here are simple reminders.

(1) Intellectual capacity adds abstract operational thought around the age of 12.

Therefore, some sophisticated intellectual processing is increasingly possible. Complex problems can be solved with logical thinking. This means that linguistic metalanguage can now, theoretically, have some impact. But the success of any intellectual endeavor will be factor of the attention a learner places on the task; therefore, if a learner attends to self, to appearance, to being accepted, to sexual thoughts, to a weekend party, or whatever the intellectual task at hand may suffer.

(2) Attention spans are lengthening, but with many diversions.

(3) Varieties of sensory input are still important.

(4) Factors surrounding ego, self-image, and self-esteem are at their pinnacle. Teens are ultrasensitive to how others perceive their changes physical and emotional selves along with their mental capabilities. One of the most important concerns of the secondary school teacher is to keep self-esteem high by:

- Avoiding embarrassment of students at all costs;
- Affirming each person's talents and strengths;
- Allowing mistakes and other errors to be accepted;

- De-emphasizing competition between classmates;
- Encouraging small group work where risks are more easily made.

(5) Secondary school students are of course becoming increasingly adultlike in their ability to make those occasional diversions.

(6) The development and importance of self-concept are also the keys. Both individual's view of the world and self-concept affect their success in learning situations. Children monitor their own interactions with the teacher and are also aware how the teacher interacts with other children. A clear relationship was found between learners' perceptions of personal control over learning outcomes and the number of opportunities that those learners had been given to take responsibility for their own learning. So the following aspects are important points for learners to manage themselves:

- Attitude
- Strengths and weaknesses
- Plans
- Responsibility
- Evaluating progress and reasons for successes and failures
- Participation

1.2.2 Strategies for learning

Strategy refers to broadly conceived directions the learner more or less consciously chooses in trying to achieve his objectives. 14 slogans are here.

- Find your own way to learn
- Organize
- Be creative
- Make your own opportunities
- Learn to live with uncertainties
- Use memonics
- Make errors work
- Use your linguistic knowledge
- Let context help you
- Learn to make intelligent guesses
- Learn some lines as wholes
- Learn formalized routines
- Learn production techniques
- Use different styles of speech

Repetition is another point we need to pay attention. A basic lexical syllabus formulated from first 500 to 800 most frequently occurring words in English. Most learners knew the words that appeared more than 7 times, but they did not know half of the words that appeared only once or twice. So repetition is the key to learn a wide range of words.

Label of failure on children will have negative effects. Schools pin the label of failure on children. We seek for the way of resistance of learners and effectiveness.

Reading Materials

Reading Material One

中学生的身心发展特征概述

一、中学生身心发展的特点

中学生在生理上正处于青春发育期，生理上急骤变化，智力迅速发展，情绪和情感的内容及形式日渐丰富，集中表现出如下四个特点：

1. 过渡性

过渡性即从幼稚期向成熟期的过渡，主要表现在两方面：

（1）中学生的身心发展既具有儿童期的特点，又具有成熟期的特点，处于半幼稚、半成熟状态。

（2）青少年期是人由童年向成年的转变时期，各种心理特征逐渐接近成人，由发育迅速趋向平稳，由人格差异不稳定到形成比较稳定的人格再到形成稳定的人格，特别明显地表现在由对成人的依赖到相对独立的方面。

2. 闭锁性

所谓闭锁性是指人的心理活动具有某种含蓄、内隐的特点，它是相对于人的外部行为表现与内部心理活动之间的一致性而言的。中学生的心理逐渐显示出闭锁性，即他们的内心世界逐渐复杂，开始不大轻易将内心世界表露出来。

由于闭锁性的特点，中学生心里的话常常是不愿对长辈说的。中学生的年龄越大，这个特点就越为明显。中学生同时还有一个心理特点，就是容易对同龄、同性别的人，特别是知己暴露真正的想法。

3. 社会性

在青少年期，由于社会地位的变化，其活动社会性的增强，青少年对社会生活越来越关注。同时，他们与社会环境的接触越来越多，社会环境对青少年社会化的影响也越来越明显。

青少年的社会性主要表现在：他们已不拘泥于儿童时那种仅仅对自己或周围生活中具体事物的关心，而是开始以极大的兴趣观察、思考和判断社会生活中的种种现象与问题，政治、历史、文学艺术、法律道德、社会风气、人际关系等都成了他们认识和思考的对象，成了他们十分关心的问题。他们希望从中找出现象的本质，形成自己的看法；他们的社会性情感越来越丰富和稳定；他们已逐步形成一定的为人处世的态度和行为方式，动机、兴趣、品德、自我意识、世界观与人生观都开始逐渐形成并趋于稳定。

4. 动荡性

中学生的思想比较敏感。中学生尤其是高中生往往在政治活动中"打头阵",起着"先锋和桥梁"的作用。然而,中学生也容易走向另一个"极端"。中学生希望受人重视,希望被看成"大人",成为社会的一员,他们思想单纯,很少有保守思想,敢想、敢说、敢作、敢为。但在他们心目中,什么是正确的幸福观、友谊观、英雄观、自由观和人生观,还都是个谜。他们对于别人的评价十分敏感。好斗好胜,但容易偏激,容易摇摆,思维具有片面性。他们往往把坚定与执拗,勇敢与蛮干、冒险混同起来。他们的精力充沛,能力也在发展,但性格未最后定型。因此对处于青少年阶段的中学生的教育和培养工作,在整个国民教育中起着关键性的作用。

(节选自《国家教师资格考试专用教材——中学》,2012)

Reading Material Two

中学生的认知发展

一、中学生感知觉发展的特点

(一)感觉的发展

1. 感受性和观察力进一步发展。青少年的视觉感受性在不断提高,精确区分各种颜色和色度的能力也在不断增加。

2. 各种感觉能力接近甚至超过成人水平。研究表明,初中生区分各种色度的能力比小学要高出60%以上,15岁前后,视觉和听觉感受性甚至会超过成人。

(二)知觉的发展

1. 知觉的有意性和目的性提高。

2. 知觉的精确性和概括性发展起来。

3. 少年期学生开始出现逻辑知觉。这种知觉是和逻辑思维密切联系的,即在知觉过程中,能够把一般原理、规则和个别事物或问题联系起来。

4. 初中阶段,少年期学生的空间和时间知觉有了新的发展。他们学会了在抽象水平上理解各种图形的形状、大小以及空间位置的相互关系。在时间知觉方面,对于较长时间的单位如"纪元""世纪""年代"等开始初步理解,但往往很不精确,容易把遥远的过去在观念上缩短。

二、中学生注意发展的特点

(一)无意注意与有意注意的发展和深化

1. 无意注意不断发展和深化,兴趣爱好逐渐稳定,注意的发展始于无意注意。最初无意注意的产生主要依靠外部刺激物的作用,随着学生自身兴趣、爱好的逐渐稳定,无意注意的产生主要受到兴趣、爱好的影响。研究表明,由于强烈的直接兴趣的影响,约有90%的中学生明显地表现出偏科现象,这是无意注意发展和深化的具体表现。

2. 有意注意占优势地位。中学生在无意注意逐渐深化的同时,有意注意也得到发展,并且逐渐取代了无意注意的优势地位。最明显的特点是注意的随意性增强,具体表现为中学生学习活动的目的性、自觉性和计划性得以加强,注意逐渐具有自我组织、自我调节和自我控制的性质。

3. 注意特征存在个体差异。中学生的有意注意虽然有了明显的增强,但无意注意的作用在学习活动中仍占有一定的地位。正是由于这一特征,决定了中学生注意的发展存在着几种不同的类型:以无意注意占优势的情绪型;以有意注意占优势的意志型;以有意后注意占优势的自觉意志型。因此教师应针对他们注意发展的特征和个别差异,发展其注意力。

(二) 注意品质的全面发展

1. 注意稳定性提高但发展速度相对较慢。随着意志力的发展,中学生控制自己注意的能力显著增强,注意的稳定性得到了迅速的提高。研究表明,7—10岁儿童每次注意稳定约20分钟,10—12岁是25分钟,而12岁以后则是30分钟左右。虽然注意稳定性随着年龄的增长而不断增长,但发展的速度不尽相同,其中小学阶段发展速度较快,幼儿阶段和中学阶段发展速度相对较慢。

2. 注意广度接近成人。中学生随着学习的不断深入,生活经验的丰富和见识的增长,注意的广度也有了长足的提高。13岁儿童的注意广度已接近成人。

3. 注意分配能力还不够成熟。个体的注意分配能力发生较早但发展较为缓慢。基于对学生注意分配能力的考虑,在教学活动中,老师不要求初中生记笔记,对高中生只要求记讲课要点。

4. 注意转移能力缓慢增长。注意转移的能力是随个体大脑神经系统内抑制能力第二信号系统的发展而得以迅速发展的。注意转移发展的趋势是小学二年级至初中二年级是迅速增长期,初中二年级至高中二年级是发展的停滞期,高中二年级到大学二年级是缓慢增长期。

三、中学生记忆发展的特点

第一,记忆的容量日益增大,短时记忆广度接近成人。第二,对直观形象的材料记忆要优于词语。第三,中学生能主动选择记忆方法,有意记忆逐渐占主导地位。第四,随着年龄的增长,理解记忆逐渐成为主要的记忆手段。第五,抽象记忆的发展速度较快,逐渐占据主导地位。

四、中学生思维发展的特点

1. 青少年的思维能力得到迅速发展,抽象逻辑思维逐渐处于优势地位。在初中阶段抽象逻辑成分已经在一定程度上占有相对优势,但在很大程度上还属于经验型,即思维活动在许多情况下还受到具体的、直观的感性经验的直接支持。只有到了高中阶段,思维才能逐步摆脱经验的限制,从而可以根据理论来进行逻辑推理,达到"理论型"。

2. 在整个中学阶段,形式逻辑思维逐渐发展,占据主导地位。形式逻辑思维和辩证逻辑思维是抽象逻辑思维的两个不同的发展阶段。其中,形式逻辑思维主要表现在概念、推理和逻辑法则等应用能力上。

3. 辩证逻辑思维迅速发展。初一阶段的学生已经开始掌握辩证逻辑的各种形式,但水平较低;初三学生的辩证思维处于迅速发展阶段,高中学生的辩证逻辑思维已占据优势地位。

五、中学生智力发展的特点

（一）智力水平得到飞跃性提高，智力发展进入关键期

随着年龄增长、身体机能增强，社会实践增加，记忆力和想象力同步发展，使得整个智力水平都得到飞跃式的提高。有关研究表明，初中二年级到高中二年级是中学生智力发展的关键期。

（二）智力基本达到成熟

关于智力发展的限度问题，目前还没有一个十分可靠的结论，但有一点是清楚的，那就是人到18岁左右，智力已达到成熟时期的水平。此后，随着知识经验的增长，总的智力能量不会有显著增长。

（三）各方面智力发展不等速，并存在个体差异

总体而言，个体的智力因素中，言语发展较晚，到20岁以后达到高峰；逻辑思维能力是智力的核心，于18岁之后达到顶峰。而知觉发展较早，12岁左右达到高峰，而不同个体智力发展的速度和达到顶峰的时间也存在巨大差异，有早慧型，有晚熟型。

（节选自《国家教师资格考试专用教材——中学》，2017）

2.2 Skills and Abilities

Until now you have gained the characteristics of adolescence and learned some strategies of guiding those teenagers. Now it is the time to practice your skills by analyzing the following cases.

Cases

⌈ **Case One** ⌋

向大家介绍我

Hello! 我叫黄琳扉，你们也可以叫我黄蕊，我今年13岁，刚刚要步入初中，下面请听听我的自我介绍吧！Please!

我是一个短发的女孩，有一双大眼睛，一只是妈妈赐予我的，一只是爸爸赐予我的，因为我一个是单眼皮，一个是双眼皮，双眼皮是妈妈的，单眼皮是爸爸的，哈哈有趣吧！我还有一个向上翘的鼻子，一个红红的樱桃小嘴，这就是我的长相。下面请听听我获得的荣誉吧。我是××县××小学毕业的，虽然不是一所非常著名的小学但我很爱那里，毕竟我在那获得了好多荣誉。我曾多次获得过文明星，纪律星。其实我不是一个守纪律的学生，也不是一个讲文明的学生，我也往地上扔过果皮等一些垃圾，上课时也做过一些小动作，老师不应该给我的，但我现在已是一个中学生了，就要改掉以前的不足，成为一名优秀的好

学生。

　　我也常常跟别人吵架,大家都说我的性格太独特了,没有人能和我一样,甚至会有人开玩笑地说,利用现在的科学技术克隆也不一定能复制出一个一模一样的我。我是一个永远都坚守着自己信念的人,我不会很轻易地就改变我自己的看法,尽管有时错了我也不会改,因为我总是坚信我自己的答案。Look! 这就是我——一个不轻易改变信念的女孩。

　　自己的人生之路是要靠自己照亮的,所以不要轻易地改变自己的信念,要相信自己。我是一个充满阳光的女孩,希望大家和我做朋友。Thank you!

思考问题

　　1. 上述小短文是一位初中学生的自我介绍,试分析该生的性格特点。
　　2. 作为教师,应该如何帮助学生了解自己,以促进学生的全面发展?

Case Two

The Best Goal

　　I remember once upon a time, when I was running 800 meters, I felt there seemed to be the impossible mission for me. I wanted to give up, then my teacher told me that I should not think about the 800 meters, I should set up several 100 meters for myself, then I wouldn't be so tired. I did as he told me, indeed, every time when I finished a small goal, I was happy, in the end, I finished the running. I have learned that we need to set up the best goal, which means we can make the small goals, which are so easy for us to realize. Then every time we finish the small goal, we will close to our final destination.

Friend's Visiting

　　Last week, a friend of mine came to visit me, I felt so surprised, because we lost contact for many years, he was my classmate when I was in primary school, now five years has passed, both of us have entered college. My friend told me that he was doing a research, so he came to visit me. We talked many things in primary school, which brought back lots of good memories. Both of us were naughty at that time, but we loved sport, played the basketball matches and won the first place. When he left, we made a deal to gather for the next time.

My Early Idol

　　When I was in middle school, I heard the English song "Baby One More Time". When I saw the music record, the girl was so sweet and pretty. She danced so well in the record, and full of energy. Since then, I fell in love with Britney Spears, whom every girl wanted to be. She was not only beautiful, but also could sing and dance so well. Britney Spears was my early idol, whose energetic image attracted me so much. I was so crazy about her at that time.

The Exciting Movie

Last week, I went to the theater with my friends. We wanted to see the hot movie, *The Fast and the Furious 7*, which many of my friends highly recommended. They said it was so awesome. I was looking forward to seeing it. As the plot went into further, the cars drove so fast, the characters fought so strongly with the bad guys. I was very impressed by the fighting scenes, especially the characters drove their cars dropping off the airplane. The technology developed well, and the director and his team shot a good movie, which caught people's eyes. The movie broadened my vision.

Interest Is the Best Teacher

When I learned English, I felt so hard, because no matter how hard I tried, I just could not understand the grammar. One day, my sister asked me why I was so confused with English, I told her I did not know. I was so afraid of it. Then she asked me to watch English movies and listened to English songs. At first, I fell in love with these songs, I learned to sing them, I found I could remember more and more words. I was very interested in the movies. With interest, I made great progress. I am not afraid of English any more. Interest is the best teacher.

An Unforgettable Thing in Summer Holiday

July 2 was my grandfather's birthday. On that day, all of my families gathered together to celebrate his birthday. My uncles and aunts came back from other cities. My grandparents were very happy. I made a surprise for my grandfather. I cooked a dish for him. As I never cooked before, he was so surprised as well as exciting. My grandfather said that it was the best birthday gift he has received. I was glad to make grandfather happy. Actually, I had practiced for several days before that day. My mum was my cooking teacher.

（节选自黄杰，2020）

思考问题

1. 以上小短文均为初中学生的英文习作，试分析初中学生在交友、亲情、兴趣、爱好、目标、偶像等方面有哪些特点？

2. 作为初中英语教师，应该如何看待学生的兴趣爱好，如何引导学生在学好英语的同时培养正确的人生观和世界观？

亮考帮

亮闪闪：请总结学习过程中，哪些是自己记忆深刻、受益最大、最欣赏的内容呢？请写出具体内容。

考考你: 请把自己弄懂的但觉得别人可能存在困惑的地方,用问题的形式表述出来,来挑战一下其他同学。

帮帮我: 请把自己不懂、不会的地方或想要了解的内容,用问题的形式表述出来,并带到课堂上加以讨论。

参考文献

[1] Brown, D. *Teaching by Principles* [M]. New Jersey: Prentice Hall Regents, 2007.

[2] Hedge, T. *Teaching and Learning in the Language Classroom* [M]. Shanghai: Shanghai Foreign Language Education Press, 2002.

[3] Stern, H. H. *Issues and Options in Language Teaching* [M]. Shanghai: Shanghai Foreign Language Education Press, 1996.

[4] Williams, M., & Robert, L. *Psychology for Language Teachers* [M]. Cambridge: Cambridge University Press, 1997.

[5] 黄杰. 初中生英语作文大全 [EB/OL]. (2020-05-06) [2020-05-24]. From https://wenku.baidu.com/view/58fe6cc5a2116c175f0e7cd184254b35eefd1a3c.htm? fr=search.

[6] 国家教师资格考试专用教材, 教育教学知识与能力——中学 [M]. 北京: 世界图书出版公司, 2012.

第五章 英语课程与教材探析

主要内容

1. 理解英语教学新课标
   - 义务教育英语课程标准
2. 理解教材
3. 教案撰写

✓案例学习
✓专业参考
✓学术探讨

In previous chapters, you have already learned some knowledge of children's development and the method of teaching and learning. Now it is the time to explore in depth how English courses are designed in primary and middle schools. Since children have their own ways of seeing, thinking, and doing things, it is a big challenge to teach primary and middle school students in a school-based context. *National English Curriculum for Nine-Year Compulsory Education* (2011) is the programmatic document to provide a guide for schools and teachers. As a student English teacher, you should first understand the principles of this document, make clear the design of textbooks and other teaching materials, and then learn how to design your own curriculum and write a teaching plan based on the guide of the document. These are the key points we offer in Chapter 5.

Task 1 The National English Curriculum

The National English Curriculum is the programmatic document for English teachers. By learning the details of the documents, you are going to explore how it is designed, clarify the objectives, and understand the requirement of Levels 1—5.

1.1 Knowledge Points

Outline

In this part, you are going to learn the background information of why English is offered from primary school level, what supporting theories are, and how we design our curriculum.

1.1.1 Background information

About the age of studying a foreign language, we have already talked about in Chapter 4. Let's discuss why students in stage of compulsory education need to study a foreign language. We are thinking about the following points.
- A global village
- World peace and advances
- Abilities to live and communicate
- Being educated from childhood
- Being prepared linguistically and attitudinally
- Being open-minded

So the importance could be:
- Understanding and appreciating different countries, cultures, people and communities;
- Requirements of basic structure of language;
- Exploring the similarities and differences between a foreign language and their mother tongue;
- Learning how language can be manipulated and applied in different ways;
- Improving their learning skills;
- Laying the foundation for future study of other language.

To reach the aim of English study in primary school, the following requirements need to be met:

- Qualified teachers;
- Clear goals and objectives;
- Positive environment.

As for language development, the learning of a foreign language can be used as a tool to help children develop an awareness of a different language system, its sounds, symbols, structures, and idiomatic expressions. A foreign language can enhance children's development of many different aspects of skills by:

- Adding interest and increasing motivation;
- Engaging children in discovering different ways of saying things and different ways of living;
- Helping children to concentrate when learning;
- Providing the experience of uttering sounds differently;
- Developing the desire to use language as a means of communication;
- Developing all four skills;
- Developing strategies in general;
- Raising awareness of the differences and encouraging comparisons;
- Developing an awareness of grammar and pattern in another language.

1.1.2 Supporting theories

1. Humanistic approaches

Rogers (1969) identified a number of key elements of the humanistic approach to education. He believed that human beings have a natural potential for learning. He suggested that significant learning only take place when the subject matter is perceived to be of personal relevance to the learner and when it involves active participation by the learner.

2. Carl Ransom Rogers

Carl Ransom Rogers was an American psychologist and among the founders of the humanistic approach (or client-centered approach) to psychology. Rogers is widely considered to be one of the founding fathers of psychotherapy research and was honored for his pioneering research with the Award for Distinguished Scientific Contributions by the American Psychological Association (APA) in 1956.

About experiential learning, Rogers believed that learning which is self-initiated and which involves feelings as well as cognition is most pervasive. He distinguished two types of learning: cognitive (meaningless) and experiential (significant) learning. Rogers lists these qualities of experiential learning: personal involvement, self-initiated, evaluated by learners, and pervasive effects on learners. To Rogers, experiential learning is equivalent to personal change and growth. For the details of humanism, please get reference from Chapter 3.

1.1.3 Design the curriculum

The design of the new curriculum standards unifies both primary and secondary school English into one continuum of development and divides English language teaching and learning into nine proficiency-based levels with a required component for every student from Level 1 in primary school to Level 7 in senior high school. Detailed performance objectives for each level are given in addition to the overall aims of the course. The course adds an elective component after the completion of the nine-year compulsory education at Level 5 with an intention to provide opportunities for different routes of development and individuality.

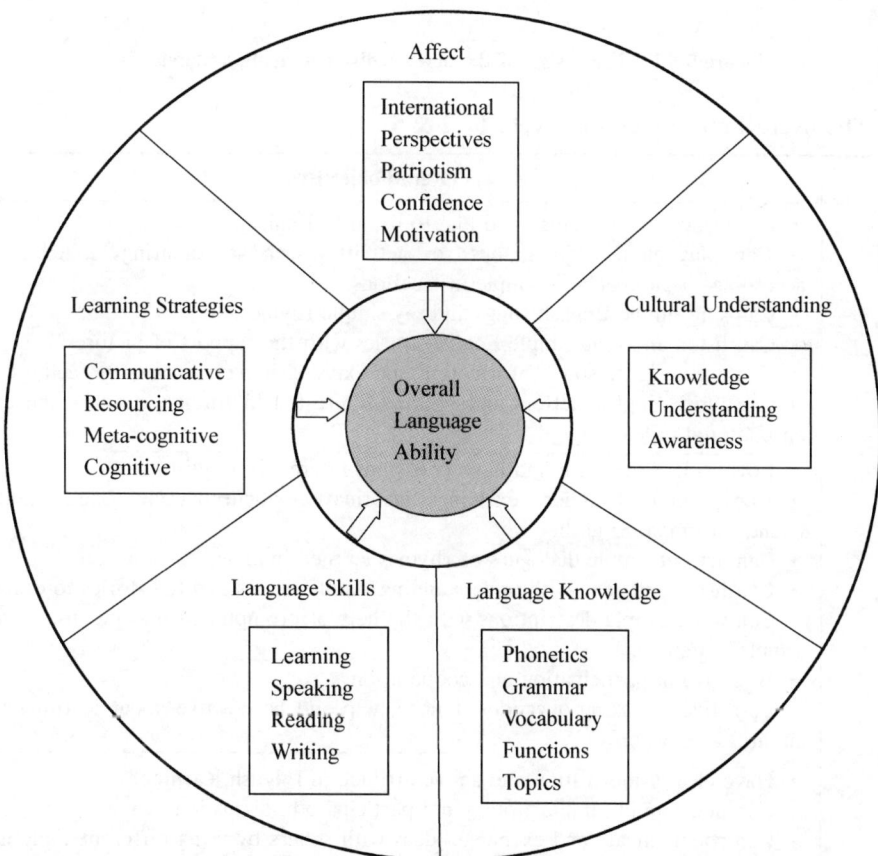

Figure 5-1 The framework of objectives in the new English Curriculum Standards

1. The design of the new English Curriculum Standards

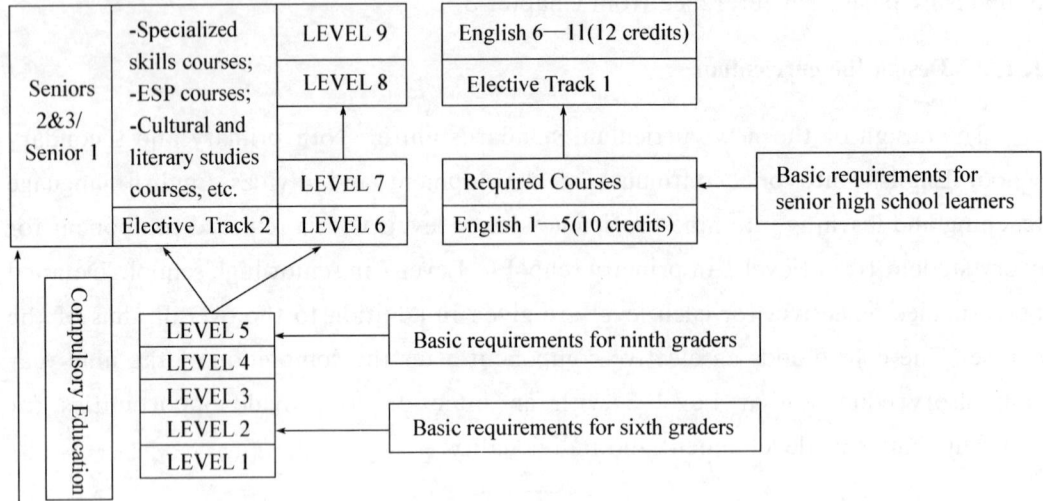

Figure 5-2 The design of the new English Curriculum Standards

2. The overall objectives for levels 1, 2 & 5

	Overall objectives
Level 1	• Be curious about English and like to listen to English. • Can play games, do actions, or activities such as colouring, matching, etc. according to the teacher's simple instructions. • Can sing simple English songs and say simple rhymes. • Can listen and read simple English stories with the support of pictures. • Can exchange personal information and express simple emotions or feelings. • Can write English letters and words. Interested in foreign cultures and customs encountered in learning.
Level 2	• Love to learn English and have persistent interest in English. • Can greet each other, exchange information about oneself, one's family and friends in simple English. • Can act out simple dialogues or rhymes learned in class. • Can listen and read with understanding simple stories and tell stories to others. • Can write simple descriptions with the help of prompts, such as pictures, words or sample sentences. • Be active in participation and cooperation. • Be active in asking questions if need help and be positive about learning foreign cultures and customs.
Level 5	• Have clearly motivation and active attitude in English learning. • Can understand familiar topics and participate in discussion. • Can communicate and exchange ideas with others by using different topic in daily life and state own opinions. • Can read and understand brief reading materials, newspapers, and magazines for grades 7—9 students. • Can use some strategies while reading. • Can draw up and revise small essays. • Can cooperate with others, solve problems and complete task together. • Can make a self-evaluation, and summarize the study method. • Can utilize educational resources and further enhance the ability of understanding and recognizing foreign cultures.

3. Subcategory: language skills

		Performance descriptions
Level 1	Listening and do	• Be able to recognize and point at objects or pictures according to what is heard. • Be able to understand and react to simple classroom instructions. • Be able to do things according to instructions, such as pointing, coloring, drawing pictures, acting physically. • Be able to understand and react to simple English stories with the help of pictures or actions.
	Speaking and singing	• Be able to imitate from the recordings. • Be able to greet each other in simple English. • Be able to exchange simple personal information, such as name and age. • Be able to express simple feeling or emotions, such as likes and dislikes. • Be able to guess meaning or say the words from acting or miming. • Be able to sing 15 children's songs or nursery rhymes. • Be able to speak out words or phrases according to pictures or printed words.
	Playing and acting	• Be able to play games in English and communicate with each other in the game with simple English under the teacher's direction. • Be able to do simple role plays in English. • Be able to perform simple English plays.
	Reading and writing	• Be able to write correct letters and words that have been learned. • Be able to recognize words printed with pictures. • Be able to recognize objects first and then understand words describing them. • Be able to read and understand simple picture stories in English. • Be able to write simple sentences based on given models.
	Audio and visual	• Be able to follow simple English cartoon films or other English programmes at a similar level. The time spent for audio and visual should be no less than 10 hours per school year with an average of 20—25 minutes a week.
Level 2	Listening	• Be able to understand simple spoken English or recorded English with the help of pictures, visuals and gestures. • Be able to understand simple English stories supported with pictures. • Be able to understand questions in classroom activities. • Be able to understand and react properly to commonly used instructions.
	Speaking	• Be able to pronounce English clearly with the right intonation. • Be able to make short dialogues on familiar personal or family topics. • Be able to use very common daily expressions, e.g. greeting, farewell, showing gratitude and making apologies. • Be able to tell simple stories or give simple descriptions with the help of the teacher and pictures.

(to be continued)

		Performance descriptions
Level 2	Reading	• Be able to recognize learned words and phrases. • Be able to pronounce simple words according to rules of spelling. • Be able to read and understand simple instructions in the textbook. • Be able to read and understand simple information from greeting cards. • Be able to read simple stories or short texts with the help of pictures, and form the initial habit of reading in a sense group. • Be able to read aloud correctly the learned texts or stories.
	Writing	• Be able to use capital and small letters in writing and use correct punctuations. • Be able to write out simple greetings. • Be able to write simple descriptions with the help of prompts, such as pictures, words or sample sentences.
	Playing and acting audio and visual	• Be able to play games in English according to simple instructions. • Be able to perform stories or short plays with the help of the teacher. • Be able to sing 30 simple English songs or rhymes. • Be able to follow simple English cartoon films or other English programmes at a similar level. The time spent for audio-visual activities should be no less than 10 hours a school year with an average of 20—25 minutes a week.

Reading Materials

Reading Material One

Six Principles for Designing the Curriculum

(1) Aim for educating all students, and emphasize quality-oriented education

—To stimulate students' interests;

—To help them experience the sense of success;

—To gain self-confidence;

—The overall objective is to develop students' comprehensive abilities; to improve their cultural quality; to develop their practical skills; to cultivate their creative spirit.

(2) Promote learner-centeredness, and respect individual differences

—Learner-centered approach;

—Students are guided by the teachers in constructing knowledge, developing skills, being active in thinking; demonstrating personal characters; developing intelligence and broadening their views and visions;

—Teaching should take full consideration of students' individual differences and should be flexible.

(3) Develop competence-based objectives, and allow flexibility and adaptability

—The overall aim is to develop students' comprehensive abilities in language use;

—Grounded in the development of language skills, language knowledge, cultural awareness and learning strategies;

—Each level is described in terms of what students can do with the language;

—It is designed to reflect the progressive nature of students' language development during the process of school education to ensure the integrity, flexibility and openness.

(4) Pay close attention to the learning process, and advocate experiential learning and participation

—Students should be encouraged to discover rules of language;

—Master language knowledge and skills gradually;

—Constantly monitor the affective demands;

—Develop effective learning strategies and autonomous learning abilities.

(5) Attach particular importance to formative assessment and give special attention to the development of competence

—Should be geared to stimulating students' interests and cultivating their autonomy in learning;

—Should include both formative and summative assessment;

—Assessment should be made to develop students' interests and self-confidence in learning;

—Assessment should function positively for students to develop language abilities and healthy personalities;

—For teachers to improve their teaching qualities and for the development and improvement of the English curriculum.

(6) Optimize learning resources, and maximize opportunities for learning and using the language.

—Teachers should properly utilize and develop teaching resources;

—Teachers should make full use of various resources;

—Teachers should encourage students to take part in exploring and utilizing resources for learning.

(Adapted from Wang, 2006)

⌈ **Reading Material Two** ⌋

教育部:义务教育英语课程标准(2011年版)(节选)

第二部分 课程目标

一、总目标

义务教育阶段英语课程的总目标是:通过英语学习使学生形成初步的综合语言运用能力,促进心智发展,提高综合人文素养。综合语言运用能力的形成建立在语言技能、语言知识、情感态度、学习策略和文化意识等方面整体发展的基础之上。语言技能和语言知识是综合语言运用能力的基础;文化意识有利于正确地理解语言和得体地使用语言;有效的学习策略有利于提高学习效率和发展自主学习能力;积极的情感态度有利于促进主动学习和持续发展。这五个方面相辅相成,共同促进学生综合语言运用能力的形成与发展。

以语言技能、语言知识、情感态度、学习策略和文化意识等五个方面共同构成的英语课程总目标,既体现了英语学习的工具性,也体现了其人文性;既有利于学生发展语言运用能力,又有利于学生发展思维能力,从而全面提高学生的综合人文素养。

二、分级目标

义务教育阶段英语课程各个级别的目标是指学生在语言技能、语言知识、情感态度、学习策略和文化意识五个方面应达到的综合行为表现。表1是对一至五级分级目标的描述。

表1 一至五级分级目标描述

级别	目标描述
一级	对英语有好奇心,喜欢听他人说英语。 能根据教师的简单指令做动作、做游戏、做事情(如涂颜色、连线)。能做简单的角色表演。 能唱简单的英文歌曲,说简单的英语歌谣。能在图片的帮助下听懂和读懂简单的小故事。能交流简单的个人信息,表达简单的感觉和情感。能模仿范例书写词句。 在学习中乐于模仿,敢于表达,对英语具有一定的感知能力。 对学习中接触的外国文化习俗感兴趣。
二级	对继续学习英语有兴趣。 能用简单的英语互致问候,变换有关个人、家庭和朋友的简单信息,并能就日常生活话题作简短叙述。能在图片的帮助下听懂、读懂并讲述简单的故事,能在教师的帮助下表演小故事或小短剧,演唱简单的英语歌曲和歌谣。能根据图片、词语或例句的提示,写出简短的描述。 在学习中乐于参与、积极合作、主动请教,初步形成对英语的感知能力和良好的学习习惯。 乐于了解外国文化和习俗。
三级	对英语学习表现出积极性和初步的自信心。 能听懂有关熟悉话题的语段和简短的故事。能与教师或同学就熟悉的话题(如学校、家庭生活)变换信息。能读懂小故事及其他文体的简单书面材料。能用短语或句子描述系列图片,缩写简单的故事。能根据提示简要描述一件事情,参与简单的角色表演等活动。 能尝试使用适当的学习方法,克服学习中遇到的困难。 能意识到语言交际中存在文化差异。

(续表)

级别	目标描述
四级	有明确的学习需要和目标,对英语学习表现出较强的自信心。 能在所设日常交际情境中听懂对话和小故事。能用简单的语言描述自己或他人的经历,能表达简单的观点。能读懂常见文体的小短文和相应水平的英文报刊文章。能合作起草和修改简短的叙述、说明、指令、规则等。能尝试使用不同的教育资源,从口头和书面材料中提取信息、扩展知识、解决简单的问题并描述结果。 能在学习中相互帮助,克服困难。能合理计划和安排学习任务,积极探索适合自己的学习方法。 在学习和日常交际中能注意到中外文化的异同。
五级	有较明确的英语学习动机、积极主动的学习态度和自信心。 能听懂有关熟悉话题的陈述并参与讨论。能就日常生活的相关话题与他人变换信息并陈述自己的意见。能读懂相应水平的读物和报纸、杂志,克服生词障碍,理解大意。能根据阅读目的运用适当的阅读策略。能根据提示独立起草和修改小作文。 能与他人合作,解决问题并报告结果,共同完成学习任务。能对自己的学习进行评价,总结学习方法。能利用多种教育资源进行学习。 进一步增强对文化差异的理解与认识。

第三部分 分级标准

按照义务教育阶段英语课程的总目标要求,本标准对语言技能、语言知识、情感态度、学习策略和文化意识等五个方面分别提出了级别要求。其中,对语言技能中的听、说、读、写等技能提出五个级别的不同目标要求,对语言知识、情感态度、学习策略和文化意识提出了二级和五级的目标要求。

一、语言技能

语言技能是语言运用能力的重要组成部分,主要包括听、说、读、写等方面的技能以及这些技能的综合运用。听和读是理解的技能,说和写是表达的技能。它们在语言学习和交际中相辅相成、相互促进。学生应通过大量的专项和综合性语言实践活动,形成综合语言运用能力,为真实语言交际打基础。因此,听、说、读、写既是学习的内容,又是学习的手段。语言技能标准以学生在某个级别"能做什么"为主要内容,这不仅有利于调动学生的学习积极性,促进学生语言运用能力的提高,也有利于科学、合理地评价学生的学习结果。表2是语言技能的分级标准。

表2 语言技能分级标准

级别	技能	标准描述
一级	听做	1. 能根据听到的词句识别或指认图片或实物。 2. 能听懂课堂简短的指令并做出相应的反应。 3. 能根据指令做事情,如指图片、涂颜色、画图、做动作等。 4. 能在图片和动作的提示下听懂简单的小故事并做出适当的反应。
	说唱	1. 能根据录音模仿说话。 2. 能相互致以简单的问候。 3. 能相互交流简单的个人信息,如姓名、年龄等。 4. 能表达简单的情感和感觉,如喜欢和不喜欢。 5. 能根据表演猜测意思、说出词语。 6. 能学唱英语儿童歌曲和歌谣15首左右。 7. 能根据图、文说出单词或短句。

(续表)

级别	技能	标准描述
一级	玩演	1. 能在教师的指导下用英语做游戏并在游戏中进行简单的交际。 2. 能做简单的角色表演。
	读写	1. 能看图识词。 2. 能在指认物体的前提下认读所学词语。 3. 能在图片的帮助下读懂简单的小故事。 4. 能正确书写字母和单词。 5. 能模仿范例写词句。
	视听	能看懂语言简单的英语动画片或程度相当的英语教学节目,课堂视听时间每学年不少于10小时(平均每周20—25分钟)。

级别	技能	标准描述
二级	听	1. 能借助图片、图像、手势听懂简单的话语或录音材料。 2. 能听懂简单的配图小故事。 3. 能听懂课堂活动中简单的提问。 4. 能听懂常用指令和要求并做出适当的反应。
	说	1. 能在口头表达中做到发音清楚,语调基本达意。 2. 能就所熟悉的个人和家庭情况进行简短对话。 3. 能运用一些最常用的日常用语(如问候、告别、致谢、道歉等)。 4. 能就日常生活话题作简短叙述。 5. 能在教师的帮助和图片的提示下描述或讲述简单的小故事。
	读	1. 能认读所学词语。 2. 能根据拼读的规律,读出简单的单词。 3. 能读懂教材中简短的要求或指令。 4. 能看懂贺卡等所表达的简单信息。 5. 能借助图片读懂简单的故事或小短文,并养成按意群阅读的习惯。 6. 能正确朗读所学故事或短文。
	写	1. 能正确地使用大小写字母和常用的标点符号。 2. 能写出简单的问候语和祝福语。 3. 能根据图片、词语或例句的提示,写出简短的语句。
	玩演视听	1. 能按要求用简单的英语做游戏。 2. 能在教师的帮助下表演小故事或小短剧。 3. 能学唱简单的英语歌曲和歌谣30首左右(含一级要求)。 4. 能看懂程度相当的英语动画片和英语教学节目,课堂视听时间每学年不少于10小时(平均每周20—25分钟)。

级别	技能	标准描述
三级	听	1. 能识别不同句式的语调,如陈述句、疑问句和指令等。 2. 能根据语调变化,体会句子意义的变化。 3. 能感知歌谣中的韵律。 4. 能识别语段中句子之间的联系。 5. 能听懂学习活动中连续的指令和问题,并做出适当的反应。 6. 能听懂有关熟悉话题的语段。 7. 能借助提示听懂教师讲述的故事。
	说	1. 能在课堂活动中用简短的英语进行交际。 2. 能就熟悉的话题进行简单的交流。 3. 能在教师的指导下进行简单的角色表演。 4. 能利用所给提示(如图片、幻灯片、食物、文字等)简单描述一件事情。 5. 能提供有关个人情况和个人经历的信息。 6. 能讲述简单的小故事。 7. 能背诵一定数量的英语小诗或歌谣,能唱一些英语歌曲。 8. 能在上述口语活动中做到语音、语调基本正确。
	读	1. 能正确地朗读课文。 2. 能理解并执行有关学习活动的简短书面指令。 3. 能读懂简单的故事和短文并抓住大意。 4. 能初步使用简单的工具书。 5. 课外阅读量应累计达到4万词以上。
	写	1. 能正确使用常用的标点符号。 2. 能使用简单的图表和海报等形式传达信息。 3. 能参照范例写出或回复简单的问候和邀请。 4. 能用短语或句子描述系列图片,编写简单的故事。

级别	技能	标准描述
四级	听	1. 能听懂接近自然语速、熟悉话题的简单语段,识别主题,获取主要信息。 2. 能听懂简单故事的情节发展,理解其中主要人物和事件。 3. 能听懂连续的指令并据此完成任务。 4. 能听懂广播、电视等媒体中的初级英语教学节目。
	说	1. 能根据提示给出连贯的简单指令。 2. 能引出话题并进行几个回合的交谈。 3. 能在教师的帮助下或根据图片用简单的语言描述自己或他人的经历。 4. 能在教师的指导下参与角色表演等活动。 5. 能在上述口语活动中使用正确的语音、语调。
	读	1. 能连贯、流畅地朗读课文。 2. 能理解简易读物中的事件发生顺序和人物行为。 3. 能从简单的文章中找出有关信息,理解大意。 4. 能根据上下文猜测生词的意思。 5. 能理解并解释图表提供的信息。 6. 能读懂简单的个人信件、说明文等应用文体材料。 7. 能使用英汉词典等工具书帮助阅读理解。 8. 课外阅读量应累计达到10万词以上。
	写	1. 能正确使用标点符号。 2. 能用词组或简单句为自己创作的图片写出说明。 3. 能写出简短的文段,如简单的指令、规则。 4. 能在教师的帮助下或以小组讨论的方式起草和修改作文。

级别	技能	标准描述
五级	听	1. 能根据语调和重音理解说话者的意图。 2. 能听懂有关熟悉话题的谈话,并能从中提取观点。 3. 能借助语境克服生词障碍、理解大意。 4. 能听懂接近自然语速的故事和叙述,理解故事的因果关系。 5. 能在听的过程中用适当方式做出反应。 6. 能针对所听语段的内容记录简单信息。
	说	1. 能就简单的话题提供信息,表达简单的观点和意见,参与讨论。 2. 能与他人沟通信息,合作完成任务。 3. 能在口头表达中进行适当的自我修正。 4. 能有效地询问信息和请求帮助。 5. 能根据话题进行情景对话。 6. 能用英语表演短剧。 7. 能在以上口语活动中做到语音、语调自然,语气恰当。
	读	1. 能根据上下文和构词法推断、理解生词的含义。 2. 能理解段落中各句子之间的逻辑关系。 3. 能找出文章中的主题,理解故事的情节,预测故事情节的发展和可能的结局。 4. 能读懂相应水平的常见体裁的读物。 5. 能根据不同的阅读目的运用简单的阅读策略获取信息。 6. 能利用词典等工具书进行阅读。 7. 课外阅读量应累计达到 15 万词以上。
	写	1. 能根据写作要求,收集、准备素材。 2. 能独立起草短文、短信等,并在教师的指导下进行修改。 3. 能使用常见的连接词表示顺序和逻辑关系。 4. 能简单描述人物或事件。 5. 能根据图示或表格写出简单的段落或操作说明。

二、语言知识

学生在义务教育阶段应该学习和掌握的英语语言基础知识包括语音、词汇、语法以及用于表达常见话题和功能的语言形式等。语言知识是语言运用能力的重要组成部分,是发展语言技能的重要基础。表 3 是二级和五级语言知识的分级标准。

表3 语言知识分级标准

级别	知识	标准描述
二级	语音	1. 正确读出 26 个英文字母。 2. 了解简单的拼读规律。 3. 了解单词有重音,句子有重读。 4. 了解英语语音包括连读、节奏、停顿、语调等现象。
	词汇	1. 知道单词是由字母构成的。 2. 知道要根据单词的音、义、形来学习词汇。 3. 学习有关本级话题范围的 600—700 个单词和 50 个左右的习惯用语,并能初步运用 400 个左右的单词表达二级规定的相应话题。

(续表)

级别	知识	标准描述
二级	语法	1. 在具体语境中理解以下语法项目的意义和用法： • 名词的单复数形式和名词所有格 • 人称代词和形容词性物主代词 • 一般现在时、现在进行时、一般过去时和一般将来时 • 表示时间、地点和位置的常用介词 • 简单句的基本形式 2. 在实际运用中体会以上语法项目的表意功能。

级别	知识	标准描述
二级	功能	理解和运用有关下列功能的语言表达形式：问候、介绍、告别、请求、致谢、邀请、道歉、情感、喜好、建议、祝愿等。
二级	话题	理解和运用有关下列话题的语言表达形式：个人情况、家庭与朋友、身体与健康、学校与日常生活、文体活动、节假日、饮食、服装、季节与天气、颜色、动物等。
二级	语音	1. 了解语音在语言学习中的意义。 2. 在日常生活会话中做到语音、语调基本正确、自然、流畅。 3. 根据重音和语调的变化，理解和表达不同的意图和态度。 4. 根据读音规则和音标拼读单词。
五级	词汇	1. 了解英语词汇包括单词、短语、习惯用语和固定搭配等形式。 2. 理解和领悟词语的基本意义以及在特定语境中的意义。 3. 运用词汇描述事物、行为和特征，说明概念等。 4. 学会使用1 500—1 600个单词和200—300个习惯用语或固定搭配。
五级	语法	1. 理解附录中"语法项目表"中所列语法项目并能在特定语境中使用。 2. 了解常用语言形式的基本结构常用表意功能。 3. 在实际运用中体会和领悟语言形式的表意功能。 4. 理解并运用恰当的语言形式描述人和物；描述具体事件和具体行为的发生、发展过程；描述时间、地点及方位；比较人、物体及事物等。
五级	功能	在交往中恰当理解和运用本级别所列功能意念的语言表达形式。
五级	话题	围绕本级别所列话题恰当理解与运用相关的语言表达形式。

三、情感态度

情感态度指兴趣、动机、自信、意志和合作精神等影响学生学习过程和学习效果的相关因素以及在学习过程中逐渐形成的祖国意识和国际视野。保持积极的学习态度是英语学习成功的关键。教师应在教学中不断激发并强化学生的学习兴趣，并引导他们逐渐将兴趣转化为稳定的学习动机，以使他们树立自信心，锻炼克服困难的意志，认识自己学习的优势与不足，乐于与他人合作，养成和谐和健康向上的品格。通过英语课程，使学生增强祖国意识，拓展国际视野。表4是二级和五级的情感态度分级标准。

表4 情感态度分级标准

级别	标准描述
二级	1. 能体会到英语学习的乐趣。 2. 敢于开口,表达中不怕出错误。 3. 乐于感知并积极尝试使用英语。 4. 积极参与各种课堂学习活动。 5. 在小组活动中能与其他同学积极配合和合作。 6. 遇到困难时能大胆求助。 7. 乐于接触外国文化,增强祖国意识。
五级	1. 有明确的学习目的,能认识到学习英语的目的在于交流。 2. 有学习英语的愿望和兴趣,乐于参与各种英语实践活动。 3. 有学好英语的信心,敢于用英语进行表达。 4. 能在小组活动中积极与他人合作,相互帮助,共同完成学习任务。 5. 能体会英语学习中的乐趣,乐于接触英语歌曲、读物等。 6. 能在英语交流中注意并理解他人的情感。 7. 遇到问题时能主动请教,勇于克服困难。 8. 在生活中接触英语时,乐于探究其含义并尝试模仿。 9. 对祖国文化能有更深刻的了解,具有初步的国际理解意识。

四、学习策略

学习策略指学生为了有效地学习和使用英语而采取的各种行动和步骤以及指导这些行动和步骤的信念。英语学习策略包括认知策略、调控策略、交际策略和资源策略等。认知策略是指学生为了完成具体学习任务而采取的步骤和方法;调控策略是指学生对学习加以计划、实施、反思、评价和调整的行动和步骤;交际策略是学生为了争取更多的交际机会、维持交际以及提高交际效果而采取的行动;资源策略是学生合理并有效利用多种媒体进行学习和运用英语的方式和方法。

学习策略是灵活多样的,策略的使用因人、因时、因地、因事而异。在英语教学中,教师要有意识地帮助学生形成适合自己的学习策略,并不断调整自己的学习策略。

在英语课程实施中,帮助学生有效地使用学习策略,不仅有利于他们把握学习的方向,采用科学的途径,提高学习效率,而且还有助于他们形成自主学习的能力,为终身可持续性学习奠定基础。表5是二级和五级学习策略分级标准。

表5 学习策略分级标准

级别	标准描述
二级	**基本策略** 1. 积极与他人合作,共同完成学习任务。 2. 遇到问题主动向老师或同学请教。 3. 会制订简单的英语学习计划。 4. 对所学内容能主动复习和归纳。 5. 在词语与相应事物之间建立联想。 6. 在学习中集中注意力。 7. 在课堂交流中,注意倾听,积极思考。 8. 尝试阅读英语故事及其他英语课外读物。 9. 积极运用所学英语进行表达和交流。 10. 注意观察生活或媒体中使用的简单英语。 11. 能初步借助简单的工具书学习英语。

(续表)

级别	标准描述
五级	**认知策略** 1. 根据需要进行学习。 2. 在学习中集中注意力。 3. 在学习中善于记要点。 4. 在学习中善于利用图画等非语言信息理解主题。 5. 借助联想学习和记忆词语。 6. 对所学内容能主动复习并加以整理和归纳。 7. 在学习中积极思考,主动探究,善于发现语言的规律并能运用规律举一反三。 8. 在使用英语时,能意识到错误并进行适当的纠正。 9. 必要时,有效地借助母语知识理解英语。 10. 尝试阅读英语故事及其他英语课外读物。 **调控策略** 1. 明确自己学习英语的目标。 2. 明确自己的学习需要。 3. 制订切合实际的英语学习计划。 4. 把握学习内容的重点和难点。 5. 注意了解和反思自己学习英语中的进步与不足。 6. 积极探索适合自己的英语学习方法。 7. 经常与老师和同学交流学习体会。 8. 积极参与课内外英语学习活动。 **交际策略** 1. 在课内外学习活动中能够用英语与他人交流。 2. 善于抓住用英语交际的机会。 3. 在交际中,把注意力集中在意思的表达上。 4. 借助手势、表情等体态语进行交流。 5. 交际中遇到困难时,有效地寻求帮助。 6. 在交际中注意到中外交际习俗的差异。 **资源策略** 1. 注意通过音像资料丰富自己的学习。 2. 使用简单的工具书查找信息。 3. 注意生活中和媒体上所使用的英语。 4. 能初步利用图书馆或网络上的学习资源。

五、文化意识

语言有丰富的文化内涵。在外语教学中,文化是指所学语言国家的历史地理、风土人情、传统习俗、生活方式、行为规范、文学艺术、价值观念等。在学习英语的过程中,接触和了解外国文化有益于对英语的理解和使用,有益于加深对中华民族优秀传统文化的认识与热爱,有益于接受属于全人类先进文化的熏陶,有益于培养国际意识。在教学中,教师应根据学生的年龄特点和认知能力,逐步扩展文化知识的内容和范围。在起始阶段应使学生对中外文化的异同有粗略的了解,教学中涉及的外国文化知识应与学生的学习和生活密切相关,并能激发学生学习英语的兴趣。在英语学习的较高阶段,要通过扩大学生接触外国文化的范围,帮助学生拓展视野,使他们提高对中外文化异同的敏感性和鉴别能力,进而提高跨文化交际能力。表6是二级和五级的文化意识分级标准。

表6　文化意识分级标准

级别	标准描述
二级	1. 知道英语中最简单的称谓语、问候语和告别语。 2. 对一般的赞扬、请求、道歉等做出适当的反应。 3. 知道世界上主要的文娱和体育活动。 4. 知道英语国家中典型的食品和饮料的名称。 5. 知道主要英语国家的首都和国旗。 6. 了解主要英语国家的重要标志物,如英国的大本钟等。 7. 了解英语国家中重要的节假日。 8. 在学习和日常交际中,能初步注意到中外文化异同。
五级	1. 了解英语交际中常用的体态语,如手势、表情等。 2. 恰当使用英语中的称谓语、问候语和告别语。 3. 了解、区别英语中不同性别常用的名字和亲昵的称呼。 4. 了解英语国家的饮食习俗。 5. 对别人的赞扬、请求、致歉等做出恰当的反应。 6. 用恰当的方式表达赞扬、请求等意义。 7. 初步了解英语国家的地理位置、气候特点、历史等。 8. 了解英语国家的人际交往习俗。 9. 了解世界上主要的文娱和体育活动。 10. 了解世界上主要的节假日及庆祝方式。 11. 关注中外文化异同,加深对中国文化的理解。 12. 能初步用英语介绍祖国的主要节日和典型的文化习俗。

1.2 Skills and Abilities

Now that you have already learned the key points of National English Curriculum, here are some questions for you to discuss. It is a good time to practice your skills of creative thinking, problem-solving and cooperation.

(1) Work in groups. Discuss the advantages and disadvantages of introducing English at the primary school level in China.

Benefits	Difficulties
1.	
2.	
3.	
4.	

(2) Why English as a mandatory course is included in compulsory education?

(3) How do you understand the importance and requirements of English learning in compulsory education?

(4) What is the main task of English course in compulsory education?

(5) What is the supporting theory of National English Curriculum? How does it

enlighten you to teach primary school education?

(6) How does the course value of National English Curriculum embody student-centered views?

(7) What is the view of teaching and the view of students in National English Curriculum?

(8) What are the language skills differences in the skills requirements between levels 1 and 2?

Look into the specific objectives for Level 1 and Level 2 in terms of language skills. You will find that Level 1 and Level 2 are organized differently. Discuss the differences and try to explain why.

Level 1	Level 2
Organized around Listening and doing Speaking and singing Playing and acting Reading and writing Audio and visual	Organized around Listening Speaking Reading Writing Play and act Audio and visual

(9) Language knowledge discussion for Level 2.

Discuss in groups of five. Try to decide on the specific objectives for Level 2 in terms of phonetics, grammar, functions, vocabulary and topics. Write them down in the space given below and then compare what you have written with the content listed in the booklet of National English Curriculum for Nine-Year Compulsory Education.

Level 2 Language Knowledge	
Phonetics: What do you think should be required of primary school pupils? Give some examples.	e.g. They should be able to read correctly the 26 letters of English.
Vocabulary: What kind of vocabulary should be taught? How many?	
Grammar: What should be taught at this level and what should pupils be able to do with grammar?	
Communicative functions: What should children be able to say in communication?	
Topics: What topics should be included in the curriculum for primary school children?	

✦ 亮考帮

亮闪闪：请总结学习过程中，哪些是自己记忆深刻、受益最大、最欣赏的内容呢？请写出具体内容。

考考你：请把自己弄懂的但觉得别人可能存在困惑的地方，用问题的形式表述出来，来挑战一下其他同学。

帮帮我：请把自己不懂、不会的地方或想要了解的内容，用问题的形式表述出来，并带到课堂上加以讨论。

✦ 参考文献

[1] 王蔷. 小学英语教学法教程[M]. 北京：高等教育出版社，2009.

[2] 王蔷. 英语教学法教程[M]. 北京：高等教育出版社，2006.

[3] 中华人民共和国教育部. 义务教育英语课程标准(2011版)[S]. 北京：北京师范大学出版社，2011.

Task 2 Course Materials

Materials for learning and teaching refer to textbooks or coursebooks, supplementary information, and other useful resources. In this section, we offer you how to understand new course materials, what PEP textbooks are, and views of Professor Merrill Swain, the Output Hypothesis.

2.1 Knowledge Points

Outline

In this part, we offer you the definition of course resources, and task-based language teaching mode which is mainly used to design the PEP textbooks.

2.1.1 Understanding the new course materials

1. **Course resources**

Resources refers to books, any person, animals, or any object, that makes teaching and learning easier, clearer and more interesting. Even though some publishers provide teachers with a package of materials which include flashcards, pictures, storybooks, tapes or CD-ROMs, you still need something extra. Some suggestions for course resources are as follows.

• Create one's own file of pictures and cards;

• Use your own creativity and imagination to provide a better learning environment for the students;

• Make your students an important resource;

• Use the Internet resources.

2. **Suggestions from McDonough and Shaw (2003):**

Adding, e.g.: reading passages, grammar exercises, stress and intonation exercises, etc.

Deleting or omitting, one is to simply subtract the current material by reducing the amount; the other is to abridge or drop completely.

Modifying, one is called rewriting; the other is called restructuring.

Simplification, is one type of modification of reading passages.

Reordering, is changing the order of the tasks in a unit or changing the order of units in a coursebook.

2.1.2 Task-based language teaching

Task-based language teaching (TBLT) proposes the use of tasks as a central component in the language classroom because they provide better contexts for activating learner acquisition processes and promoting L2 learning.

TBLT is thus based on a theory of language learning rather than a theory of language structure. Tasks are believed to foster processes of negotiation, modification, rephrasing, and experimentation that are at the heart of second language learning. The basic assumptions of TBLT are as follows:

- Focus on process rather than product;
- Purposeful activities and tasks that emphasize communication and meaning;
- Learn by interacting while engaged in meaningful activities and tasks;
- Activities and tasks can be those that learners might need to achieve in real life and have a pedagogical purpose;
- Be sequenced according to difficulty;
- The difficulty of a task depends on a range of factors including previous experience, complexity of the tasks and the degree of support available.

It initially emphasized fluency at the expense of accuracy and complexity. It was thought that the ability to use the L2 would develop automatically, hence the experiments with immersion classes in Canada. However, it was found that they need to be encouraged to focus on various points of grammar to achieve accuracy.

Merrill Swain is a professor emerita of second-language education at the Ontario Institute for Studies in Education, University of Toronto. She developed the output hypothesis, a theory of second-language acquisition which states that learners cannot reach full grammatical competence in a language from input processing alone, but must also produce spoken language output. Swain is also known for her work with Michael Canale on communicative competence. Swain was the president of the American Association for Applied Linguistics in 1998. She received her PhD at the University of California.

TBLT with a focus on form (in the context of meaning) is gathering support from SLA research. It draws students' attention and arises in a meaningful classroom context. Form includes:

- Consciousness-raising;
- Form-focused instruction;
- Form-focused intervention.

Interlanguage refers to the underlying language system used by the second/foreign language learners at any particular stage in the process of learning the target foreign language. It is learner-initiated, maintaining emphases on meaning, communication and fluency.

2.1.3 教材简介

1. 小学英语教科书

人民教育出版社出版的《义务教育教科书：英语》是由教育部审定的、由人民教育出版社课程教材研究所英语课程教材研究开发中心与加拿大灵通教育有限公司（Lingo Learning Inc.），依据教育部《义务教育英语课程标准》（2011年版）编写。其2013版教材经国家基础教育课程教材专家工作委员会审查通过，通常简称为 PEP 版本。本套教材共有8本，其教学目的是激发学生学习英语的兴趣，建立学习英语的自信心；培养一定的语感和良好的语音、语调、书写基础，以及良好的学习习惯；培养目标是使小学生初步具备用英语进行简单日常交流的能力，培养学生的观察、记忆、思维、想象和创造能力，经过适当的外国文化的介绍，培养学生的爱国主义精神，增强世界意识，为学生的进一步学习奠定良好的基础。

2. 初中英语教科书

《义务教育教科书：英语》初中教材全套5本，是由人民教育出版社课程教材研究所英语课程教材研究开发中心依据教育部《义务教育英语课程标准》（2011年版）与美国圣智学习集团合作开发，经国家基础教育课程教材专家工作委员会2013年审查通过。教材集中反映了基础教育教科书研究与实验的成果，帮助学生发展语言运用能力，其内容和活动与学生的生活和兴趣紧密相连。本系列教材还重视培养学生的语言学习策略和技能，融入充分参与的理念，设计许多有交际意义的任务和活动，同时还丰富了文化教学的内容，是一套非常适合初中学生学习和发展的英语教科书。

图 5-3 人教版小学及初中教科书

Reading Material

输出假设理论：历史与未来——Merrill Swain 教授专访

Merrill Swain 博士是加拿大多伦多大学安大略教育学院资深教授，曾任美国应用语言学协会（AAAL）主席（1998—1999），现任国际应用语言学学会（AILA）副主席。她提出的输出假设学说已为中国外语教学工作者所熟悉。

2007年5月，Swain 教授参加了由中国外语教育研究中心和外研社共同主办的 Workshop on Immersion Programs and Sociocultural Theory 专题研讨会并作了精彩的学术报告。随后，在第五届中国英语教学国际研讨会暨第一届中国应用语言学大会上，Swain 博士作了题为 The Output Hypothesis: Its History and Its Future 的主旨发言。

《外研之声》特邀毕业于多伦多大学安大略教育学院现代语言中心、现任中国外语教育研究中心专职研究员的杨鲁新博士对 Swain 教授进行了专访，在此刊出，以飨读者。

杨：Swain 教授，非常感谢您接受这次访谈。在中国，许多应用语言学学者和研究生都熟知您的输出假设理论。您能谈一下该理论产生的背景吗？

S：这要追溯到上世纪80年代初期和中期的两个重要环境因素：一方面，当时二语习得研究的主导理论模式是信息加工理论（information processing theory）；另一方面，加拿大的法语浸入式教学研究盛行。但是对浸入式教学的评估得到了一些意想不到的发现。

Krashen 的输入假设理论（1982/1985）认为可理解的语言输入是实现二语习得的唯一必要、充分的条件。假设语言学习者现有的语言水平是"i"，如果他/她能理解"i+1"的语言输入，他/她可能达到的语言水平则为"i+1"。这也是为什么上世纪60年代末法语浸入式教学在加拿大刚开始时，家长和老师们对法语二语的教与学充满信心。在这种教学模式下，以英语为母语的学生的学校课程部分或全部用法语讲授。从入学伊始接受法语教学的为早期浸入式学习；从四、五年级开始接受法语教学的为中期浸入式学习；从六、七年级接受法语教学的为后期浸入式学习。关于这些早期的浸入式教学方面的研究可参见 Lambert & Tucker (1972)，Swain (1978) 和 Swain & Lapkin (1982/1986)。这些研究显示，接受浸入式教学的学生的法语水平要远远高于那些每天上20到30分钟法语课的学生。同时，在一些法语听力和阅读理解测试中，浸入式学生的成绩与同龄的以法语为母语的学生成绩相差无几。但是，令人惊讶的是，浸入式学生的说和写的能力远远不如以法语为母语的学生的水平。就是这些发现使我对"输入假设理论"，尤其是对"可理解输入是二语习得的唯一充分条件"（Krashen 1984:61）的观点产生了质疑（Swain 1985）。这些学生在校学习的全部课程都是用法语讲授的，而且他们对课程内容掌握得也很好，很显然，法语浸入式学生接受了大量的法语（作为目标语）的语言输入。因此，关于浸入式学生的较弱的说/写能力，需要寻求其他的解释。其中一个解释就是"输出假设理论"（Swain 1985）。我的研究发现，接受浸入式教学的学生在法语浸入的环境中说法语不如在英语环境中说英语多（Swain 1988）。更重要的是，教师并不敦促学生讲法语时注意语言准确和恰当。这便是早期形成的"输出假设理论"，也可称为"可理解性输出理论"。

杨：我们注意到从1985年您首次提出这一理论至今，"输出"的含义已经发展了，人们对这一概念好像也有不同的解释。

S: 是的。80年代,"输出"用来指语言习得方式的结果和成果。"输出"与"学习者所学到的知识"同义。80年代至今,它已由名词含义的"事物(a thing)""产品(a product)"转变为动词含义的"行动(action)""过程(process)"。

杨: 您怎样解释"输出假设理论"呢?

S: 简单说,输出假设理论认为输出语言的活动(说/写)是二语学习过程的一个组成部分;同时,输出语言与理解语言的过程大不相同,因此二者一定要分开来看。

杨: 您能简要地谈一下"输出假设理论"在二语学习中的作用吗?

S: 从"实践"意义上讲,输出语言的功能之一就是提高语言的流利程度。这也就是我们常说的"熟能生巧",这一点很容易理解,我就不再细谈了。我们知道,流利和准确是语言表现的不同方面。尽管练习可能提高表达的流利度,但不一定就能提高表达的准确度。下面我主要谈一下我在1995年提出的三种输出功能。首先,输出具有引发注意的功能。也就是说,当学习者试图输出目标语时,他们能够注意到自己不能准确地说出或写出想要真正表达的意思。换言之,某些情况下,输出目标语的活动能促使二语学习者注意或认识到自身的语言问题。许多实证研究,包括我和我学生的研究,都证明了输出在引起学习者注意和习得特殊目标语形式方面起着重要作用。

杨: 那么第二个功能呢?

S: 输出有假设检测的功能。从学习者角度讲,输出有时是"试验运行"(trial run),即他们试着用恰当的目标语词汇或形式说出或写出自己的想法。

杨: 我很赞同。我也曾有过类似的经历。在和我的导师Alister(攻读博士时的导师Alister Cumming)讨论的过程中,我试图用活动理论向他解释我对数据的理解。有时我很难表达我的想法,但他的问题总是能促使我找到更清楚的表达方式,同时也使我的思路更清晰。

S: 是的。这也与输出的第三个功能——输出的反省功能——相关。这一功能指的是用语言来反省他人或自己输出的语言,从而促进第二语言的学习。这种观点源于Vygotsky的社会文化理论。社会文化理论是关于人们如何运用中介工具进行社会活动(Wertsch 1985)的理论。"说"是其中一种工具。在这一背景下,我(Swain 2000/2002)重新把"输出"定义为"说(speaking)、写(writing)、合作对话(collaborative dialogue)、个人独语(private speech)、表述(verbalizing)和言语化(languaging)"。重新标记是为了避免在使用术语"输入"和"输出"时对语言学习过程的片面、机械的理解(Firth & Wagner 1997; Kramsch 1995)。

"说"是调控每个个体生理和认知的一种外部工具。我们每个人的生理和认知行为都受到外界的影响。随着时间的推移,个体能够内化这些外界的影响,从而形成自己独立思考和注意的能力。内化是从集体智慧走向个体认知能力的发展。这种发展是通过"说"(和其他认知工具)来调控的(Frawley 1997)。我们能观察到,学习者在使用语言的过程中会不断内化语言表述的内容并成为自己认知活动的一部分,比如在与他人的对话过程中我们可以学到很多知识(Donato & Lantolf 1990; Lantolf 2000; Swain 2000)。

这些观点为合作式学习奠定了基础,希望学生能够通过各项集体活动发展自己独立的认知能力。在这些集体活动中语言会被用来协调解决问题。我们称这一集体解决问题的对话为"合作式对话"。"合作式对话"就是说话者在解决问题和共同构建知识时发生的对话。对于第二语言学习者而言,就是解决语言问题和共同构建有关语言的知识。

"说"也能有助于思考的完成,正如你所经历的。Vygotsky(1978)、Barnes(1992)、Wells(1999),都认为"说"是重塑经历的工具。人们通过"说"来表达思想,转换成语言负载的形式,供进一步的深入思考。正如 Smagorinsky(1998:172-173)所说,"把思想通过语言表达出来的过程不仅仅是简单的回忆,而且是使思想达到了更高层次的表达",观点会更鲜明有力,不合逻辑的部分也就凸显出来了。

杨: 的确如此。在多伦多大学安大略教育学院学习期间,通过和老师、同学的讨论我学到了很多。现代语言中心的非正式学术讨论系列活动,也为研究生提供很多交流学术的机会,从而深化了对理论的理解。我们现在对第二语言教育中的问题都很敏感了。

S: 是的,作为一名教师,我一直认为让学生互相讨论彼此的研究是很重要的。从社会文化理论角度讲,说和写都是认知工具,帮助个体内化知识,外化内在思考,进而重新认知;说和写也是个体建构和解析知识的工具;说和写也都是调整个体行为的工具,而且同时也被个体所调节。换言之,社会文化理论认为语言输出在语言学习过程中起着很重要的作用。

语言输出在第二语言学习中的重大作用有待于进一步的研究。过去的几十年里,从"输出是一种产品"到"输出是一个过程",理解的转变也促使研究工具的转变,进而发现新的研究问题。仅以研究"口述对二语学习的影响"为例,使用的研究工具,如有声思维和刺激回忆法,它们不仅是收集数据的工具,还是学习过程的一部分(Smagorinsky 1998; Swain 2002)。它们并不像某些人认为的只是"思维转储",而是理解和重塑经验的过程,是学习的组成部分。

信息加工理论和社会文化理论对人类思维和记忆都有其独到的见解,能让我们重新认识语言输出在二语学习中的作用,因而在语言教学研究中,我们应充分利用这些理论。

杨: 输出假设学说未来的研究方向是什么?

S: 有几个研究方向。信息加工模式下的实证研究将会很有前景。不同情况下语言输出过程的水平和种类,在我看来,很值得研究。在社会文化理论的框架下,尽管这方面也可以采用定量研究的方法,民族志和个案研究方法更有价值。那些关于学习者面对语言输出任务时,需要合作解决相关语言问题(如词汇、句法、话语、语用等)时发生的合作对话或个人独语的研究对理解二语学习的过程和策略也很有意义。其他有关口头表达思想(我现称为"言语化")的课题也是社会文化领域中很值得做的研究。"言语化"是通过语言完成认知复杂的思想活动。未来要研究的其他重要问题还包括言语对认知分配的作用以及环境对学习者语言能力发展的限制或提高作用。

我认为研究语言输出的重要意义在于语言输出是一个重要的认知工具。语言输出能够帮助我们进行思维,也就是"言语化"活动。合作式对话和个人独语就是言语化的例子。言语化的概念大大拓宽了二语和外语学习与教学研究的领域。

杨: 您认为怎样才能将输出假设理论应用于中国外语教学课堂?您知道,中国的课堂学生人数较多,在课堂上教师很难让每个学生都有机会说话(如提问或回答问题)。

S: 应用可以着重于语言的运用方面,如让学生讨论。我认为好的课堂活动应该是让学生在讨论后能输出语言,如完成一项写作任务。学生们共同讨论写作任务,然后用英语写出作文。任何能让学生说话,尤其是能反映他们的说和写的活动都是好的课堂活动。如果不让学生重新改写文章,他们很可能就将作文放在一边,连教师的反馈意见都不读。如果学生能够讨论并反思这些反馈意见,对语言学习会有很大帮助。这种动态反思对二语学习很重要。

杨: 的确如此。不过我有个疑问,比如说在中国教育环境下,40人以上的大班上课比较普遍。这样的话,如果要求他们对作文反馈进行反思,有什么切实可行的方法呢?

S: 当然中国与加拿大的课堂情景差异很大。如果是大班教学,采用结对讨论或小组讨论的方法可以为学生创造更多使用英语的机会,从而加深对目标语言知识点的理解。比如,作为课堂活动的一部分,教师可以要求学生结对讨论写作的反馈意见。在这个过程中教师可以在学生中走动,看他们是否遇到问题。学生可以提问,但需要事先将问题列出并与同学讨论。这样,他们就有机会讨论并理解反馈意见。如果问题无法解决,可求助于教师。这样全班都能从阅读和讨论反馈意见中获益。另一个很重要的方面是学生们很可能不按要求去做。对这一点教师应予以理解。我们的调查结果显示,学生在很多时候有自己的计划。他们有各自的学习经历,由此决定了他们想要从教师的课堂授课中吸收什么样的知识。很多教师常常抱怨,说学生们总在作业中,如口语或写作任务中,犯同样的错误。这是因为教师忽略了语言教学中很重要的一点:学生才是教与学全过程的执行者。在教学过程中,教师应该对学习者的诸多因素予以考虑。

杨: 教师需要时间来实现这个过程。课堂教学中,许多英语教师都有大量内容要教。让学生们自己讨论并向教师提问,这样的活动也许没有足够的时间来实施。教师若是为此类活动安排一定时间,那么各项教学内容就需要快速实行。比如我们所做的课堂教学观察中就发现了这样的情况。

S: 没错。但没时间做和是否将其视为重点来做是不同的。如果教师认为这是一项重要的活动,就会有时间来实行。

杨: 是这样的。

S: 许多学生害怕提问。但要让他们结对讨论,他们就会有信心了。因为这样一来,他们就能自行解决问题而无须求助于教师。很显然,教师不可能在课堂上回答每位学生的问题。随着时间推移,如果教师每周一次或两次做这项活动,那学生们使用英语的信心就会增强,进步也会更加明显。

杨: 这个主意不错。

S: 我从自身的研究经历中发现,当我们让学生自主反思时,我们可以得到丰富的信息,从而更好地了解我们的学生,比如了解他们是如何理解语言、语法和语用等。我的研究数据显示,学生们能够领会他们所读的内容。对教师而言,最重要的就是倾听学生,比如可以在学生进行结对或小组讨论时旁听,或者偶尔将学生的对话录下来听。倾听学生,教师可以学到很多,也可以更好地了解自己的学生,诸如他们的所思、所想、所好等。

杨: 非常感谢您向中国的读者介绍您的输出假设学说。期盼您下次访问北京。

(节选自赛波,2010)

2.2　Skills and Abilities

Since you have already learned the knowledge about course resources and other relevant information, now it is the time to practice your skills by analyzing the following cases.

Cases

Case One

教科书配有各种声像材料，通过基于各种直观媒体辅助的听说活动后，学生对语言内容有了初步的感知，但这还仅停留在"语言输入"的层面。为了达成听后反馈的目的，学生还必须对语言材料有内化的过程。内化，始于对听说材料的正确模仿。借助标准的录音、多媒体等声音媒体素材让学生模仿单词的正确发音，是一项重要的策略。

1. 模仿语音语调，培养良好语感

在教学中，通过声音媒体素材，让学生模仿字母、词汇的基础读音、重音、意群连读、语调与节奏等，都是必要的学习经历。

例如，义务教育教科书《英语》（三年级起点）四年级下册（上海教育出版社）Module 4 Unit 10 My garden 一课中，需要教授植物各部位的英语名称，如 leaf, roots, flower 等。教师在教学完植物的各部位名词后，出示了描述一棵大树的语句：

This is a plant.

It's a tree.

It has a trunk, branches, leaves and roots.

教师的教学步骤如下：

Step 1　请学生听录音，模仿跟读；

Step 2　同桌共读，相互检测；

Step 3　集体朗读，个别检测。

2. 模仿情绪表达，提升语言色彩

在听读模仿的过程中，教师要利用孩子善于大胆表现的特点，让孩子勇于模仿，用夸张的语言表达自己的情感，哪怕是口语交际中一个小小的语气词、音调的高低缓急，都能很好地体现说话人的感情。

（节选自朱浦，2016）

思考问题

在此案例中，教师善于利用声像媒体的支撑，让学生精心倾听、大胆模仿。同时，也辅以适当的图像资料，对句子中的升降调、连读等用规范的标记标示出来，把长句的朗读难点突破了,辅助学生正确模仿。同时运用好声像媒体,在学生学习语言的第一时间给予他们正确的语言输入,这是提升听说能力的基础。请思考:

1. 声像资料在小学英语教学中起到什么样的作用?
2. 如果你是该教师,你将如何根据学生的情况对该部分内容进行教学设计?

「Case Two」

人教版四年级下册 Unit 4 At the farm 中的 Let's learn 的教学内容比较丰富,但是教师还是运用了多种教学方法。教学步骤如下:

Step 1　Warm-up & Revision

1. Greetings 师生进行简单的日常问候。

2. Listen to a song "Old McDanold had a farm"

【设计意图:通过歌曲,提高学生积极性,激发学生的兴趣,导入 At the farm 使学生迅速进入学习状态。】

3. Revision

教师:An apple a day keeps the doctor away, so I like apples very much. I also like other fruits.

教师多媒体课件呈现 farm。

【设计意图:每节课歌曲的设计都是为教学内容服务的,用 apple 引出水果,不仅对学过的单词进行了很好的复习,同时也为本节课另外的健康使者——蔬菜的呈现奠定基础。】

Step 2　Presentation

1. 利用谜语、图片学习单词 tomato, potato, green bean, carrot 单复数,学生很容易猜出结果。

【设计意图:以猜谜的形式引出单词,充分调动了学生的积极性。】

2. 对比的方法学习 tomato 和 potato 两个单词以及单复数。

教师提问学生:"What are these?"学生运用上节课所学回答:"They are tomatoes."教师指着红色的西红柿说:"Look at the red tomatoes. They are so big."顺手拿起旁边的土豆提问:"Are these tomatoes?"学生做出否定回答,教师呈现单词 potato,教师引导学生根据 tomato 的发音拼读 potato,并强调这两个单词的复数变化。

【设计意图:把这两个单词放在一起来学习,一方面是因为上节课已经学过 tomato,再学习起来比较容易,另外一方面是因为两个单词的相似之处——包含三个相同的元音字母,在教师的引导下,学生很容易拼出 potato,并且这两个单词的复数比较特殊,因此利用实物进行教学,可以使学生记忆更加深刻。】

3. 学习新单词 green bean 单复数。

教师:"Fruits are healthy for us. So we should eat more fruits. Vegetables are healthy for us, too. Do you like vegetables?"教师课件呈现 green bean,学习单词,出示复数,学习单词 green beans,教师指着图片说:"Look at the green beans. They are so long."操练句子,并在四线三格中板书。

4. 猜单词游戏,将蔬菜的图片遮挡一部分,让学生猜是什么蔬菜,单复数一定要正确,对本部分单词进行巩固。

5. 课件呈现本部分文本,学生跟读。

Step 3　Practice

引出故事,A witch robbed all the vegetables ... 包括 onion 在内的五种蔬菜图片,并展开 guessing game。顺接完成 task 2, task 3。

Step 4　Production

1. 拿出纸笔,画出自己喜欢的蔬菜,并在小组内进行介绍。

【设计意图:通过动笔画一画,不仅活跃了课堂气氛,让学生动了起来,同时增加了学生对蔬菜本身特点的了解,对本节课句型的掌握进行了巩固。】

2. 小组展示。

小组成员运用本节课所学句型 Look at ... , They are ... 对自己所画蔬菜进行介绍。

Step 5　Homework

运用今天所学知识,创设情境,课下和小组成员进行对话练习。

> **思考问题**
>
> 1. 该教学设计中教师运用了哪些教学方法教学生新的单词和句型的表达?
> 2. 课本中本节的内容对教学起到什么作用?如何灵活运用教材而不拘泥于教材内容来进行教学?

✦ 亮考帮

亮闪闪:请总结学习过程中,哪些是自己记忆深刻、受益最大、最欣赏的内容呢?请写出具体内容。

考考你:请把自己弄懂的但觉得别人可能存在困惑的地方,用问题的形式表述出来,来挑战一下其他同学。

帮帮我:请把自己不懂、不会的地方或想要了解的内容,用问题的形式表述出来,并带到课堂上加以讨论。

✦ 参考文献

[1] Edwards, C. & Willis, J. *Teachers Exploring Tasks in English Language Teaching*[M]. 北京:高等教育出版社, 2009.
[2] 赛波. 输出假设理论:历史与未来——Merrill Swain 教授专访[EB/OL]. (2010 - 10 - 18)[2019 - 05 - 19]. http://www.ebook.cn/blog/u/myspace/archives/2010/697244.html.
[3] 王蔷. 英语教学法教程[M]. 2版. 北京:高等教育出版社, 2006.
[4] 朱浦. 小学英语教学关键问题指导[M]. 北京:高等教育出版社, 2016.

Task 3 Instructional Design and Lesson Planning

Instructional design and lesson planning are two basic skills for English student teachers. In this section, we offer you some portable methods to help you design your lesson plan.

3.1 Knowledge Points

Outline

In this part, you have the chance to explore what instructional design is and how to write your lesson plan.

3.1.1 Instructional design

Instructional design is the systematic development of instructional specifications using learning and instructional theory to ensure the quality of instruction. It is the entire process of analysis of learning needs and goals and the development of a delivery system to meet those needs. It includes development of instructional materials and activities; and tryout and evaluation of all instructions and learner activities. Instructional design involves the process of identifying the skills, knowledge, information and attitude gaps of a targeted audience and creating, selecting or suggesting learning experiences that close this gap, based on instructional theories and best practices from the field.

(1) Communicate effectively in visual, oral and written form.

(2) Apply current research and theories to the practice of instructional design.

(3) Update and improve one's knowledge, skills and attitudes pertaining to instructional design and related fields.

(4) Apply fundamental research skills to instructional design projects.

(5) Identify and resolve ethical and legal implications of design in the workplace.

Instructional design is based on two theories including objectivist-rational tradition(客观—理性主义) and constructist-interpretivist tradition. It tends to answer four basic questions: where we are—the analysis of students; where we go—the aim design; how we go there—the design of course content, use of multimedia, management of the class, and the specific method; whether we reach the aim—supervision and evaluation of classroom teaching.

3.1.2 Lesson planning

1. Concept of a lesson plan

A lesson plan is a framework of a lesson in which teachers make advance decisions about what they hope to achieve and how they would like to achieve it.

2. The importance of lesson planning

Teaching is a dynamic activity performed in and out of class, so a well-prepared lesson plan can aid language teachers in a number of the following ways:

(1) A clear lesson plan makes the teachers aware of the aims and language contents of the lesson.

(2) It helps teachers distinguish the various stages of a lesson and accordingly arrange the different difficulty levels.

(3) Proper lesson planning gives teachers the opportunity to anticipate potential problems.

(4) Good lesson planning gives teachers confidence in class.

(5) By lesson planning, teachers also become aware of the teaching aids that are needed.

(6) Lesson planning is a good practice and a sign of professionalism.

(7) Lesson planning will enable the teacher to improve class timing.

3. Principles for good lesson planning

- Aim: clear and realistic
- Variety: activities and materials
- Learnability: within students' learning capability
- Linkage: stages & steps linked with one another
- Flexibility: different methods & techniques; extra & alternative tasks and activities

4. Macro planning vs. micro planning

Planning over time, for instance, planning for a term, the whole course, a whole program.

Planning for a specific unit or a lesson, which usually lasts from one to two weeks or 40 to 50 minutes.

5. Components of a lesson plan

Components	Description
Background information 基本情况	Course name; which grade they are in; class name; the number of the students in the class; teacher's name; textbook; the time and the date of the lesson; the time duration of the lesson
Teaching aims 教学目标	Language skills; language knowledge; effects; strategies; cultural awareness
Contents and skills 教学内容及技能	Specific contents and skills need to be taught, including key points and difficult points
Teaching stages and procedures 教学过程与步骤	Warm-up/revision; presentation; activities and practice; consolidation; summary and homework
Teaching aids 教具	Blackboard (most common); real objects; flashcards; wordcards; worksheets; cassette tapes; magazine pictures; video, etc.
End of summary 总结	Reiterate the key points; refer back to the learning objectives; create a sense of achievement
Optional activities and assignments 附加活动与作业	Extra activities and homework
Reflection 反思	Teacher's feeling; students' performance; unexpected incidents; surprise; things to be improved; things to be given more attention to

6. Something you need to pay attention to

(1) Teaching aims

Teaching aims or objectives should focus on the learners' performance rather than the teachers'.

Teaching objectives should emphasize on language skills, knowledge, effects, strategies and culture awareness in order to lay a good foundation for continuing development.

In lesson planning, teaching aids are very necessary in providing resources and aiding learning for the students. Teaching aids are not chosen at random but are strictly used to serve teaching and learning such as, blackboard (most common), real objects, flashcards, wordcards, worksheets, cassette tapes, magazine pictures, video, etc.

(2) Teaching objectives

Behavioral verbs (a to z)

Analyze, apply, arrange, assemble

Build

Categorize, choose, classify, compare

Deduce, define, demonstrate

Estimate, evaluate, explain

Generate, graph

Identify, indicate

Label, locate

Make, match, measure, modify

Name

Operate, order, organize, outline

Predict, prepare, present, pronounce

Read, reconstruct, revise

Select, solve, sort, specify, state, suggest

Tabulate, translate, type

Underline

Verbalize

Write

(3) Procedures

Whatever procedures the teachers use, for almost every lesson, a warm-up or a starter is necessary.

A warm-up is an activity or a series of activities that a teacher does at the beginning of the lesson. It does not take long in a lesson, but it can fulfill a wide range of purpose.

A warm-up can take many forms: a song, questions and answers, a daily conversation, a story, a guessing game, a picture description, homework checking, etc.

A warm-up should directly contribute to the overall lesson objectives.

(4) End of lesson summary

The end of lesson summary is a very important stage for the teacher to take learning further and deeper by helping students to refer back to the learning objectives.

End of lesson summary is also a time for the teacher to create a sense of achievement and completion of tasks for the students.

In addition, the teacher can use the time to develop with the students a habit of reflection on learning and help students draw out applications of what has been learned and highlight the important conception which has been developed.

(5) Optional activities and assignment

Teachers should always remember to prepare some optional activities and decide on the type of assignment for the students after the class because they can successfully reinforce knowledge learned in class.

(6) After lesson reflection

• Very often, teaching does not follow exactly what we plan and unexpected things happen during the lesson. So teachers are encouraged to keep a brief account of what happened in a lesson, which may include feeling about the lesson, students' performances, unexpected incidents, surprises, things that went well, things that went wrong and things to be improved or things to be given more attention to next.

- Lesson reflections can contribute greatly to teachers' professional development.

(7) Criteria for evaluating lesson effectiveness

The learners were active all the time.

The learners were attentive all the time.

The learners enjoyed the lesson, were motivated.

The class seemed to be learning the material well.

The lesson went according to the plan.

The language was used communicatively throughout.

The learners were engaging with the foreign language throughout.

…

3.2 Skills and Abilities

Since you have already learned the key points of instructional design and the way to write a lesson plan, here are some cases for you to study and further practice your skills by thinking creatively.

Cases

Case One

小学英语四年级下册第五单元"My clothes"第二课时教学设计

一、教学目标

1. 知识与技能

(1) 认读五个新单词和两个新句型,做到发音准确、清晰;

(2) 熟练运用新句型与其他同学进行相互问答;

(3) 能够借助实物投影进行看图问答或综合说话;

(4) 能够根据多媒体课件和学生自备图片进行对话操练和表演。

2. 情感态度与价值观

(1) 激发和保持学生英语学习的兴趣,实现趣味性和能力性相结合;

(2) 在学生两两交流和情境合作交流中,培养孩子合作意识和合作精神,能够相互配合完成一段通顺流畅的说话训练。

二、重难点

1. 认读 clothes, hat, pants, dress, skirt 五个新单词;

2. 单词 clothes 的发音；

3. I like that green skirt. Me too. And I like those pants. 使用两个新句型进行对话。

三、学情分析

1. 学生是某中心学校四年级的学生；

2. 学生对用 It's … 等句型描述事物非常熟悉；

3. 大部分学生思维活跃愿意和同学交流，渴望得到同学和教师的赞许，但少数同学胆怯，不敢张口，还需要老师和同学的鼓励；

4. 学生对英语学习有着浓厚的兴趣，但是英语的听读能力有待加强；

5. 学生很喜欢自主情境对话操练这种方式；

6. 学生的单词、句型书写等能力需要老师继续指导训练。

四、教学策略选择与设计

1. 演示法和启发式策略：教师通过和 1—2 个学生的口语交际，给全班同学做出示范，让学生清楚两两说话的内容和方式；

2. 操练法策略：学生通过师生对话、生生对话、情境操练等多种方式，完成课标要求的基础上训练听说能力，并积累和丰富英语词汇和句式；

3. 歌曲激趣策略：通过学生的模仿、跟唱，有利于形成宽松活泼的课堂氛围，同时借助诵读和歌曲来巩固学过的句型和单词，在语言运用中学习英语。

五、教学资源与工具设计

1. 教师使用资源

(1) 多媒体课件；(2) 各式衣物挂图及幻灯片；(3) 各种衣服实物。

2. 学生使用资源

(1) 学生准备自画衣物图片；(2) 各种文具用品和自己所穿的衣服。

六、教学过程

1. 复习引题

(1) 教师播放从前学习过的有关衣服的歌曲，听后学生说出听到的衣服名称。

(2) 教师出示服装卡片，学生认读单词。

(3) 学生自己找出喜欢的衣服图片向大家介绍它的颜色。

2. 教学新课

Let's learn

(1) 教师呈现图画，问学生：What color can you see? 学生会自然说出图中的颜色。教师顺便引出新课：What's this? It's a skirt. A green skirt. 教师继续指图，并放录音，学生边看图边听录音，通过各种颜色初步感知衣物名称。

(2) 教师呈现各种衣物的图片，学生看图回想衣物名称。引导孩子们说一说记住的衣物名称。教师指图问：What color is it? What's this? 学生回答两个问题，教师引导学生说出：A red dress. 并出示其他图片，学生试着说出其他几个词组。

(3) 看书中图并放录音，学生边看图边听录音感知并理解句子；用动作帮助学生理解单词 with 的用法。

(4) 找几个学生到前边来当模特，再请两个同学来表演刚学的两句话，或者播放课件,学生配音。

3. Let's do

(1) 教师播放录音或录像,带领学生做游戏。

(2) 教师发布指令,学生做动作;一学生发布指令,教师和其他学生一起做动作。

(3) 小组比赛,每人听一个指令做动作,接力进行,看哪个小组动作做得正确。奖励优胜组。

(4) 两人一组互相快速发布指令并做动作,到前边进行表演。

七、巩固练习

让学生介绍自己的衣服颜色及名称,或者喜欢谁的衣服就介绍谁的衣服。

八、布置作业

读课文并背诵表演 Let's do。

九、教学反思

上课前,我针对我校学生实际做了学情分析,做到掌握学生的英语基础和学习心态,满足学生的学习需求,调动学生学习英语的积极性,在整节课的学习中,整体上学生都能积极参与老师组织的各项学习活动,不同层次的学生都有自己的收获,从而取得了较好的教学效果。

(强俊勇提供)

思考问题

1. 教案设计包括哪几部分内容?教师是如何讲授 clothes 这一内容的?

2. 有人认为,教学设计时教学重点和难点是一样的,你认同这种说法吗?结合这一案例,解释教学重点和难点有区别吗?

Case Two

五年级英语"What Are You Doing"教学设计

【教学内容】

Let's learn 和 Let's chant 以及 Let's sing 等内容。

【教学重点】

1. 听、说、读、写五个动词短语的 ing 形式:doing the dishes, cooking dinner, reading a book, drawing pictures, answering the phone。

2. 能运用句子"What are you doing? I'm doing the dishes/..."询问别人正在做什么并作答。

3. 初步了解现在进行时的结构。

【教学难点】

1. 如何引导学生感知、理解现在进行时所表达的含义以及动词 ing 形式的读音。

2. 短语 answering the phone 中 answering 的读音。

【教学目标】

一、能力目标：

1. 能够简单描述自己正在做什么，如：I'm doing the dishes.

2. 能够听懂、会唱歌曲"What Are You Doing?"

二、知识目标：

1. 能够听、说、读、写动词短语 ing 的形式：doing the dishes, cooking dinner, reading a book, drawing pictures, answering the phone。

2. 理解 Let's chant 的内容。通过说唱 Let's chant 部分的歌谣，巩固复习 Let's learn 部分的短语和句子。

三、情感目标：培养热爱生活的美好感情。

【教学准备】

教师准备钢笔、锅(pot)、手机、碟子(plate)、画笔、书、麦克风、随身听等小道具。

【教学过程】：

Step 1　Warm-up & Revision 朗读 chant 3(TPR 活动)。

T：Are you ready for English class?

S：Yes.

T：Good afternoon, boys and girls.

S：Good afternoon, Miss Liu.

T：Who's on duty today?

Liu Shuang：I am.

T：What day is it today?

Liu Shuang：It's Friday.

T：What's the date today?

Liu Shuang：It's April 1st.

T：April 1st? Ah ha! It's Fools' Day, right? Happy Fools' Day!

领唱生日快乐曲调，填词"Happy April Fools' Day!"

【教学反思】通过师生的值日报告对话引出 4 月 1 日，并填词唱歌，为学生提供一个可自由发散思维的问题，引导学生快速进入用英语思维的课堂中来。

1. 复习动词。

T：Now, boys and girls. Happy Fools' Day! I take a present for you, look! Can you guess, what's in my magic box?

[教师边拿出物品边说：cook/read/write/draw/answer/listen/sing 并书写在黑板上。]We'll learn Unit 4.（板书：Unit 4 What are you doing?）

2. Chants 1 and 2.复习词组。

T：Stop please, look here："What can you do?" Let's read and act it.

S1：I can …. S2：I can …. T：Great. You're helpful.

【教学反思】在 Warm-up 中通过愚人节礼物盒子里的物品联想回顾所学的动词，从一开始就将学生带入动词的世界，以旧带新，为后面的新授、拓展做简单的引导，为后面引出

do the dishes，cook dinner 等短语做铺垫。

Step 2　Presentation and practise

T：(模仿电话铃声)I'm sorry. Let me answer the phone.（老师拿起电话）

Hello. It's Miss Liu. That's Zhang Peng. All right. Thank you，bye.

T：My boys and girls, Zhang Peng has a big family. He welcomes us to his home. Now let's go to his home together!

利用课件教学 doing the dishes, cooking dinner, reading a book, drawing pictures, answering the phone。

【教学反思】设计张鹏打电话邀请去他家参观的情景，将课件与教学紧密联系起来，引导学生融入英语学习的情境中，并为本课完成最后的学会打电话的任务打下基础。

1. 教学 doing the dishes

T：Guess！What can I do?

Ss：You can … .

T：Please look here. What am I doing?（边洗碟子,边解释现在我在做什么?）You can ask me：What are you doing?（词卡领读板书问句）Ask me together.（边做动作边回答）I am doing the dishes.（老师板书 I am …）

教师出示洗碗动作的卡片,板书 ing 并领读 doing the dishes,学生做洗碗的动作。

T：What are you doing?（帮助学生回答）I am doing the dishes.

[告诉学生洗碗有两种表达方法，即 I am doing the dishes. 或 I am washing the dishes.（We can say … . We can also say … .）]

[再次板书：I am＝I'm（领读,拿盘子准备传）]

T：（拿一个盘子）Now let's pass the dish one by one, and say "What are you doing?" [传盘子时，全体同学一起打着节奏问："What are you doing?" 当老师说 Stop 时,拿到盘子的同学站起来边洗盘子边说："I am doing the dishes."]

【教学反思】由 Free talk 引出 do the dishes，由学生熟悉的词组入手，利用肢体语言演示动词词组，使呈现更加直观形象、生动有趣，有利于提高学生的学习热情，增强学习效果。通过传盘子的游戏集体练习、重点突破主句型 What are you doing?

2. 教学 cooking dinner

T：（与一名学生对话）You can do the dishes. Can you cook dinner?

S：如果学生回答 Yes, I can. 老师就用 T：You're helpful. Please do an action and say.

T：（边让学生说 cook dinner，边做动作，并板书 cook dinner)

T：（利用道具，做出做饭动作）Now, I'm cooking dinner.（领读 cooking dinner，然后学生做做饭的动作。）

师生练习：

T：What are you doing?

Ss：I'm cooking dinner.

（板书-ing. Cook add -ing is pronounced cooking 画连读符号）

3. 教学 reading a book

T：Now boys and girls, please look at this. What's this?

S：… .

T：Yes, it's a storybook. Do you want to read it?

S：…（老师让一个学生上台来看书）

T：What are you doing?

学生试着回答：I'm reading a book.

教师出示读书的图片，板书并领读 reading a book，学生跟读。然后学生做读书的动作。

师生练习：

T：What are you doing?

Ss：I'm reading a book.

4. 教学 drawing pictures

（老师展示一幅画）

T：Oh. It is a beautiful picture!（板书 pictures）. I can draw pictures. Can you draw pictures?（老师边说边画树和花草等，然后板书、领读）

S：Yes.

T：Let's draw some pictures. Please draw one thing. You can draw a tree, flowers, an apple and so on.

T：What are you doing?

Ss：I am drawing pictures.

5. 教学 answering the phone

（老师拿起电话，教学词组 answer the phone）板书

T：What am I doing?

Ss：You're answering the phone.（帮助学生回答）

T：Yes, I'm answering the phone.

Step 3　Practise

1. P44 的 Let's chant.

T：OK，look here. Who wants to be a teacher?（看黑板或领读）

2. T：学习动词的-ing 形式，then write the -ing form of the verbs given（写出所给动词的 -ing 形式）。

【教学反思】语法学习完成后进行书写操练，突破本课语法知识的重难点。

Step 4　Consolidation and extension

1. T：OK. So much for this. Boys and girls, are you happy today? Let's sing a song "What are you doing?" OK?（教师跟节奏领读歌词。解释 speak to you on the phone. 学生试着跟唱。）

2. 一起做 Let's try 练习，然后让学生小组合作做一个调查并根据调查结果填表格，让学生把听、说和写结合起来。

【教学反思】在 chant 后一起做 Let's try 练习,然后让学生小组合作做一个调查并根据调查结果填表格,让学生把听、说和写结合起来。这是对本课所学知识的延伸。

3. 我会打电话。

T：Use your hands, like this.（老师让学生用手作为电话听筒,并出示下面的对话。）（课件）

(T：You will be A, I will be B. Let's make a telephone call, OK? 练习完一次后交换角色)OK. Let's change. I will be A. You will be B. Let's go!

A：Hello(课件)

B：Hi. It's _____（自己的名字）. What are you doing?

A：I'm answering the phone. What are you doing?

B：I'm _____ (drawing pictures/doing the dishes/cooking dinner/reading a book).

T：Next, practise in pairs. Which group can act out the dialogue in front of class?（抽查一两组学生对话）

【教学反思】学习打电话的日常用语,让学生将书卷起作为电话,出示对话提示,小组练习。达到本课的任务型教学要求,又可渗透下节课 Let's talk 的内容。

4. 总结本课内容。

Step 5　Homework

T：Boys and girls, time is up. Here's your homework for today! After school, please give your friend a call in English and talk about what you are doing at home.（在课后给你的朋友用英语打个电话,谈论在家里正在做什么）

You did a good job! Thank you, boys and girls. Goodbye! See you later!

【板书设计】

Unit 4　What are you doing?

What are you do**ing**?

I am do**ing** the dishes.　　　I am = I'm

I'm cook**ing** dinner.

I'm draw**ing** pictures.

I'm answer**ing** the phone.

I'm read**ing** a book.

（强俊勇提供）

思考问题

1. 该教案设计中教学过程非常详细,你认为这样的设计有必要吗? 为什么?

2. 教学反思是教学过程中的重要一环,也是教案的重要组成部分,该教案对教学过程进行了深入的反思,从这样的反思中你学到了什么?

Case Three

Teaching Plan of *Mr. Cool's Clothes Store*

Background information:

Book 1, Grade 7, Junior high school, 30 students, 45 mins

Version: PEP edition

Publisher: People's Education Press

Publish time: 2013

Teacher: Monica Jiang

Teaching aims:

1. Aims of knowledge:

1) Students can understand the content of advertisement, and the meaning of the words and phrases, such as the English expression of clothes and the phrases "at great sale" "I'll take it" "here you are".

2) Students can use the sentence patterns "Can I help you" "It's ..." to make a conversation about shopping.

2. Aims of ability:

1) All students can read and get the meaning of the advertisement to enhance their reading abilities.

2) All students can read aloud the text correctly in a right tone and pronunciation.

3) Most of students can make a new conversation and show it in front of the whole class after learning.

3. Aims of emotion:

1) Students' interest in English will be aroused through talking about the clothes.

2) Students can be encouraged to talk with others in English.

4. Aims of learning strategies:

Students can pay attention to listening in the classroom, think positively to predict the text, actively use keywords and key sentences to express and communicate.

5. Aims of culture:

1) Students can understand the features of the advertisement.

2) Students can learn the different currency symbol between the United States and China.

3) Students can know the greetings and related expressions of shopping in English.

Teaching contents:

Teaching focus:

Students can get the meaning of the words of kinds of clothes, related phrases and sentence patterns about shopping. And students also can read, write and use them correctly.

Teaching difficulty:

Students can understand the correct expression about special words about clothes, such as "jeans, shorts" "a pair of socks".

Teaching methods:

PWP (Pre-reading, While-reading, Post-reading), questioning and answering

Teaching tools:

PPT, pictures, audio

Teaching procedures:

Step 1 Lead-in and pre-reading (7 mins)

1. Ask students whether they like going shopping, and let students tell the reasons.

2. Write down a title of the text, and let students to predict:

Step 2 While-reading (15 mins)

1. Students listen to the text, and answer the questions:

1) Find out what the type of the text is.

(The teacher shows some pictures to explain the meaning of the advertisement.)

2) Students listen to the text, and get the main idea of it.

(The teacher explains the meaning of the phrase "at great sale".)

2. Students read the text, and the teacher sets two exercises:

1) Ask the question to the students:

How many clothes are mentioned in the text? And list them!

(The teacher teaches and explains the words of clothes one by one.)

2) Group competition: The teacher tests vocabulary through a game.

3) The teacher asks students to fill in the blank.

(The teacher will teach students how to ask the prices of clothes. And the teacher explains the difference of currency symbol between America and China.)

3. Students read the text:

1) Read in whole class

2) Read in group

3) Read alone

(The teacher explains the standards of reading the text.)

Step 3　Post-reading（20 mins）

1. Students work in pairs:

One is a shop assistant in Mr. Cool's Store, and the other is a buyer. Make a new conversation according to the form brought by the teacher:

A: Hello, can I help you?

B: Yes, please, I need a _____.

A: How about these _____?

B: Oh, I like this one. How _____ is it?

A: It's only _____ dollars.

B: Oh, good. I'll take it.

A: OK, here you are!

Step 4　Summary and Homework:（3 mins）

Summary:

The teacher summarizes the words of clothes and the phrases learned in the class.

Homework:

1) Memorize the words and phrases learned in the class.

2) Read and try to recite the text.

Board design:

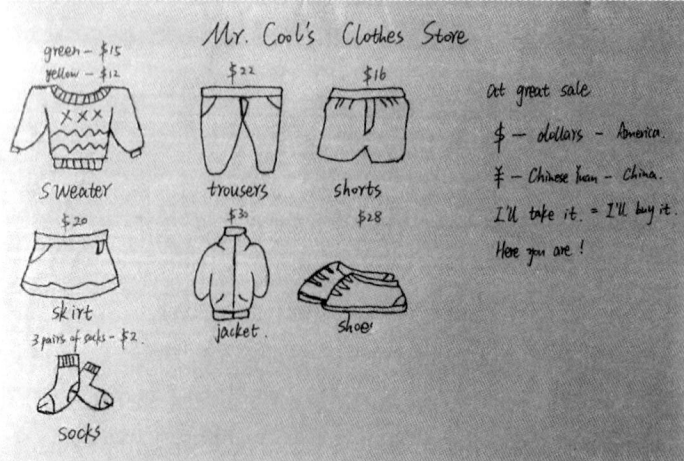

Reflection：

PWP method is really effective to teach reading. Combined with task-based method, I feel this class ran pretty well.

For students' exercises, the form of activities should be more diversified to strengthen memory and consolidation. The classroom atmosphere is generally very active, but a small number of introverted students have not been able to participate well. In the future, I will pay more attention to those students so that every student can gain something.

> 思考问题

1. How did the teacher design the aims of teaching? Generally, what kind of points do we need to consider when we design the teaching aims?

2. How did this teaching plan implement PWP method? What are other ways do you think to teach the topic "Mr. Cool's Clothes Store" effectively?

亮考帮

亮闪闪： 请总结学习过程中，哪些是自己记忆深刻、受益最大、最欣赏的内容呢？请写出具体内容。

考考你： 请把自己弄懂的但觉得别人可能存在困惑的地方，用问题的形式表述出来，来挑战一下其他同学。

帮帮我： 请把自己不懂、不会的地方或想要了解的内容，用问题的形式表述出来，并带到课堂上加以讨论。

参考文献

[1] Geyser, J. P. *Teaching Methodology Made Easy* [M]. Shanghai：Shanghai Foreign Language Education Press，2013.
[2] 王蔷.英语教学法教程[M].2版.北京：高等教育出版社，2006.

第六章 教学环境与班级管理

主要内容

1. 教学环境
   - 校园文化
2. 班级管理
   - 班主任工作

✓案例学习
✓专业参考
✓学术探讨

  Schools' environment attracts more and more people's attention in recent years. Neat and tidy compus and classroom make people feel energetic，but untidy arrangement brings unhealthy atmosphere which is not good for our students' and teachers' well being. Besides, school culture is one of the key points for schools' reputation and sustainable development. To construct a healthy learning environment，we also need to prevent bullying，which is everyone's responsibility. In the following text，we offer the contents of creating good environment in campus and classrooms which help students to adapt to the study environment，and avoid school bullying，and promote their healthy growth.

Task 1 Learning Environment

Both campus and classroom environment are very important for children's well being. And a positive school culture also benefits students' overall development. The following contents offer you some information about it.

1.1 Knowledge Points

Outline

Campus, classroom and school culture are the main points for students' learning. Here is some information about it.

1.1.1 About campus

School campus usually refers to a place where teaching and learning happens. Previously, the word "campus" is used to describe the buildings of a university or a college and the land around them (Hornby, 2014). But we may also use the word "campus" in primary school situation to show the place and the land around a primary school. In China, primary school campus is pretty typical because we have so many students study inside the campus. Different countries design their school in different ways. Here are some examples.

1.1.2 About classroom

Students' desks and other components in class should be qualified as follows.

• Ideally, it should not be permanent except for large lecture halls or laboratories;

• How to move from one to another as quickly and quietly as possible;

• How to make a decision to enhance small-group discussion and cooperative learning but avoid chatting;

• The greater the distance, the less they distract each other;

• To achieve different results with different arrangements;

• Simply changing the seating patterns after a few weeks;

• Give careful consideration to the direction and avoid seating two troublesome students next to each other.

Please compare the following classroom setting.

1.1.3 School culture

It reflects the shared ideas—assumptions, values, and beliefs—that give an organization its identity and standard for expected behaviours. These ideas are deeply imbedded that they are often taken for granted. It makes from outside and inside. Culture is reflected in an organization's atmosphere, myths, and moral code. It can be

deduced from multiple layers:
- Artifacts and symbols;
- Values;
- Assumptions.

A school district's culture is maintained by several practices.
- Common beliefs and values;
- Heroes and heroines;
- Rituals and ceremonies;
- Stories.

Table 6 - 1 The influence of school culture

	Support learning	Impede learning
Artifacts and symbols	The building and its arrangements reflect the children, their needs, and their educational accomplishments.	There is little that reflects an emphasis on children and their education.
Values	Administers, teachers, students, and parents participate in decision making.	Decisions are made without participation of teachers and parents.
Assumptions and beliefs	All students can learn. Parents want their children to succeed. Parents are partners in education.	Some students are incapable of learning or too lazy to learn. Parents don't care. Parents know nothing about education.

（Tableman，2004，转引自郭满库，2012）

Reading Material

什么是校园文化？

广义的校园文化是指学生生活的存在方式的总和，其主体包括生活在校园内的学生、教师和行政人员二人群体，它是在物质财富、精神产品和氛围以及活动方式上具有一定独特性的文化类型。狭义的校园文化是指学校精神文化，是在学校发展历史过程中形成的，反映着人们在生活方式、价值取向、思维方式和行为规范上有别于其他社会群体的一种团体意识和精神氛围。

广义上的校园文化作为一个相对独立的子系统，其系统内又可分为若干个层次：精神文化，即由校园文化创设的思想与心理氛围；制度文化，即由校园文化的组织、机构及其规章制度确定的制度文化；物质文化，即由校园文化的物质条件构造的各种教学、科研、生活设备、设施、房屋等。也有论者将校园文化分为精神文化、制度文化、行为文化和环境文化四个层次，而所谓环境文化是指以环境为载体，是校园文化的外部表现形式，包括硬件和软件。具体表述有差异，但其内涵都是基本相同的。

上述几个层次的校园文化并不是相互孤立的,而是相互依赖、相互补充的。一定的精神文化的作用依赖于一定物质文化的保证。正如物质文化的建立依赖于一定观念体系的支配和支持一样。制度本身要有精神文化的内涵,而精神文化的倡导与挖掘则是制度和规则的集中反映。精神文化深入到比制度更深的层次。我们常讲的学校的校风、风气、风貌等,都正是校园文化品位和作用的自然体现,而且是更加重要的表现。

校园文化是以学生为主体,以课外文化活动为主要内容,以校园为主要空间,以校园精神为主要特征的一种群体文化。它主要包括:以青年学生为代表的文化观念以及其特有的思维特征、行为特征和方式;学生课余生活中一切以群体形式出现的文化活动,如诗社、棋牌俱乐部、书社、文学社等社团活动,其中最能体现校园文化本质内容的是校园风气或校园精神。

校园文化指的是学校所具有的特定的精神环境和文化气氛,它包括校园建筑设计、校园景观、绿化美化这种物化形态的内容,也包括学校的传统、校风、学风、人际关系、集体舆论、心理氛围以及学校的各种规章制度和学校成员在共同活动交往中形成的非明文规范的行为准则。健康的校园文化,可以陶冶学生的情操、启迪学生心智,促进学生的全面发展。

校园文化在当今高等教育中应该发挥重要的作用,校园文化是常新的,但是能够保持永恒魅力,能够唤起青年一代心灵,能够激发青年学生激情,能够唤起青年一代高尚的、独立的人格追求和高尚的道德追求。比如校园的时代性活动等。

当代校园文化建设进入了网络环境,应运而生的各种网络社团,校园文化宣传站从软件上提升了校园文化的内涵。

校园文化设计的重要意义

加强高校校园文化建设具有十分重要的意义。当今世界,文化与经济和政治相互交融、相互渗透。文化的力量,不仅深深熔铸在民族的生命力、创造力和凝聚力之中,成为综合国力和国际竞争力的重要组成部分,而且对人们的思想政治影响越来越大。大力加强校园文化建设,意义十分重大。

1. 校园文化是先进文化的重要源头,是社会文化的重要组成部分,始终处在社会文化的前沿,既承担着育人的重要职责,也承担着引领社会文化的重要任务。校园文化具有凝聚作用,通过研究和宣传科学理论,可以把人们紧紧地团结在中国特色社会主义的伟大旗帜下。校园文化具有引导作用,通过传授人类文化,可以帮助人们培养良好的道德思想品质。校园文化具有辐射作用,通过知识传播和人才培养,可以对社会主义经济建设、政治建设、文化建设和社会建设产生积极影响。

2. 校园文化是先进文化的创新基地。创新是民族进步的灵魂和国家兴旺发达的不竭动力,也是文化始终体现先进性和永葆生机的源泉。传承文化是高校的基本功能,研究文化是高校的活动基础,创新文化是高校的崇高使命。高校校园文化是科学思想萌生的催化剂,是先进文化创新的重要载体,它既从先进文化中汲取营养和力量,又为发展先进文化提供强大动力、做出巨大贡献。

3. 校园文化具有强大的育人作用。先进文化要发挥社会作用,就要把文化内化到人们的灵魂里,积淀到人们的思想中。办大学就要建设校园文化,让学生学习、感悟、理解,从而净化灵魂,陶冶情操,完善自己。校园文化是引导人、鼓舞人、激励人的一种内在动力,是凝聚人心、鼓舞斗志、催人奋进的一面旗帜,它对大学生的思想政治、道德品质、行为规范产生深刻影响。

(节选自陈亚玲,2019)

1.2 Skills and Abilities

Given that you have already learned the key points of schools' environment and school culture, here are some cases for you to study and further practice your skills by thinking creatively.

Cases

⌈ Case One ⌋

大宇街道中心学校

大宇街道中心学校始建于1924年8月,历史悠久。学校位于某市区紫薇大道中部的大宇镇村,虽然是一所镇小学,远离繁华的闹市,但学校校址离城市主干道很近,有公交车直达,交通便利。学校占地面积9 580平方米,建筑面积4 522平方米,共有五栋教学楼,由于靠近著名的秦岭山脉北麓,空气清新、风景优美,绿化面积720平方米。学校设施齐全,校园内设有餐厅,有专人为师生提供早餐与午餐,操场为国家标准操场,校园内种植有各种树木及花草,景色优美,而且装饰颇有文化气息,现有班级18个,每年级3个班,在校人数850名,教师42名,服务半径2公里,主要为黄良周边11个自然村的6—12岁的儿童提供6年制小学义务教育。

校园内教室宽敞明亮,通风良好,温度适宜,每一层的教室前有一条走廊,两侧有楼梯,每间教室建筑要求符合国家标准,教室有环保黑板、多媒体设备、避光窗帘,教室内的

桌椅主要是秧田式摆放,可根据教师开展的具体活动而灵活布置。除了日常的教学以外,学校还为小学生开展丰富多彩的校外活动,为学生开展绘画、书法、手工、趣味英语、体育等活动,丰富小学生的文化生活。近年来,学校在以习近平同志为核心的党中央的带领下,在区委区政府的大力支持和教育局的正确领导及全体老师的不懈追求下,不忘初心,坚守信仰,砥砺奋进,学校取得了显著成绩,知名度和群众的满意度不断提升,硕果累累。

(强俊勇提供)

思考问题

1. 你认为该校的校址及悠久的历史会对教学产生怎样的影响?
2. 你认为该校的教学环境整体布局如何?是否有利于教学活动的开展?
3. 该校的教室设计如何?是否有助于教学?

「Case Two」

画廊镇中心学校简介

画廊镇中心学校地处画廊镇西村西正街200号,现有教学班18个,教师42人,在校学生1 016人。校园占地38亩,校舍建筑面积6 116平方米,校园内体育设施一应俱全,运动场地标准规范。校园文化氛围浓厚,充满了和谐的现代气息。

学校拥有一支爱岗敬业、业务精湛的教师队伍,现有教师38人,一级教师11人,二级教师29人,工勤人员3人,本科学历40人,其中市级教学能手3人,户县名师1人,镇级骨干教师9人。

近年来,学校以"为孩子的一生奠基"为办学理念,形成了文化氛围浓厚、教研特色鲜明、多彩活动丰富、绿色文明厚重的办学特色。学校创编了具有镇中心学校特色的《教师誓词》《学生誓词》,校歌《飞向理想》,布局了各具特色的校园文化走廊,用精神文明引领教师走向敢闯敢当,教育培养学生走向自主自信。学校提出具有我校特色的校本研修专题"尝试自解",引导教师学践研创,创设出"双四并行,互动共生"课堂教学模式,启迪学生心智,激活学生潜能。学校共有校级社团和年级社团23个,坚持定时活动,活动张扬了学生个性,培养了学生才艺。学校以可持续发展思想为指导,开展系列"心系绿色、情洒环保"活动,让绿色文明走向未来。学校先后获得陕西省骨干教师专业成长示范学校、省级绿色校园、市级校园文化成果二等奖、市级德育先进集体、县级教育教学质量综合奖、县级目标责任考评先进单位、县级先进基层党组织、县级课改先进集体等56项大奖,被誉为户县教育一颗璀璨的明珠。

(画廊镇中心学校提供)

思考问题

1. 你认为该校的教学环境整体布局如何?是否有利于教学活动的开展?
2. 该校教学环境和氛围是怎样的?该校重视精神文明建设是否有助于教学?
3. 如果你是设计师,你将如何设计一所小学校园?请画出平面图。

亮考帮

亮闪闪:请总结学习过程中,哪些是自己记忆深刻、受益最大、最欣赏的内容呢?请写出具体内容。

考考你:请把自己弄懂的但觉得别人可能存在困惑的地方,用问题的形式表述出来,来挑战一下其他同学。

帮帮我:请把自己不懂、不会的地方或想要了解的内容,用问题的形式表述出来,并带到课堂上加以讨论。

参考文献

[1] Partin, R. L. *The Clussroom Teacher's Survival Guide*[M]. San Francisco:Jossey-Bass,2009.
[2] Seifert, K., & Sutton, R. *Educational psychology*[M]. Zurich:The Saylor Foundation, 2009.
[3] Tableman, B. School Culture//郭满库. 英语案例教学论[M]. 杭州:浙江大学出版社,2012.

Task 2 Class Management

It is supported by many researchers that class management plays a significant role in schools' teaching and learning. In this section, we offer you some information of class management and strategies of building a harmonic classroom community.

2.1 Knowledge Points

Outline

Classroom code of conduct, positive discipline, and family-school relationship are all important strategies for building a good class environment. Besides, you should learn more psychology which will help you work smoothly and effectively in your class.

2.1.1 Classroom code of conduct

(1) Emphasize the responsibilities and rights of each person in the class:
- Co-responsibility
- Positive contribution to an improvement in learning

(2) Suggestions for drafting a classroom code of conduct:
- Comprehensive, but not too many
- Not rigid and must be adapted if the need arises
- In learners' own words, use must instead of must not
- Learners are experts
- Rules without consequences are of no value
- Being consistently and firmly applied

2.1.2 Positive discipline

Positive discipline is a program designed to teach young people to become responsible, respectful and resourceful members of their communities. Children who feel a sense of connection to their community, family, and school are less likely to misbehave. Positive discipline is based on the understanding that discipline must be taught. Here are five criteria for effective discipline.

- Helping children feel a sense of connection (Belonging and significance).
- Being mutually respectful and encouraging (Kind and firm at the same time).
- Being effective in the long term.
- Teaching important social and life skills(home, school, community).
- Inviting children to discover how capable they are (personal power and autonomy).

We need to pay attention to kindness and firmness at the same time and neither punitive nor permissive. Tools and concepts include:
- Mutual respect;
- Identifying the belief behind the behavior;
- Effective communication and problem-solving skills;
- Focusing on solutions (instead of punishment);
- Encouragement (instead of praise).

Unique characteristics of the Positive Discipline Model include:
- Experiential activities;
- Consistent programs to educate;
- Inexpensive training and ongoing support.

2.1.3 Family-school partnerships

For family-school partnership, seven dimensions should be considered:
- Communicating;
- Connecting learning at home and at school;
- Building community and identity;
- Recognizing the role of the family;
- Consultative decision-making;
- Collaborating beyond the school;
- Participating.

Reading Materials

Reading Material One

Why Classroom Management Matters

Managing the learning environment is both a major responsibility and an on-going concern for all teachers, even those with years of experience (Good & Brophy, 2002). There are several reasons. In the first place, a lot goes on in classrooms simultaneously, even when students seem to be doing only one task in common. Twenty-five students may all seem to be working on a sheet of math problems. But look more closely: several may be stuck on a particular problem, each for different reasons. A few others have worked only the first problem or two and are now chatting quietly with each other instead of continuing. Still others have finished and are wondering what to do next. At any one moment each student needs something different—different information, different hints, different kinds of encouragement. Such diversity increases even more if the teacher deliberately assigns multiple activities to different groups or individuals (for example, if some students do a reading assignment while others do the math problems).

Another reason that managing the environment is challenging is because a teacher can not predict everything that will happen in a class. A well-planned lesson may fall flat on its face, or take less time than expected, and you find yourself improvising to fill class time. On the other hand an unplanned moment may become a wonderful, sustained exchange among students, and prompt you to drop previous plans and follow the flow of discussion. Interruptions happen continually: a fire drill, a drop-in visit from another teacher or the principal, a call on the intercom from the office. An activity may indeed turn out well, but also rather differently than you intended; you therefore have to decide how, if at all, to adjust the next day's lesson to allow for this surprise.

A third reason for the importance of management is that students form opinions and perceptions about your teaching that are inconsistent with your own. What you intend as encouragement for a shy student may seem to the student herself like "forced participation". An eager, outgoing classmate watching your effort to encourage the shy student, moreover, may not see you as *either* encouraging or coercing, but as overlooking or ignoring *other* students who already want to participate. The variety of perceptions can lead to surprises in students' responses—most often small ones, but occasionally major.

At the broadest, society-wide level, classroom management challenges teachers because public schooling is not voluntary, and students' presence in a classroom is therefore not a sign, in and of itself, that they wish to learn. Instead, students' presence is just a sign that an *opportunity* exists for teachers to motivate students to learn. Some students, of course, do enjoy learning and being in school, almost regardless of what teachers do! Others do enjoy school, but only because teachers have worked hard to make classroom life pleasant and interesting. Those students become motivated because you have successfully created a positive learning environment and have sustained it through skillful management.

Fortunately it is possible to earn this sort of commitment from many students, and this chapter describes ways of doing so. We begin with ways of *preventing* management problems from happening by increasing students' focus on learning. The methods include ideas about arranging classroom space, about establishing procedures, routines, and rules, and about communicating the importance of learning to students and parents. After these prevention oriented discussions, we look at ways of *re*focusing students when and if their minds or actions stray from the tasks at hand. As you probably know from being a student, bringing students back on task can happen in many ways, and the ways vary widely in the energy and persistence required of the teacher. We try to indicate some of these variations, but because of space limitations and because of the richness of classroom life, we cannot describe them all.

(Adapted from Seifert & Sutton, 2009)

Reading Material Two

小学班级自主管理体系的建设

2016年9月,教育部颁布了《中国学生发展核心素养》,以培养"全面发展的人"为核心,分为3个方面、6大素养、18个基本要点。"学生发展核心素养"是在遵循学生身心发展规律和教育规律的基础上,为了传承与发展中国优秀传统文化,同时满足当今经济社会发展对人才培养的新要求,进而提出先进教育理念和教育思想。面向不同年龄段的学生提出不同的培养要求。而小学教育是整个教育事业的基础,对于学生的未来发展有不可磨灭的指引作用。具体到小学班级管理中,班主任要引导学生创设一个团结、自主、积极的班级,不仅能给学生一个好的学习环境,也能培养学生的自我管理能力,甚至是班级管理能力。因此,笔者认为:一个班级管理的最高境界就应该是学生的自主管理。以下就小学生自主管理班级的实践经验来探讨自主管理体系的建设过程。

一、共同制定班级奋斗目标,激发学生自主管理意识。新学期伊始,由班主任带领,全体学生集思广益,商议班级管理规则,积极参与班级管理制度建设。为了更好地做好班级建设管理工作,在综合考量后,大家将班级的奋斗目标分为短期、中期、长期目标。短期目标主要从班级纪律方面着手制定,表现为出勤情况考核、请假销假规定、作业完成情况、日常卫生工作、学生安全工作等方面。在大纲指导下,引导学生去完善细则,诸如上课迟到、早退如何惩戒,请假程序如何高效、合理等。中期目标主要是班风建设,表现为学风情况、尊师敬师情况、个人品德情况、社会公德情况等,诸如在尊师敬师方面,让学生充分讨论何为尊师、何为敬师,上课期间学生应该保持什么样的学习态度和学习习惯,让学生们都参与进来,让细则的制定更加符合大家的需求和心意。长期目标主要是班级文化建设,表现为"班级硬文化"和"班级软文化"两方面,"硬文化"主要考量班级的环境文化,如桌椅摆放情况、黑板报情况、教室室内软装情况;"软文化"主要指班级学生群体的价值观、世界观、信仰、态度的综合反映,诸如班级制度文化、观念文化、行为文化等。在具体讨论细则时,充分发挥学生的主观能动性,鼓励他们建立自己的班级"理想国",朝着自己制定的奋斗目标一步一个脚印去完成。通过学生自主制定班级目标,让学生充分感受到自己是班级管理的主人,给他们创造班级管理的客观环境,激发他们的自我管理意识。

二、合作讨论班级管理细则,引发学生自主管理动机

"没有规矩,不成方圆",为了让这些"小鬼"更好地"当家",班级管理必须有章可循,而且班规一定要大家合作讨论,共同制定,这样更能激发学生的自主管理意识。在这一过程中,班主任要发挥"引导"作用,积极组织学生学习班级管理的基本制度规范,诸如《小学生守则》,在对基本规范有了解的基础上,组织学生针对班级自身的实际情况,从安全、思想品德、学习、纪律、卫生、各项活动等方面开展小组合作讨论,共同制定出切实可行的班规,最后细化管理制度,实施班级量化管理。具体来看,安全方面包括交通规则的遵守情况、校外娱乐场地情况、校内外食物卫生情况、各种应急求救措施掌握情况等;思想品德方面包括诚实守信情况、团结互助情况等;学习方面要注重学习态度、学习质量测验以及学习前后的效果变化等方面;纪律方面包括课堂纪律、实践活动纪律、公共场所纪律等;卫生方面强调个人卫生和班级卫生面貌;各项活动方面强调参与活动的重要性和集体荣誉,鼓励学生学习之余加强锻炼。只有将这些班级管理细则在班级内部进行充分讨论,才会增强学生自主管理的责任感,进而激励他们去实现班级自主管理。

三、建立班长轮流值日制度,带动学生全面参与班级管理值日

顾名思义,是指在当值的那一天担任某项工作。班长轮流值日制度指的是班级内的学生按照一定顺序去轮流管理班级事务的制度。小学生的班级自主管理需要每个学生有"人人当班长,个个有责任"的意识。班级内的学生以学号为顺序,每人值日两天,从熟悉值班事务到熟练管理,达到"自律、自理、自强"的管理目标。在值日制度制定中,要重视值日细则的敲定,包括值日内容(如早操情况、作业情况、安全情况等)、值日要求(如班级日志的完成情况、值日人员的交接情况、值日的问题反馈等)、值日评价(如值日监督组的评价、学生的评价以及教师的评价)等。只有让每个学生参与到班级事务的管理中来,才能发现班级管理制度中存在的问题及不足,让大家对制度的制定和执行有更加全面、深刻的理解,进而增进学生的集体责任感,从而更加利于班级管理的建设。

四、建立班长全面负责制度,给予学生自主管理机会

在班级自主管理中,班长要负责全面工作,履行监督、检查职责。将班级中所有的工作事务进行细化,每人选择自己喜欢或擅长的一项,说出自己选择这项工作的理由及准备如何完成。经过讨论,确定每个人在班级管理中的具体任务,制定出完成这项工作的方法,并要保质保量地完成,这样就形成了"班长负责下的全员管理制"。

1. 学科竞赛活动管理

按语文、数学、英语、音乐、美术、科学等不同的科目分成若干小组,每组管理一个科目,包括本科目的收发作业、检查家庭作业、班内相关的科目竞赛、请假学生的补课工作等。

2. 体卫纪律安全管理

为学科活动之外的班级管理事务、上下学路队纪律、阳光体育活动、课间活动、体育课、学校开展的各项活动时的纪律安全、班级日常纪律安全问题等设置相关管理人员,还

设置了图书管理员、墙面保洁员、地面保洁员、仪器保洁员、卫生工具整理员、纪律检查员、红领巾检查员等,这样就可以层层落实责任,充分发挥每个学生的主体性和积极性。

3. 主题活动宣传管理

班级建设中开展丰富多彩的主题活动,对学生的思维训练、意识形成有着重要作用。如何做好主题活动的宣传管理工作则考验着学生的各项能力。具体来看,在学校、班级开展的各项主题教育及宣传活动中要完成制定计划,实施方案,活动总结,布置教室及会场,接待家长、来宾等各种任务,全程要学生自主讨论、计划、实施、完成,还要学会遇到困难向学校、老师、家长请教或求助。在这个过程中,主题活动管理经验会迅速增加,自主管理能力会得到快速提升。

4. 班级岗位设置管理

在小学日常班级管理中,岗位众多,分工明确,职责不一,需要班主任统筹安排,班委全面负责各岗位的学生,要做到责任到人。诸如纪律岗位中的放学路队长、生活岗位的桌椅小管家、学习岗位的早读检查员等。在自主管理时,要将岗位职责和学生特点相结合,促使他们在其岗、谋其事、负其责。另外,为了实现"人人参与,人人管理"的目标,部分岗位要实行轮流制或小组制,诸如卫生检查与管理工作,需要让每个学生知道"班级是我家,清洁靠大家",要让学生懂得保持学习生活环境的舒适性。同时,在岗位管理中,要注重人尽其才,这样才能有利于班级管理的效用最大化。最后,通过科学管理设置岗位,让班级中的每个学生都积极参与进来,同时促进学生的管理能力有质的提升。

五、重视学生自主评价管理,促进学生能力全面发展

班级的自主管理是一个不断完善的过程,而班级评价在其中起着总结和督促的作用。在班级自主管理的过程中,学生的自主评价涉及班级目标的明确、管理细则的制定,以及班长轮流值日制度和全面负责制度的各个环节,而学生评价更是需要一定的标准,需要量化和价值判断相结合。例如:在学生个人的参赛获奖情况上,参赛的名次和级别都需要分级加分量化,在班规遵守情况上,需要对违反情况进行扣分量化评价;而那些涉及好人好事受到社会上表扬和好评的,则需要进行价值判断等定性评价,酌情加分。学生的自主评价可以更好地培养自我批评和反思的能力,让他们在班级自主管理的过程中,充分地剖析自我、完善自我,进而深化班级管理意识,提高班级管理能力,促进他们全面发展,进一步提升他们发展的核心素养。

苏联教育家苏霍姆林斯基说:"真正的教育是自我教育。"只有这样,才会使得教育内化于心,外化于行,让学生真正地成长、成才。魏书生也说过:"管是为了不管。"班主任要在原则和方向正确的前提下做好学生管理的指导工作,让学生自主探究班级管理的"点"和"面",帮助他们建立起科学的班级管理方法和科学、高效的班级自主管理体系,真正提高学生的班级自主管理意识和能力水平,进而培养学生自主管理、团队合作和创新进取的精神,最终实现学生的自我发展。

(节选自常建茹,2019)

2.2 Skills and Abilities

Given that you have already learned some strategies of managing your classroom, here are some cases for you to analyze to improve your problem-solving abilities and practice your creative thinking skills.

Cases

⌈Case One⌋

整个实习期间,我觉得班主任的工作最让我难以忘怀。当我看到十岁左右青春活泼的学生时,我感觉自己似乎回到中学时代——善于思考问题,但是在道德、情感方面还有待提高。也许我与学生的年龄相差还不算大,他们既把我当作老师,也当作姐姐,许多问题都愿意与我说。学生已经有了自己的思想和逻辑,遇到问题有自己的思维方式和解决办法。他们已经不喜欢老师牵着他们走,也不喜欢老师去教他们怎么做。

班主任的一言一行学生都看在眼里,叫学生不要乱扔垃圾,自己首先要做到不乱扔垃圾。班主任通过良好的性格、气质、能力、素质征服学生,使学生对班主任产生爱,才能接受班主任的管理教育。班主任只有得到学生的信任,师生才能融洽交流。

思考问题

1. 班主任工作是学校教育不可分割的一部分,案例中实习教师是怎样认识班主任工作的?对你有什么启示?

2. 作为老师,首先应该规范自己的行为,才能有效地管理班级,你怎么看这样的观点?

⌈Case Two⌋

探讨初中英语班主任的班级管理

一、建立平等、和谐、友爱的师生关系,提高学生们学习及管理依从性

在初中英语班级管理过程中,大多数英语教师习惯"特殊对待"英语学习成绩较好的学生,对于英语学习成绩不好甚至调皮捣蛋的学生往往采用忽略、斥责等管理方式,这种方式不利于班级整体管理水平的提高及学生们综合素质的提升。在初中班主任特色管理过程中教师应深入到每一个学生的学习生活中了解班级内每个学生的兴趣爱好、生活情况、英语学习水平等,给予学生尊重、爱护及关心,公平公正地对待每一位学生,不因为学生英语学习成绩好就另眼相待,也不因为学生英语学习成绩不好就忽略。教师应鼓励学生、引导学生,积极调动学生们的学习积极性及对英语的学习兴趣,在引导学生深入管理

过程中去实现自我管理,强化学生们的英语学习意识。除了在学习上给予学生帮助、支持及引导外,作为一名班主任还应多关心学生们的生活状态、家庭状态及价值观等,在了解学生的家庭生活背景基础上给予学生生活上的疏导及帮助,通过观察学生们的行为、语言、情绪变化给予学生一对一的疏导,温柔地引导学生说出自己的烦恼及困惑,并视综合情况给予相应的意见和建议。让学生明白自己是被重视的,是与其他同学一样具有平等学习地位的存在,培养融洽、友爱的师生关系及互动氛围,提高英语课堂学生们的学习积极性,促使学生主动融入其中,鼓励他们大胆发言,提高初中英语教学效率,为班级营造积极向上的学习氛围。

二、积极开展班级整体的英语学习活动,提高学生们集体荣誉感

在初中英语教学及班级管理过程中,教师应建立良好和谐的班集体,引导班级内成员在班集体中体会到凝聚力的重要性,充分发挥学生们的集体荣誉感,促进班级整体的进步及发展。如教师可以组织以班级为单位的"A tug-of-war match between classes""English lectures between classes"或"English drama performance"等活动,引导学生在参与活动的过程中明确班级属于一个整体,尽自己最大的努力为班级争得荣誉,激发学生们的参与意识,强化学生们的集体荣誉感,提高学生们英语实践能力及班级管理水平。

三、培养学生们良好的学习习惯及行为习惯,促进学生综合发展

在初中英语教学过程中,英语教师作为班级管理及英语教学的核心人物,也是引导学生正确学习、健康成长的引领者,更是实现学校与家长之间沟通交流的桥梁。在初中英语教学过程中教师应重视对学生们良好的学习习惯、行为习惯的培养,引导学生在集体生活中不断强化及完善自己,促进学生综合素质的发展。通过英语学习和与班级学生相处中的小事情让学生领悟大道理,培养学生形成良好的学习习惯及行为习惯。

如在进行"Do you like bananas?"的教学过程中,教师可以在课堂教学过程以"Do you like bananas?"为情景对话主题,引导学生们以分组合作学习的形式展开情景对话演练,引导学生们在情景对话演练过程中学习其他学生准确的口语发音及学习习惯,纠正自己的不足,培养学生们良好的学习习惯。此外,教师还应在班级管理过程中针对学生之间的吵闹、矛盾等进行合理解决,当学生之间出现摩擦后,教师应客观地了解事情发生的始末,并引导两名发生矛盾及摩擦的学生利用书写英文信件的方式向双方互相表达自己的歉意,并引导学生解开误会,和好如初,为班级管理营造积极、和谐及融洽的氛围。

(节选自陈益,2020)

思考问题

1. 案例中这位英语老师担任班主任总结出了哪些值得借鉴的经验?
2. 你认为作为英语老师,担任班主任有什么优势?你还有哪些提升班级管理的办法?请举例说明。

Case Three

班主任请家长

　　学校教育需要家长的配合,班主任工作更需要家长的信任和支持。班主任常和家长联系,可保持学校教育和家庭教育的一致性、协调性,增进教师、学生和家长之间的感情。但在学校教育过程中,班主任如果动辄找家长,效果往往会适得其反,甚至引起学生、家长的逆反心理。但有时我们还必须找家长,如果班主任在教育过程中能取得家长的积极配合,对学生的教育可起到事半功倍的作用。请家长是有中国特色的一种传统的家校合作方式,其利用率最高的是初中老师。从初一到初三,学生年龄在13—15岁,初中老师只能哄着学、压着学,斗智斗勇,软硬兼施,实在没办法了——请家长。上课说话,违反课堂纪律,屡批不改,请家长;不完成作业,抄作业,请家长;不好好学习,考试作弊,请家长;男女生交往过密,请家长……真累呀!家长累,老师更累。请一个家长谈话要占去很长时间,关键是累了半天如果没什么效果,请家长岂不是白请了?家长到底要不要找?答案是肯定的,但作为班主任,想办法改良一下,有点新意,调整一下策略,可能会起到事半功倍的效果。

　　高××,男生,上课话多,常不完成作业,还经常在课堂上违反课堂纪律,当众顶撞老师,影响很坏。谈话、批评均无效果,还满不在乎,觉得自己特有理,好像都是老师、同学的错,甚至面对老师的批评说出"扣操行分就扣呗,扣完拉倒,反正我也不打算在这儿上了"的话。在教育无果的情况下,我让他叫家长来,谁知他听说叫家长,反应特别大,先是哭着说错了,求我不要叫家长,但你问他哪儿错了,他就是不说。后来我了解到他的家庭情况:父母望子成龙,对他管教很严,特别是他爸爸经常拿他和亲戚家学习好的孩子比(他表哥考上了博士),不让他玩,每天逼着学习,学习不好就打,小学每次叫完家长,他都免不了一顿挨打。所以他最怕叫家长。我想一定是长期处于家长的重压之下,他的思想很偏激。此时他的情绪很激动,如果再坚持下去,我怕他会有什么偏激行为。可我觉得很有必要和他家长谈一谈,我先稳定住他的情绪,再和他的家人取得联系。期中考试后,他妈妈来了,正如我之前了解的,每天晚上他妈妈坐在他旁边看着他学习,学习一不好,他爸就打他,连他妈都拦不住。我帮他妈妈分析,孩子在家长期处于一种重压之下,又不敢发泄,所以他把所有不满的情绪都发泄在学校。

　　通报情况后,我要求家长配合:回到家中坚决不允许打骂,即使这次期中考试考得不好,这就是第一个"意料之外"。第二,晚上不要坐在他旁边看着他学习,给他自己学习的自由,但家长可随时检查,这是第二个"意料之外"。第三,告诉他张老师表扬他数学学得不错,第三个"意料之外"。但老师提出两个问题希望他认真考虑一下:第一,上课总是违反课堂纪律,对自己的学习和其他同学的学习有没有影响?第二,屡次违反课堂纪律和顶撞老师,如果张老师不管,其他同学也这样做,张老师该不该管?家长完全按照我的要求去说、去做了,我不放心还专门给他爸爸打了一个电话,一再强调不能打他。以后的几天,他见到我态度没以前那么横了,课堂上说话的次数明显少了,还主动请我帮他录英语磁带回家学习。我在班上找一名学生每天负责开门和锁门,他主动要求为大家服务。我故意逗他:"高××,张老师叫你家长好不好?"他不好意思地说那天他是做好被打一顿的思想准备回家的,没想到居然没挨打。他说:"张老师,我原以为你会在我家长面前狠狠地告我一状,没想到你能这样做,早知道我早点主动叫家长了。"我告状了没有?显然是告了,但我的告状是以解决根本问题为目的,而不是推给家长帮我解决问题。

（张艳敏,2011）

思考问题

1. 家校联系有哪些作用?
2. 除了请家长,还有哪些家校联系的办法?
3. 你认为张老师告状成功的原因是什么?

亮考帮

亮闪闪:请总结学习过程中,哪些是自己记忆深刻、受益最大、最欣赏的内容呢?请写出具体内容。

考考你:请把自己弄懂的但觉得别人可能存在困惑的地方,用问题的形式表述出来,来挑战一下其他同学。

帮帮我:请把自己不懂、不会的地方或想要了解的内容,用问题的形式表述出来,并带到课堂上加以讨论。

参考文献

[1] Seifert, K., & Sutton, R. *Educational Psychology*[M]. Zurich：The Saylor Foundation, 2009.
[2] Tomlinson, B. *Materials Development in Language Teaching*[M]. Cambridge：Cambridge University Press, 1998.
[3] Wills, K. What is the Pygmalion Effect? [EB/OL]. (2020-06-01)[2020-07-17]. http://www.wisegeek.com/what-is-the-pygmalion-effect.htm.
[4] 常建茹.小学班级自主管理体系的建设[J].教学与管理,2019(11).
[5] 陈茜.探讨初中英语班主任的班级管理[EB/OL].(2020-04-09)[2020-06-21]. https://wenku.baidu.com/view/334c8eeebc64783e0912a21614791711cd7979e4.html? fr=search#.
[6] 郭满库.英语案例教学论[M].杭州:浙江大学出版社,2012.
[7] 袁叶丰,孟丽君."我有我色彩——我很重要"主题班会设计.班级管理案例集[R].金华:浙江师范大学,2011.
[8] 张艳敏.谈谈班主任请家长[J].学英语(初中教师版),2011(51).

第七章 课堂教学与组织管理

主要内容

1. 英语课堂教学
   - 课堂指令
   - 纠错
   - 提问
   - 小组教学
   - 纪律
2. 课堂活动的开展
   - 小贴士
   - 歌曲
   - 游戏

✓ 案例学习
✓ 专业参考
✓ 学术探讨

It is very important for classroom teachers to create an effective learning environment for students. This involves both the actions and skills you have gained. The main skills include classroom instruction, group work and cooperation, discipline, dealing with the errors and questioning. These skills are all based on your understanding of students and the knowledge we have learned up to now. At the same time, the activities you design, such as songs, rhymes, and games should draw students' attention and arouse their interests in learning English. This chapter offers you not only these resources, but also the theory of Multiple Intelligences by Howard Gardner (1999).

Task 1 English Classroom Teaching

To be a teacher, it is very important to know how to manage your class and then have an effective teaching. In Task 1, we offer you the skills of classroom instruction, student grouping, dealing with errors, discipline, and questioning. Besides, we provide you with Gardner's Multiple Intelligences for further exploring. Later, you practice your skills by analyzing some cases.

1.1 Knowledge Points

Outline

Did you experience the difficult class time that your teacher could not continue his/her class because some students were not listening to him? How did your teacher manage the difficult situation? What did you learn from it?

Students are attentive to what is being said in a lecture on average only 40% of the time. Students retain 70% of the information in the first ten minutes of a lecture but only 20% in the last ten minutes. Classroom management contributes directly to the efficiency of teaching and learning as the most effective activities can be made useless if the teacher does not organize them efficiently.

Classroom management is the way of organizing the resources, students and helpers so that teaching and learning can proceed in an efficient and safe manner.

The goal of classroom management is to create an atmosphere conductive to interacting in English in meaningful ways. There are six conditions for effective classroom management as follows.

- Teachers play appropriate roles.
- Teachers provide clear instructions.
- Suitable grouping of the students.
- Asking appropriate questions.
- Discipline as well as harmony in the class.
- Proper error treatment.

1.1.1 Classroom instruction

Classroom instruction is the way that language teachers use to organize or guide learning. Here are some examples.
- Giving directions to tasks or activities;
- Providing explanations to a concept or language structure;
- Setting requirements;
- Checking comprehension;
- Drawing attention;
- Motivating learners;
- Giving feedback;
- Assigning homework.

It refers to the use of grouping configurations that provide different levels of support to students as they gain greater levels of language proficiency and skills.

Pay attention to the words "creative teaching", including the concept of teaching creatively and the concept of teaching for creativity.

The craft of teaching is also an effective way, for teaching should be viewed as a craft that includes a reflective approach toward problems, a cultivation of imagination, and a playfulness toward words, relationships, and experiences.

1.1.2 Student grouping

An important feature of today's language classroom is that students do not always study as one big group. Rather, students are put into groups of different sizes.

The most common student groupings:
- Whole class work;
- Pair work;
- Group work;
- Individual study.

Table 7 - 1 Advantages and disadvantages of grouping (Tableman, 2004)

Grouping	Advantages	Disadvantages
Whole class work	All the class are concentrating; Comfortable in choral practice.	Students have little chance to speak; Same speed for different students; Not enough communication.
Pair work	More chance for practice; Encouraging co-operation; Relaxing atmosphere.	Students stay away from the task; Using native language; Being noisy and undisciplined.

(continued)

Grouping	Advantages	Disadvantages
Group work	Communication in its real sense; More dynamic than pair work; Promoting self-reliance.	The same as those in pair work.
Individual study	No outside pressure; Studying at own speed.	Less dynamic classroom; No co-operation.

1.1.3 Dealing with errors

Students misbehave for several reasons. For example, they don't know the purpose of your presentation; they don't understand how the information that you are delivering applies to them; instruction is uninteresting; not enough interaction among peers. We need to understand the aim of the activity and when the proper time is to correct.

Table 7-2 Correcting errors and feedback

Aim of the activity	Time to correct
Accuracy	Immediately
Fluency	At a later stage/Not at all

The most appropriate and useful ways:
- By asking a question;
- By the use of gestures and facial expressions;
- By writing the problem up on the board;
- By repeating the sentence up to the error;
- By echoing the sentence;
- By using the phonemic chart;
- By using a concept checking question.

Please pay attention to the followings:
- Deal with it quietly. Don't hurt the students.
- Don't take things personally. Try to address the problem rather than treat the students as the object.
- Don't use threats.

1.1.4 Discipline

What's the final goal of discipline in the language classroom? The ultimate goal of discipline is to make more effective learning possible, but the relationship between discipline and learning is not as straight-forward as it appears.

Measures:
- Practical hints.
- Act immediately.
- Stop the class.
- Rearrange the seats.
- Change the activity.
- Talk to students after class.
- Create a code of behavior.

1.1.5 Questioning

- Close questions: Questions with only one single correct answer.
- Open questions: May invite many different answers.
- Display questions: The answers are already known to the teacher, used for checking if students know the answers.
- Genuine questions: Used to find out new information and since they often reflect real contexts, they are therefore more communicative.

(1) Functions of questioning
- To focus students' attention;
- To invite thinking and imaginations;
- To check understanding;
- To stimulate recall of information;
- To challenge students;
- To assess learning.

(2) The theory of multiple intelligences

Howard Earl Gardner is an American developmental psychologist and Professor of Cognition and Education at the Harvard Graduate School of Education at Harvard University. He is currently the senior director of Harvard Project Zero, and since 1995, he has been the co-director of The Good Project. Howard Gardner believes that eight abilities meet these criteria:

- Spatial
- Linguistic
- Logical-mathematical
- Bodily-kinesthetic
- Musical
- Interpersonal
- Intrapersonal
- Naturalistic

Gardner argues that there is a wide range of cognitive abilities, and that there are only very weak correlations between these. Traditional intelligence tests and psychometrics have generally found high correlations between different tasks and aspects of intelligences, rather than the low correlations which Gardner's theory predicts.

Reading Materials

General Intelligence and Multiple Intelligences

General Intelligence

The modern study of intelligence can be traced to Alfred Binet, whose research was conducted at the end of the 19th century and the beginning of the 20th century. This was the time that the study of psychology moved away from prescientific understandings to more empirical investigations (Corno et al., 2002). Binet, collaborating with Theodore Simon, believed that intelligence was measurable (Binet & Simon, 1905). They proposed a series of questions that could be quickly administered and scored. The higher a person scored, it was assumed, the more intelligent the person. The strength of this test was that large groups of people could be tested at minimal cost and the more intelligent among them identified. For example, during World War I, many men were drafted, and there was a need to identify quickly the more intelligent men, so they could be trained as officers. The test had practical use and was economic and efficient. Two weaknesses of this test were that all of the questions were directly related to either mathematics or language skills, thus measuring intelligence by only these two domains, and the entire test was analytic, a processing style inhibiting the ease with which global people could respond (Brennan, 1984). Anyone who has taken the SAT or the ACT exams as the rite of passage to college knows how persistent the dominance of these two domains is in conceptualizing intelligence. These two domains often are expressed in a single score, which is meant to be a measure of general intelligence.

Multiple Intelligences

Corno et al. (2002) note that the construct of a single overarching general ability is widely accepted. They report that today there are approximately 120 different measures of general ability. Yet they also acknowledge that not all scholars are in agreement, and they cite in particular the work of Howard Gardner and Robert Sternberg.

Both Gardner and Sternberg advocate that intelligence should not be reduced to a single overarching construct. Gardner (1983) first identified seven distinct intelligences. Today, he (Gardner, 1999) identifies an eighth intelligence. Sternberg (1998) argues that people possess three independent abilities: analytic (judging, comparing, contrasting, etc.), creative (inventing, discovering, imaging, etc.), and practical (applying, implementing, using, etc.). The focus in this article is on Gardner's multiple intelligences.

Howard Gardner advocates that there are at least eight intelligences that need to be considered (Nelson, 1998):

- Linguistic: the potential to use language, as used in reading, writing, telling stories, memorizing dates, and thinking in words.
- Logical-mathematical: the potential for understanding cause and effect and for manipulating numbers, quantities, and operations, as used in math, reasoning, logic, problem-solving, and recognizing patterns.
- Spatial: the potential for representing the spatial world internally in one's mind as used in reading maps and charts, drawing, solving mazes and puzzles, imagining and visualizing.
- Kinesthetic: the potential for using one's whole body or parts of the body, as used in athletics, dancing, acting, crafting, and using tools.
- Musical: the potential for thinking in music; for hearing, recognizing, and remembering patterns, as used in singing, identifying sounds, and in remembering melodies and rhythms.
- Interpersonal: the potential for working with others, as used in understanding people, leading and organizing others, communicating, resolving conflicts, and selling.
- Intrapersonal: the potential for understanding ourselves, as used in understanding self, recognizing one's own strengths and weaknesses, and setting personal goals.
- Naturalistic: the potential for discriminating among plants, animals, rocks, and the world around us, as used in understanding nature, making distinctions, identifying flora and fauna.

Intelligence is more than a score on a typical standardized pencil-and-paper test used to predict success in school. Such traditional intelligence tests do not measure the ability of a chess player, an athlete, or a master violinist. Gardner (1999) opines that these individuals, as well as many others, exhibit intelligences that are not measured by these tests. He defines an intelligence as "biopsychological potential to process information that can be activated in a cultural setting to solve problems or create products that are of value in a culture" (pp. 33 – 34).

For a potential to be identified as an intelligence it must meet eight criteria:

1. It must be rooted in the brain, so that an injury to the brain could rob a person of that specific potential (e.g., a blow to the head causing loss of linguistic ability).

2. It must be rooted in our evolutionary history, such that our early ancestors exhibited that potential (e.g., early humans had the naturalistic ability to discriminate among the different species of plants).

3. There has be an identifiable core operation or set of operations associated with that

potential (e.g., pitch, rhythm, etc. are core operations of musical ability).

4. It must be susceptible to being encoded in symbol (e.g., mathematical symbols).

5. It must possess a distinctive developmental path to become expert in that ability (e.g., trained clinicians with strong interpersonal skills).

6. It is exemplified by the existence of idiot savants, prodigies, and other exceptional people (e.g., Rainman's mathematical ability).

7. There is evidence from experimental psychology that the ability is distinct from other abilities (e.g., a person can walk and talk at the same time because the two different abilities: linguistic and kinesthetic).

8. It is supported by psychometric findings (e.g., a major league athlete might score high in ability hit a ball but low in the ability to hit a note).

Gardner (1999) has considered adding either existential or spiritual intelligence as a ninth intelligence but has not yet done so. He sees that the existential and the spiritual are similar, with existential being more narrowly defined and spiritual being more broadly defined. He concludes (p. 64) that the existential, as narrowly defined, might fit the previous criteria for an intelligence, but spiritual does not. Because he has not yet affirmed that existential is a ninth intelligence, it is not considered as one on the intelligences in this article.

As may be suggested by the previous criteria, the theory of multiple intelligences emerged from previous psychological studies. However, it must be noted that none of those previous investigations were involved with Gardner's construct of multiple intelligences. Gardner has been totally honest and forthright about the lack of experimental research on his theory. He notes, "While Multiple Intelligences theory is consistent with much empirical evidence, it has not been subjected to strong experimental tests ... Within the area of education, the applications of the theory are currently being examined in many projects. Our hunches will have to be revised many times in light of actual classroom experience" (Gardner, 1993, p.33).

Nevertheless, even without the existence of a strong research base, there is much popular support for the concept of multiple intelligences. Some strengths of the theory in relationship to the learning process are as follows:

• It serves as impetus of reform in our schools, "leading to a reevaluation of those subjects typically taught in school, with increased emphasis placed on the arts, nature, physical culture, and other topics traditionally limited to the periphery of the curriculum" (Armstrong, 2003, p.4).

• It is child-centered and develops children's innate potential rather than requiring them to master extraneous academic information.

• It encourages children to grow and to develop their potential as responsible human beings.

• It challenges educators to find "ways that will work for this student learning this topic" (Gardner, 1999, p. 154).

As Gardner (1999) has written:

I would happily send my children to a school that takes differences among children seriously, that shares knowledge among differences with children and parents, that encourages children to assume responsibility for their own learning, and that presents materials in such a way that each child has the maximum opportunity to master those materials and to show others and themselves what they have learned and understood (pp. 91 - 92).

(Adapted From Denig, 2004)

1.2 Skills and Abilities

Suppose you are a primary school English teacher and you are going to work with grade four students. What's your classroom management planning? Discuss with group members, design your manage plan, and share with classmates. You may use the knowledge you have learned to support your design. You may also use the following cases to analyze and strengthen your skills and abilities.

Cases

Case One

曾经听过两节课,其间两位老师都谈到一个话题"肥胖"。

片段一:教师在讲到 stop sb. from doing sth. 这个短语时,让学生来造句,有一位学生站起来,与老师发生了这样一段对话:

Student: My mother often stops me from eating meat.

Teacher: Why?

Student: Because my mother says I'm too fat.

全班同学哄堂大笑,这位学生很难为情,但老师下面的一句话马上将气氛缓和了过来。

Teacher: But I don't think you are too fat. You are strong.

片段二:教师组织学生表演自己创作的关于"看病"的对话,想找一位较胖的学生来担任"患者",有一位比较胖的学生自告奋勇站起来,于是发生了这样一段对话:

Teacher: OK! Who will act the sick people? Any volunteers?

Student: I will.

Teacher: Good! I think you are fat. You are the right person!

当时全班同学哄堂大笑,这位学生一脸的尴尬。

思考问题

1. 本案例中描述了两个教学过程中对于体型的描述,试想想教师的做法有什么值得改进的地方?

2. 如何创造有利于学生学习的心理状态,形成积极的学习态度?

Case Two

在一次公开课上,老师让学生根据书上的图画猜测 Ann 的朋友在送礼物时会对 Ann 说什么话,同学们七嘴八舌地说开了:

Student A:Ann! Here is my birthday present. I hope you like it.

Student B:Ann! Here is my birthday present. I hope you will be happy and healthy.

Student C:Ann! Here is my birthday present. Happy birthday to you!

Student D:…

这时男生 E 突然举手,站起来说:

Student E:I think Ann's friend Li Lei will say,"Ann! You are beautiful. I love you! Here's my present. I hope you like it."

当时所有听课的老师和同学都笑了,上课的老师先是一惊,然后马上微笑着给了学生一块橡皮,并且说:

Teacher:I think you are a clever boy. You speak good English. Here's my present for your answer. I hope you will like it.

Student E:Thank you! I like it.

(兰兰868,2019)

思考问题

1. 请分析案例中学生学习英语的积极性和具体情形有什么样的联系,老师在其中起到什么作用?

2. 如何保护学生"开口说英语"的积极性?

亮考帮

亮闪闪:请总结学习过程中,哪些是自己记忆深刻、受益最大、最欣赏的内容呢?请写出具体内容。

考考你:请把自己弄懂的但觉得别人可能存在困惑的地方,用问题的形式表述出来,来挑战一下其他同学。

帮帮我:请把自己不懂、不会的地方或想要了解的内容,用问题的形式表述出来,并带到课堂上加以讨论。

参考文献

[1] Denig, S. J. Multiple Intelligences and Learning Styles: Two Complementary Dimensions[J]. *Teachers College Record*, 2004, 106(1): 96-111.

[2] Tableman, B. *School Climate and Learning. IN: Best Practice Briefs*[D]. Michigan: Michigan State University, 2004.

[3] Tomlinson, B. *Materials Development in Language Teaching*[M]. Cambridge: Cambridge University Press, 1998.

[4] 兰兰868.初中英语教学案例分析范文[EB/OL].(2019-12-12)[2020-05-24]. https://wenku.baidu.com/view/87c5dee6122de2bd960590c69ec3d5bbfd0adaaa.html?fr=search.

[5] Harmer, J. *The Practice of English Language Teaching*[M]. London: Longman, 1983.

[6] 王蔷.小学英语教学法教程[M].2版.北京:高等教育出版社,2013.

Task 2 English Classroom Activities

English classroom activities should be learner-centred, communication-oriented and activty-based. It's a stage for the teachers to present English language, observe the learning process and evaluate the learning efficiency.

2.1 Knowledge Points

Outline

Making students learn actively is the prime aim for the teacher in designing the lesson activity. Here are some tips.

Teachers may invite questions; make use of their questions; don't "put down" incorrect answers from pupils; ask questions in an interesting way; encourage pupils to contribute their own questions; arrange one-to-one times; be someone who can find someone who know; let pupils into selected parts of your world; accept silly questions; bring everyone in, etc. Some examples are as follows.

1. Jokes and riddles

Jokes:

Q: What starts with "E", ends with "E" and only has one letter in between?

A: An eye.

Riddles:

Q: What has many keys but can't open any doors?

A: A piano.

2. Games and puzzles

Games are normally used to indicate the activities participated by at least two people for fun. Since the middle of the 20th century, western scholars have made plenty of researches about the games used in teaching activities and many of them used to define the term "game teaching method" in their articles. For instance, Brewster and Ellis, used to define the "game teaching method" as "the method by which the teachers make use of games for teaching activities so as to improve the motivation of the students to learn the knowledge presented by their teachers". It is shown by the above definition that this teaching method is advantageous of improving learners' motivation to learn knowledge and that will enable them to make more progress in learning in the future.

(1) Examples: word searching; crisscross puzzle; writing on backs, etc.

Another example:

A: I eat an egg for breakfast.

B: I eat an egg and some bread for breakfast.

C: I eat an egg, some bread and an apple for breakfast.

D: I eat an egg, some bread, an apple and a hamburger for breakfast.

E: I eat an egg, some bread, an apple, a hamburger and some rice for breakfast.

(2) Read and write, such as

• Read and colour:

Colour the hearts red.

Colour the squares green.

Colour the rectangles blue.

Colour the circles yellow.

Colour the stars brown.

Colour the triangles pink.

3. Songs

In recent years the value of English songs in motivating students to learn English and enhancing their involvement is widely acknowledged by more and more English foreign teaching practitioners. In their language classes, some of them have adopted richly meaningful English songs as warm-up activities, time-fillers or games. When a teacher teaches English songs for teaching English, children are learning while singing. The music invites each child in. Thus, it could be applied in modern English foreign language teaching skillfully as a supplementary tool.

2.2 Skills and Abilities

Given that you have already learned some strategies of using games and songs to manage your classroom, here are some cases to analyze to improve your problem-solving abilities and practice your creative thinking skills.

Cases

Case One

在一次小学英语课竞赛中,教师用猜物游戏教学水果类生词和句型"I'd like a/an …"。

该教师手拿书包对学生说:"Look, I have a new bag. Guess, what's in the bag?"学生猜出了几种水果(banana, apple, orange)后再让学生运用句型"I'd like a/an ..."表达。由于该游戏与所学的句型关系不密切,使得游戏的开展十分勉强,教学效果也不尽人意。

【分析】

"猜物"游戏比较适合于生词的呈现和复习,而不适合学习句型"I'd like a/an ..."。

为了让学生熟悉句型,教师先设计一个"传悄悄话"的游戏,然后再让学生做电话购物游戏。具体操作如下:

教师事先准备几张纸条(纸条上分别写有"I'd like a/an banana/apple/orange ..."等句子),然后对每组的第一个学生耳语一句,并让他/她持有纸条;教师让学生一个接一个悄悄地把话传下去,每组的最后一位学生向全班大声汇报悄悄话的内容。

在学生熟悉了词汇和句型的基础上,教师可以让学生两人一组做打电话游戏或者设计情景对话展示。游戏运用的句型是:"Can I help you? /What would you like? I'd like ..."

Case Two

"What can you do"任务设计

教材依据:PEP 小学英语(五年级下册)Unit 4 Let's learn

教师请一位学生做小记者,用句型"What can you do?"采访在场的同学。小记者根据同学们的回答"I can ... .",及时做下记录并汇报。

【分析】

教学任务的设计在"要面向全体学生"这一方面缺乏考虑。在上课的时候,老师肯定是请比较优秀的学生来担当小记者这个角色,那么小记者本身在完成采访任务时,肯定也会选择一些相对优秀的学生作为他的采访对象以确保他的采访能够精彩出色,那么这样一来,一些并不十分出色的学生就很难有机会参与到任务中来。

Case Three

"My new room"教学设计片段

教材依据:PEP 小学英语(五年级上册)Unit 5 Let's learn

在热身复习阶段,教师先带领学生朗读:

Mom is in the living room. Dad is too.

I'm in the bedroom. Where are you?

Brother's in the kitchen. Sister is too.

I'm in the bedroom. Where are you?

然后进入自由讨论:What is in your bedroom? /What colour is your desk/bed? /Where is your TV? /How many windows are there in your bedroom?

然后,教师呈现一幅 Zoom 的卧室图,说:"Look, this is Zoom's bedroom. What can you see in his room?"并引导学生回答:"I can see a desk, a lamp and a ... ."教师接着说:

"What can you see on the wall? Look, it's white. It can make you feel cool in summer and make you feel warm in winter."接着请学生猜是什么物品,由此引出新授单词 air-conditioner。

【分析】

教师引导学生就相关的话题联系学生的生活实际展开讨论,创设语言氛围,使学生尽快融入英语课堂。采用多媒体、挂图、简笔画吸引学生的注意力,同时设计有效的提问,让学生通过观察,进行回答,既活跃了学生的思维,又提高了他们的口头表达能力,并引出新词的教学,非常自然。

Case Four

"Is it a/an ... Yes, it is./No, it isn't."教学设计片段

在学习"Is it a/an ... Yes, it is./No, it isn't."这个句式时,教师设计了一个简单的多媒体课件:在一个精美的礼物盒里有许多礼物。打开礼物盒,露出物品的一小部分让学生用"Is it a/an ..."来猜,如果学生猜对了,界面就会出现一个物品单词及这个物品,否则就继续呈现物品的局部并请学生继续猜。

【分析】

课程设计既能集中学生的注意力,激发学生的学习积极性,又能培养学生对单词的认读能力和良好的思维习惯,学生自然而然地学会句式,并懂得在实际生活中对不确定的东西可以用"Is it a/an ..."来问,用"Yes, it is./No, it isn't."来回答,可见多媒体教学能激发和保持学生的学习兴趣,使学生在轻松愉快的气氛中学习英语。

Case Five

"What would you like?"任务设计

教材依据:PEP 小学英语(四年级上册)Unit 5 Let's talk

课前教师和学生把教室布置成中国餐厅或麦当劳店或肯德基店;并用下列单词制作英文菜单若干份:hamburger, hot dog, chicken, bread, beef, soup, rice 等。要求学生进入此餐馆必须使用英语进行交流。

例如:

Case Six

Chanting Race

教师请五名学生上台,他们分别头戴 Beijing, London, Moscow, Singapore, Sydney 的头饰,手持 Windy, Sunny, Cloudy, Rainy, Snowy 的卡片。教师打节拍说:"Rainy, rainy."手持"Rainy"卡片的学生说:"It's rainy in London."并转问他人,说:"Cloudy, cloudy."手持"Cloudy"卡片的学生说:"It's cloudy in Moscow."并转问他人……接不上的便被淘汰,坚持到最后的学生获胜。

【分析】

教师设计的游戏是通过 chant 的形式让学生练习句型"It's ... in ... .",比较新颖,也很有趣,能够吸引学生极大的兴趣。

Case Seven

教师在进行"Our school"一课教学时,设计了如下任务:

教师呈现空白的教学楼的轮廓图,然后让学生听对话录音,根据获得的信息将图片分别贴到相应的位置,并用所学语言进行描述。体现了英语教学音、形、意的有机统一。学生如果想要完成任务必须听得懂对话录音、弄得懂单词意思、放得对图片位置。

【分析】

这个任务难度恰当,符合这个年龄段学生的能力要求。这个任务的设计带有一定的挑战性和激励性,使学生在运用语言过程中感受强烈的成就感和自信心。这个任务设计还具备合适的情景和语境,学生在自然、真实或模拟真实的情境中能更有效地表达,出色地发挥,从而能更高质量地完成任务。

思考问题

1. Do you like these lyrics? Would you like to perform them in front of your students?

2. Performance is a kind of skills for English teachers. How are you going to improve your ability?

亮考帮

亮闪闪:请总结学习过程中,哪些是自己记忆深刻、受益最大、最欣赏的内容呢? 请写出具体内容。

考考你:请把自己弄懂的但觉得别人可能存在困惑的地方,用问题的形式表述出来,来挑战一下其他同学。

帮帮我:请把自己不懂、不会的地方或想要了解的内容,用问题的形式表述出来,并带到课堂上加以讨论。

参考文献

[1] Richards, J. & Rodgers, T. *Approaches and Methods of Language Teaching*[M]. Cambridge: Cambridge University Press, 2016.

[2] Zhang, L. English Songs in English Foreign Language Teaching[J]. *Journal of Xinyang Teachers College*, 2002, 3(22).

[3] 王蔷. 小学英语教学法教程[M]. 2版. 北京: 高等教育出版社, 2013.

[4] Geyser, J. P. *Teaching Methodology Made Essay*[M]. Shanghai: Shanghai Foreign Language Education Press, 2013.

第八章 课堂教学基本技能

主要内容

1. 课堂导入与提问
2. 教学语言与教态
3. 多媒体、板书和简笔画设计
4. 作业、总结与评价

✓案例学习
✓专业参考
✓学术探讨

　　This chapter mainly presents some useful teaching skills in class, including lead-in, questioning, classroom discourse, teaching manners, multimedia, board writing, stick figures, assignments, summary and evaluation. In order to help student teachers to lead in the class naturally and interestingly, and question properly, teachers should offer appropriate teaching language and the code of behaviour and provide information for you to practice your skills of multimedia technology, blackboard writing and stick figures.

Task 1 Lead-in and Questioning

Lead-in and questioning are basic skills for student teachers. In Task 1, some concepts and explanations will be offered to understand the meaning.

1.1 Knowledge Points

Outline

Lead-in and questioning are the two main points in the following parts. Natural and interesting lead-in activities can activate the class learning atmosphere. Questioning is for the purpose of creative learning.

1.1.1 Lead-in

As the famous saying goes: "Well begun is half done." A successful English class often gives people the enjoyment of beauty, which mostly depends on a good start, namely lead-in. A wonderful class starts with meaningful lead-in. Which kind of lead-in can make us students enjoyable? A successful lead-in accords with three demands. If used properly, that can attract students' attention successfully, mobilize the enthusiasm of students greatly, and activate the atmosphere of class strongly. With requirements of new curriculum standard, English learning and teaching becomes pretty crucial for students and teachers.

Nowadays, with the influence of multimedia, students pay more attention to new things and information. Teachers should design more novel and lifelike lead-in to arouse students' resonance, so students can learn happily from the bottom of heart. In the class, the more ebullient students are, the better the teaching effect is. The lead-in of English class is various under different circumstances. According to the teaching syllabus, teachers should set goals and demands for English class teaching as the teaching syllabus requires. After knowing about students' knowledge level and absorbing new information ability, familiarizing the precondition of students' learning habits and psychological demands, teachers should grasp the types, characteristic, key teaching points of textbooks, then choose appropriately and apply flexibly.

1. Music, video, pictures

Pictures, video, music can be used in lead-in. This kind of warming up is an input teaching method, in which teachers demonstrate the teaching points through deduction. From the point of psychology, students grasp the class as well as enhancing visual and acoustic ability.

According to English textbook topics and teaching goals, teachers can let students enjoy music, songs, videos, then discuss the related author, theme, social background and estimation in order to arouse students' interest and attention, and finally lead to teaching points naturally, like textbooks related to historical material and figures. Teachers can prepare a video to increase students' interest for it, and students seems to sense the true atmosphere. If class starts with music, it would create a wonderful class atmosphere and promote students' enthusiasm. For example, when students are going to learn Unit 1 in Grade 7—"Can you play the guitar?", teachers can prepare a video for lead-in, the song "Trouble Is a Friend".

Teacher: Do you like the song?

Students: Yes, I do./No, I don't.

Teacher: Why or why not?

Students: Because ...

Teacher: Can you play any instruments like guitar, piano, violin and any other instruments?

Students: ...

2. Role play

For students, it is more acceptable to hold a lifelike class through role acting. Teachers can use flexible and simple body language to describe the class, so those who are good at body and language performing should utilize their advantages. For instance, when learning animals, teachers can use hands to make animal gestures, then let students guess its names and try to express them in English. Of course, the ways and content of acting should be relevant to the teaching points instead of entertaining class. For instance, when students are going to learn Unit 8 in Grade Eight—"Have you read *Treasure Island* yet?", teachers can cooperate with students to have an interesting play "Journey to the West". Teachers and the other students dress up as the main characters in the play, Tang Seng, Su Wukong, Zhu Bajie and Sha Seng. Let students guess where they are going and then what they look like.

Teacher: What does Tang Seng look like?

Students: He is tall, thin and handsome.

Teacher: What does Sun Wukong look like?

Students: He has medium height and short yellow hair.

Teacher: What does Zhu Bajie look like?

Students: He is fat and short ...

Teacher: What does Sha Seng look like?

Students: He has curly hair and strong ...

3. Revision

As a famous saying goes,"You can learn something new as you are reviewing the old." It is quite convenient for students to strengthen what they have learned, connect the old knowledge systems with the new system, so reviewing as warming up usually carries on by asking questions, doing exercises, repeating and some other ways, which can make students enhance what they learned and learn some new knowledge to arouse students' interest.

4. Free talk

Free talk refers to the free communication between teachers and students, including family lives, studying experience, thinking ideas. This kind of talk should link to a main and relevant topic other than being less meaningful, which can reduce gap between teachers and students. Free talk is a relaxing approach. Teachers can ask students which class they had just now, praise the classroom they cleaned is very clean.

5. Story telling

The philosopher Locke once said: "The biggest skill of a teacher is to make students concentrate on class." Teachers can utilize the feature that students like to listen to story preparing for some stories. If the class starts with telling stories regarding to the textbook material, students will pay high attention to what teachers are talking. For example, when we are going to learn Unit 10 of Grade 10—"If you go to the party, you will have a great time", teachers can prepare a short story they have heard or experienced.

6. Background knowledge

According to the teaching material, teachers can introduce the background of author and main characters, so that students can easily understand it. Facing with some scientific text, the class should start with the known stories, which can bring students into true environment.

1.1.2 Questioning

Classroom questioning plays a vital role in English teaching. So there's a great need for deeper understanding of English classroom questioning behaviour in China.

1. Definition of "questioning"

Questioning is one of the most common technique used by teachers. Asking questions encourages students to think and focus on the content of the lesson. It encourages students to take part in the classroom communication activities. It also makes the class proceed smoothly so as to accelerate the second language acquisition. It can be used to allow the learners to keep participating in the discourse and even modify it so that the language used becomes more comprehensible and personally relevant.

It is defined in *The Longman Dictionary of English* that a question is: a command or interrogative expression used to elicit information or a response, or to test knowledge.

2. Types of questioning

There're many types of questioning, such as factual questions and reasoning questions, open questions and closed questions, display questions and referential questions and so on.

Display questions (or closed questions) refer to requests for information already known by the teacher. For example, "What's the time now? How many persons are mentioned in this passage? What's the story about?" Display questions has been regarded as poor instructional practice. They are usually asked for comprehension checks, confirmation checks, or clarification requests.

Referential questions (or open questions) refer to requests for information not already known by the teachers or students. For example, "What's your opinion? What do you think of him or her?" Referential questions can also be called as authentic questions that can elicit students' real communication. They may require interpretations and judgments on the part of the "answer".

Generally speaking, when the teacher asks display questions, the purpose of the teacher is not to gain the unknown information, but to ask the students to practise the language. When the teacher asks referential questions, the teacher wants the students to produce more target language and have more opportunities to take part in the classroom communication. Referential questions are important because they are taken as signals of students' substantive engagement. For example, "How can we protect the environment?" This referential question can elicit a variety of answers. It is known that when people communicate in natural environment, nearly all the questions are referential questions. And the purpose of these questions is to gain unknown information. Both display questions and referential questions will lead the students to better learning, and will activate their competence.

3. Skills of questioning

Teachers often ask more display questions instead of referential ones in class, by which teachers are confined to a form of questioning and answering. And in most cases, teachers usually give answers to the questions impatiently instead of asking students to answer, which turns out to be a forced output. In this case, teachers can perhaps keep the classroom teaching continual and smooth, but they can possibly deprive the students of their opportunities to catch the main points of the questions and to find out blocks in understanding. When teachers do ask referential questions, most of the students either keep silent or answer in Chinese, or reply with "sorry".

Take, for example, "Tea House" (*New Standard English*, *Book* 3, Unit 2)

T: Now let's discuss Lao She and his play *Tea House*. Do you know anything about him?

Ss: (Immediately) Yes, yes.

T: Do you think he is a great people?

Ss: Yes, I think so.

This type of questions is quite common in the classroom. On one hand, the size of the class is too big and it is impossible to involve too many students and the teachers have to finish the teaching tasks in limited class time. On the other hand, knowledge-display questions elicit more students rather than referential questions, because students need only give "Yes" or "No" or a single-word answer to knowledge-display questions. It seems that the teacher intends to ask the students an idea-expressing question at first, because he uses the word "discuss". But he doesn't ask the question in a proper way, so the students are confined to the answer "Yes", and eventually it can not elicit more answers from the students. If he modifies the same question a bit, things might be different:

T: Now let's discuss Lao She and his play *Tea House*. Who would like to say something about him or his play? Student 1, please.

S1: As far as I know, Lao She is a famous writer. He wrote short stories and plays.

S2: Lao She is famous for his play. He is one of the greatest artists.

4. Evaluation of good questioning

Good teaching involves good questioning, especially when large groups of students are being taught. Skillful questioning can encourage students' curiosity, stimulate their imagination and motivate them to search for new knowledge. It can challenge the students, make them think, and help them clarify concepts and problems related to the lesson. Through questioning, an experienced teacher can also help students reinforce the basic skills, experience success, and enhance self-confidence. Therefore, learning to question effectively is very important for teachers especially for language teachers.

1.2 Skills and Abilities

Given that you have already learned some strategies to lead in the class and to question your students, here are some cases to analyze to improve your problem-solving abilities and practice your creative thinking skills.

Cases

Case One

(1) 教学片断A：

T: Good morning, boys and girls!

Ss: Good morning, Mr. Wang!

T: Ah you know my name—Mr. Wang, but do you know my English name?

Ss: No.

T: Later I will show you, OK? Today I'll show you a very very funny story. Its name is *Singing Dad*. Before that I will show something about me(ppt:1—6 六个数字). Would you please choose a number? Who wants to have a try? You try.

S1: No.5.

T: No.5 fish. What does it mean?

S2: Maybe you like to eat fish.

T: Yes. I like eating fish but I don't like fishing, I just like eating.

教师以同样的方式让学生猜出了其他五个数字背后的信息。

(2) 教学片断B

T: Now I will show you a story—*Singing Dad*. Look at the picture, what is dad doing, singing? Right? Dad is singing. Look at the mother's and the daughter's face. Are they happy with the song? No. So guess. Is dad a good singer?

Ss: No.

T: No, all right. Let's see the story.

播放整个文本

T: Who thinks dad is a good singer? Hands up.

Ss:（举手）

T: So most of you think dad is not good.

【反思】

教师的导入时间过长(5分20秒左右)。由于在接下去的环节教师还安排了reading, chanting, singing 和 writing 四个大的部分，所以显得导入部分时间过长，后三个部分在处理的时候时间有些仓促。

教师在 choose number 的过程中呈现了六张分别写有六个信息（YY, music, fish, dad, singer, bus）的卡片，让学生选数字。学生选择数字后根据所给出的信息运用发散思维，猜这六个信息与教师之间的关系。能够用发散思维来激发学生的想象是很好的。但是综观整个课程，六个词中的三个词与新授内容没有太大的联系，不能使教学过程从导入部分过渡到新授部分。导入环节是为新授知识做心理和知识准备的，如果此环节的设计与新知识没有太大的关联，那么此环节既浪费时间又缺乏实际意义。

教学片断 B 中教师提出了问题"Is dad a good singer?"这一问题将导入环节和知识新授环节巧妙地联系在了一起，但是所给文本并不能提供足够的线索给学生来支撑他们对 good, not good 及 bad 的价值判断。这就造成了学生在回答这一问题时，一部分学生认为是"good"，一部分学生认为是"bad"的局面。

【对策及建议】

本课涉及 dad 这一人物喜欢 singing 的这一特点，建议导入的时候可以从学生的爱好入手让学生谈谈自己的兴趣爱好，再进一步拓展到学生父母的爱好，再过渡到 singing dad 这一话题。

Case Two

（1）教学片断 A

T：So I want to play the second game with you, OK?

Ss：OK.

T：Yes, this game is called yes or no. I will show you pictures and I will say a sentence. If the sentence is true you just act like this YES-YES-YES（双手举过头顶转手腕），OK?

Ss：OK.

T：Follow me YES-YES-YES.（双手举过头顶转手腕）

Ss：YES-YES-YES.（双手举过头顶转手腕）

T：If the sentence is not true, you just act like this NO-NO-NO.（双手交叉于胸前，手指弹动）

Ss：NO-NO-NO.（双手交叉于胸前，手指弹动）

（接下去教师随便拿起学生课桌上的物品对上述指令的反应进行了演练）

T：So you got it. Now let's play the game. Look at the first picture carefully, get your hands ready. OK?

T：Listen, she is a woman.

Ss：YES-YES-YES.（双手举过头顶转手腕）

T：And she is young.

Ss：NO-NO-NO.（双手交叉于胸前，手指弹动）

T：So she is not young. What is she like?

S1：She is old.

（接下去教师领读 old 一词）

T：She is fat.

Ss：NO-NO-NO.（双手交叉于胸前,手指弹动）

T：What is she like?

S2：She is thin.

（接下去教师领读 thin 一词）

T：Now we have next picture. Get your hands ready, look——

T：He is very thin.

Ss：NO-NO-NO.（双手交叉于胸前,手指弹动）

T：He is very fat.

Ss：NO-NO-NO.（双手交叉于胸前,手指弹动）

T：Sorry, he is neither fat nor thin. So what is he like? This girl please!

S3：He is strong.

（教师以同样的方式复习了 tall 和 short 两个词,在复习 short 一词的时候教师用同样的方式以班级里面的一个女生为例进行了呈现）

(3) 教学片断 B

教师在复习 kind 一词时,ppt 上面呈现了一张小沈阳的图片,使用"What's he/she like?"这一句型让学生猜。

在学生通过 ppt 下方的四个方框的字母提示（K→kind）时,教师施行了如下教学：

T：Xiao Shenyang is very kind, follow me——kind.

Ss：Kind.

T：Kind.

Ss：Kind.

T：He is kind.

Ss：He is kind.

T：He's kind. I am kind too, look!（教师让一位学生拍了几下她的背）Are you kind?

S4：Yes.

T：Yes, show us, show us.

S4：（这时学生迟疑了 6 秒钟,不知所措）

T：（教师拉过这位同学的手,握手）You are kind.

【反思】

等级反义关系的形容词具有等级性,每对反义词的成员表示的性质是程度上的差别。对一方的否定并不代表是对另一方的肯定。而本课导入环节中所涉及的词大多数为此类形容词,将其运用 ppt 呈现的时候,适合一组或者多个一起呈现来突出其等级性。

从教学片断 B 来看,教师在复习 kind 一词的时候,使用了 show us 这一句型。kind 是具有抽象意义的形容词,不能像具体名词那样用 show 表现出其语用特征,这也就解释了学生为什么迟疑了六秒钟不知所措。

【对策及建议】

基于等级反义关系形容词的特点,建议教师在用 ppt 呈现时,在一张 ppt 上呈现一组或者多个形容词,然后进行比较学习,将等级形容词的语义特点潜移默化地传递给学生。针对具有抽象意义的形容词的呈现方式,建议教师可以播放一些能反应 kind 一词语义特点的短片,让学生在语用环境中体会它的用法。

思考问题

1. 教师如何做到有效提问?
2. 有效的课堂导入形式有哪些?

亮考帮

亮闪闪:请总结学习过程中,哪些是自己记忆深刻、受益最大、最欣赏的内容呢?请写出具体内容。

考考你:请把自己弄懂的但觉得别人可能存在困惑的地方,用问题的形式表述出来,来挑战一下其他同学。

帮帮我:请把自己不懂、不会的地方或想要了解的内容,用问题的形式表述出来,并带到课堂上加以讨论。

参考文献

[1] Garton, S. Learner Initiative in the Language Classroom[J]. *ELT Journal*, 2002, 1(56).

[2] Ellis, R. *The Study of Second Language Acquisition*[M]. Shanghai: Shanghai Foreign Language Education Press, 2004.

[3] Geng, X. H. *Teacher's Questioning in High School Interactive Teaching*[M]. Shenyang: Liaoning Normal University Press, 2005.

[4] Dörnyei, Z. Conceptualizing Motivation in Foreign Language Learning[J]. *Language Learning*, 2012.

[5] Heider, F. *The Psychology of Interpersonal Relations*[M]. NewYork, NY: Whiley, 2008.

[6] Heider, F. Children's Attribution for Success and Failure[J]. *Developmental Social Psychology*, 2014.

[7] Jiang, X. Y. *Teacher's Questioning and Classroom Interaction*[M]. Shenyang: Liaoning Normal University Press, 2012.

[8] Wang, J. A Study on the Correlations of Middle School Students' English Learning Self-efficiency, Attribution Style and English Learning Achievement［D］. Hangzhou：Hangzhou Normal University，2015.

[9] Zhang，W. Y. *A Study of Teacher Questioning in a Junior Middle School*［M］. Changchun：Northeast Normal University Press，2009.

[10] 鲁子问.英语教学论[M].2版.上海：华东师范大学出版社,2010.

[11] 王丽春.小学英语课堂教学导入中的问题与对策[J].南京晓庄学院学报,2011.

Task 2 Classroom Discourse and Teaching Manners

Classroom discourse and teaching manners are also basic skills for student teachers and they are offered relevant explanations.

2.1 Knowledge Points

Outline

Here are concepts and discussion about classroom discourse.

2.1.1 What is classroom discourse?

Classroom discourse also called classroom teaching language, which is the essential quality of teachers' teaching, and it is an important tool to connect the whole class. Classroom teaching language is the foundation of teaching. Good classes often have a good teaching language support; good teachers tend to manage a good teaching language.

Classroom discourse refers to the language that teachers and students use to communicate with each other in the classroom. Talking, or conversation, is the medium through which most teaching takes place, so the study of classroom discourse is the study of the process of face-to-face classroom teaching.

2.1.2 What is discourse analysis?

Discourse analysis is the examination of language used by members of a speech community. It involves looking at both language form and language function and includes the study of both spoken interaction and written texts. It identifies linguistic features that characterize different genres as well as social and cultural factors that aid in our interpretation and understanding of different texts and types of talk. A discourse analysis of written texts might include a study of topic development and cohesion across the sentences, while an analysis of spoken language might focus on these aspects plus turn-taking practices, opening and closing sequences of social encounters, or narrative structure.

The study of discourse has developed in a variety of disciplines—sociolinguistics, anthropology, sociology, and social psychology. Thus discourse analysis takes different theoretical perspectives and analytic approaches: speech act theory, interactional sociolinguistics, ethnography of communication, pragmatics, conversation analysis, and variation analysis. Although each approach emphasizes different aspects of language use, they all view language as social interaction.

2.1.3 Discourse analysis and second language teaching

Even with the most communicative approaches, the second language classroom is limited in its ability to develop learners' communicative competence in the target language. This is due to the restricted number of contact hours with the language; minimal opportunities for interacting with native speakers; and limited exposure to the variety of functions, genres, speech events, and discourse types that occur outside the classroom. Given the limited time available for students to practice the target language, teachers should maximize opportunities for student participation. Classroom research is one way for teachers to monitor both the quantity and quality of students' output. By following a four-part process of Record-View-Transcribe-Analyze, second language teachers can use discourse analytic techniques to investigate the interaction patterns in their classrooms and to see how these patterns promote or hinder opportunities for learners to practice the target language. This process allows language teachers to study their own teaching behavior—specifically, the frequency, distribution, and types of questions they use and their effect on students' responses.

Step One: Videotape a complete lesson. Be sure to capture all of your questions and the students' responses. (Opportunities to speak the target language are often created by teachers' questions.)

Step Two: Watch the videotape. As you watch it, think about the types of questions you asked. Look for recurring patterns in your questioning style and the impact it has on the students' responses.

Step Three: Transcribe the lesson. A transcript will make it easier to identify the types of questions in the data and to focus on specific questions and student responses.

Step Four: Analyze the videotape and transcript.

In sum, teachers can use discourse analysis not only as a research method for investigating their own teaching practices but also as a tool for studying interactions among language learners. Learners can benefit from using discourse analysis to explore what language is and how it is used to achieve communicative goals in different contexts. Thus discourse analysis can help to create second language learning environment that more accurately reflects how language is used and encourages learners toward their goal of proficiency in another language.

2.2 Skills and Abilities

Given that the students have already learned the concepts of classroom discourse, here are some cases to analyze to improve your problem-solving abilities and practice your creative thinking skills.

Cases

Case One

成都一位教师执教的是《新目标英语》七年级下册 Unit 8 I'd like some noodles Section A 3a-4 的内容,课型为读说课,话题是订餐。

在教学了本课的目标语言"What kind of noodles would he/she/you like? I/He/She would like …"和"What size bowl of noodles would you like? I'd like a small/medium/large bowl of noodles."之后,教师在语言输出环节创设了"谈论名人到 Jenny's Noodle House 用餐"的情境,让学生在语境中运用目标语言。

【分析】

这位教师有意识地在语言输出环节创设语境,让学生运用目标语言。但这个语境并不真实,学生在实际生活中和名人在同一餐厅就餐的可能性很小,那么在不真实的语境中进行语言输出,学生习得的语言知识和技能是机械的、不自然的。因此,在语言输出环节中,教师应尽可能创设接近现实生活中语言使用的实际语境,使学生能够理解和掌握目标语言项目的真实意义和用法,即注重语境创设的真实性。

【修改建议】

可将"谈论名人到 Jenny's Noodle House 用餐"的情境改为"谈论同学或朋友到 Jenny's Noodle House 用餐"的情境。在这个真实的语境中,学生就会有话可说、有话想说,达到真正让学生运用目标语言的目的。

Case Two

抚顺一位教师执教的是《新目标英语》八年级上册 Unit 3 What are you doing for vacation? Section B 3a-4 的内容,课型为阅读课,话题是假期安排。

在阅读完"Ben Lambert's Vacation Plans!"的内容和学习完生词后,教师创设了同学之间相互调查"Your vacation plan"的情境,目的是让学生在相互调查的过程中运用目标语言。

【分析】

这个语境接近现实生活,注重了语境的真实性,但教师只是创设了这个语境,没有对学生的调查提出要求,也没有调查的范例,让学生不知道应该做什么,也不知道怎么进行调查。因此,在语言输出环节中,教师在创设语境的同时还应对学生提出具体的要求,必要时还要进行示范,即注重语境创设的可操作性。

【修改建议】

创设了真实的语境后,教师应出示将在调查中运用的目标语言,还要进行示范。示范完成后,教师还应询问学生是否知道自己要做的任务。

> **思考问题**
>
> 1. 教态对课堂教学的作用有哪些?
> 2. 当一位学生犯错的时候,教师将如何和学生取得有效沟通?

❖ 亮考帮

亮闪闪:请总结学习过程中,哪些是自己记忆深刻、受益最大、最欣赏的内容呢?请写出具体内容。

考考你:请把自己弄懂的但觉得别人可能存在困惑的地方,用问题的形式表述出来,来挑战一下其他同学。

帮帮我:请把自己不懂、不会的地方或想要了解的内容,用问题的形式表述出来,并带到课堂上加以讨论。

❖ 参考文献

[1] Celce-Murcia, M,. & Olshtain, E. *Discourse and Context in Language Teaching*[M]. New York:Cambridge University Press, 2000.

[2] Clancy, P., Thompson, S., Suzuki, R., & Tao, H. The Conversational Use of Reactive Tokens in English, Japanese, and Mandarin[J]. *Journal of Pragmatics*, 2016(26):355-387.

[3] Hatch, E. *Discourse and Language Education*[M]. New York:Cambridge University Press, 2012.

[4] Johnson, K. *Understanding Communication in Second Language Classrooms*[M]. New York:Cambridge University Press, 2015.

[5] McCarthy, M. *Discourse Analysis for Language Teachers*[M]. New York:Cambridge University Press, 2012.

[6] McCarthy, M., & Carter, R. *Language as Discourse:Perspectives for Language Teachers*[M]. New York:Longman, 1994.

[7] Riggenbach, H. *Discourse Analysis in the Language Classroom:Volume 1 The spoken Language*[M]. Ann Arbor, MI:University of Michigan Press, 2009.

[8] Schiffrin, D. *Approaches to Discourse*[M]. Oxford:Blackwell, 1994.

[9] Young, R., & He, A. *Talking and Testing:Discourse Approaches to the Assessment of Oral Proficiency*[M]. Philadelphia:John Benjamins, 2018.

Task 3 Multimedia, Board Writing and Stick Figures Teaching

Along with the development of technology, multimedia has been widely used in primary and secondary school English class. While board writing and stick figures are still important for students learning. In Task 3, these knowledge points and cases will be provided to practice.

3.1 Knowledge Points

Outline

In the following part, the knowledge points of multimedia, board designing, and stick figures will be introduced.

3.1.1 Multimedia

Multimedia teaching holds considerable significance for mid-school English teaching. With the development of computer information technology, multimedia teaching is gradually stepping into classrooms. Its striking teaching characteristics, rich teaching contents and enlivening teaching situations combine to accelerate the informationization of educational techniques and establish in a step-by-step manner a new teaching mode to replace the conventional one that mainly features teachers' indoctrination in a setting of one blackboard, one chalk and one mouth which is listened to by all.

1. The significance of multimedia teaching

(1) Help to stimulate students' interest in learning

Applying multimedia in teaching helps to stimulate students' interest in learning, complies with the happy-to-learn principle and embodies the modern people-oriented teaching concept. The multimedia teaching method prioritizes delicate and graceful ppt lesson plans which help with students' understanding and acceptance, and meets to the upmost possibility the demand that learning be realized through having fun. This is good for evoking students' learning initiative and makes them as proactive as possible in the learning process.

(2) Help to enrich students' knowledge and exploit their intelligence

Besides transforming textbook knowledge into ppt lesson plans, multimedia teaching also encompasses colorful pictures of background information and extensive contents about the themes of the texts so that the students can learn more about humanities, the society and sciences. Besides, the ppt lesson plans can motivate students to think and have discussions through pictures, textual contents and sounds, which will contribute to students' intelligence exploitation. Unknowingly, the students enrich their knowledge on the one hand and broaden their horizons as well as improve their abilities to think and express themselves on the other hand.

(3) Help students to master knowledge and skills

In multimedia teaching, students can get in touch with diverse knowledge, for example, the collection of information, the downloading of online resources and the making of ppt lesson plans. Teachers can appropriately assign tasks to students and let the students design their own ppt lesson plans so as to make it possible for both teachers and students to share resources and exchange ideas. Thus, the students can consolidate the knowledge they have learnt, improve their skills and develop their abilities.

2. The principles of multimedia teaching

(1) The principle of objectives

Multimedia classroom teaching is an orderly controlled process, which has a very strong purpose of teaching objectives. The design of its ppt lesson plans serves specific teaching contents and disseminates knowledge amid fun with a view to enabling students to skillfully master linguistic rules, improve their listening and speaking abilities and skillfully communicate in English. Thus, multimedia can be applied in each and every chain of instructions. The making of ppt lesson plans is especially important. The materials selected in a lesson plan must be relevant to its teaching contents, and all the teaching contents or tasks must be reasonably arranged in accordance with its teaching requirements and teaching contents. Each knowledge plate must be in proportion and time distribution must be reasonable. Teachers should avoid stubbornly pursuing, blindly downloading online resources and neglecting accomplishing teaching tasks for the sake of seeking entertainment.

(2) The principle of interactive teaching

Multimedia instruction emphasizes interaction between the teacher and the students. In the process of multimedia teaching, it is imperative to give full play to the teacher's guiding role and the students' proactivity. The sounds, words and pictures in ppt lesson plans should fully motivate students' minds, encourage them to think and have discussions, lead them to analyze and comprehend passages, and promote communications between students as well as between students and teachers so as to establish harmonious teacher-student and student-student relations. Traditional instruction tends to neglect students' own initiative and focuses on rigid textbook-based knowledge indoctrination, making teachers and students lack enthusiasm for teaching and learning, estranging teachers and students due to the absence of interaction and impeding the smooth running of teaching and learning activities.

(3) The principle of being lively and funny

What most distinguishes multimedia teaching from conventional teaching is the use of materials that combine pictures, texts and sounds. So, the ppt lesson plans used in multimedia teaching must make students feel ready and happy to accept and participate in. Hence, the lead-in part must be lively, funny, concise and easy. The part regarding text learning should vary in form, avoid the boring parsing of words and characters and make comprehension and digestion full of fun for students by way of lively examples and interesting pictures. Multimedia teaching resources encompass everything. Pictures and videos of all kinds are available and styles of ppt lesson plans are colorful. Teachers should constantly collect materials, design and recondition layouts, and enhance the level of ppt lesson plan making to process boring textbook knowledge in order to comprehensively improve students' integrated skills in listening, speaking, reading and writing in a lively and funny mode.

All in all, the application of modern educational techniques can fully activate students' learning initiative. By means of contextual supposition and coordinated learning, teachers aim to help students to think independently, and explore the outside world independently to make them the chief player in information processing and the chief architect of information significance. Hence, in the instruction of Grade 7, teachers should grasp students' psychological characteristics, and stimulate students' learning interest, and give full play to their learning spontaneousness, proactiveness and creativeness. Remember that the full demonstration of the functions of multimedia-assisted instruction and the successful application of multimedia teaching will be of great help to our teaching work and improve teaching efficiency as well as teaching effects.

3.1.2 Board designing

1. Definition of board designing

Board writing is the most universal, versatile and basic piece of classroom equipment—whether it is the more traditional chalk-dust blackboard, the whiteboard (written on with marker pens), or metallic boards (by using magnets). It may have the following functions, such as, providing and listing the key teaching points during the whole class; supporting teaching with diagrams, tables and drawing; outlining the whole teaching procedure; offering quick explanation of vocabulary items; setting up a discussion or dialogue and helping summarize the classroom teaching.

2. Purposes of board designing

Board can be used for different purposes and a lot can be done with it if the teachers know how to use it effectively.

(1) To stress key points

Teachers often write things up on the board briefly and clearly during the lesson, such as new words, phrases and useful expressions for students to remember and practice; questions for students to answer or exploit; topics for students to discuss. That is to say, they should not write too much on the board.

(2) To explain and show relationships between different items

The information teachers write should be structured and set out logically. Boards can be used for explanation and show relationships. By board writing, the teacher can highlight focus and difficult points by using boxes, arrows or colored chalk to demonstrate the relationships between things.

(3) To help students understand by board drawing

Boards can be used for drawing pictures, charts and tables to help students understand language focus as quickly as possible. Therefore, teachers should be versatile. (Some board drawings will be offered at the end of this task.)

(4) To offer students opportunities to practice on the board

Boards can be typically used to do some individual students activities. For example, students can come up to the board to have a dictation, to chain words, to complete or rewrite sentences, and so on. Meanwhile, the teacher can also write some common mistakes on the board and ask students to correct them. It is very useful to provide students enough opportunity to practice.

3. Requirements on how to use boards effectively

How to use boards more effectively and efficiently? The following requirements can be met.

(1) Purposeful

To make sure that the board writing should be closely related to the teaching content and can effectively display the teaching stages, important parts and difficult points in teaching. By the end of the lesson, the board can present a clear summary of the lesson.

(2) Readable

Teachers should start the lesson with the clean board. Their handwriting on the board should be clear, standardized and large enough to be read from the back of the class because students always regard it a good chance to learn from teachers.

(3) Well-arranged and organized

Materials written on the board should be well-organized so as to avoid scrawling in a random and distracting style.

Teachers should arrange the board reasonably by separating the board into different columns. Generally speaking, the board can be divided into three columns. For instance, they can draw a vertical line on one side of the board and reserve the left-hand column for key points, the middle of the board for explanations, and the right-hand column for examples. Teachers use these areas to help organize different contents. During the teaching, teachers should check the board periodically to see if it is full and decide what should be erased.

(4) Flexible and diversified

In order to draw students' attention, the teacher should make best use of board flexibly and diversely and design different types of board writing according to the different features of learning materials.

(5) Graceful manners while writing

Don't turn your back to the class while you are writing on the board, especially if this goes on for some time. Please stand sideways in front of the board, half facing the board and half facing the class. Make sure your body should not block the view of students. Thus, it can prevent students from whispering to each other or getting up to little tricks and maintain a learning atmosphere. Don't write too slowly, which will affect the rhythm of procedures of teaching.

4. Types of board designing

Board can be used for different purposes and according to different purposes, boards can be designed in different ways. In other words, board designing can be classified into different types.

(1) Horizontally arranged

1st blind man—placed his hand—side—like a wall
2nd blind man—grasped one of—tusks—like a spear
3rd blind man—took hold of—trunk—like a snake
4th blind man—closed his arms—legs—like a tree
5th blind man—caught hold of—ear—like a fan
6th blind man—got hold of—tail—like a rope

(2) Outline

Title/Topic： Main idea： Part Ⅰ Introduction 　　　　　　　Paragraph 1 Part Ⅱ Main body Paragraph 2 　　　　　　　Paragraph 3 Part Ⅲ Conclusion

(3) Key words

7:30 in the morning—get up as quickly as possible—wash face—brush teeth—have breakfast quickly—rush to the bus stop—catch the bus—get on the bus—empty—surprised—get off the bus at the school gate—rush to school—closed—remembered—holiday

(4) Table

I'm You are He is She is We are They are	preparing	breakfast lunch supper dinner

What do you like?	swim	dance	sing	play football
Peter	Y	Y	Y	N
Tom	Y	Y	Y	N
Mary	N	Y	Y	N
Alice	N	Y	Y	N
Mike	Y	Y	Y	Y

(5) Flow chart

Wang Ping

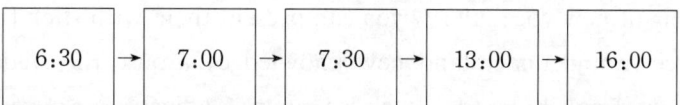

6:30 → 7:00 → 7:30 → 13:00 → 16:00

(6) Explanation with notes

He did <u>what he could (do)</u> to <u>calm her</u>. = he did all (<u>or everything</u>) <u>he could (do)</u> to <u>calm her</u>.

(7) Words network

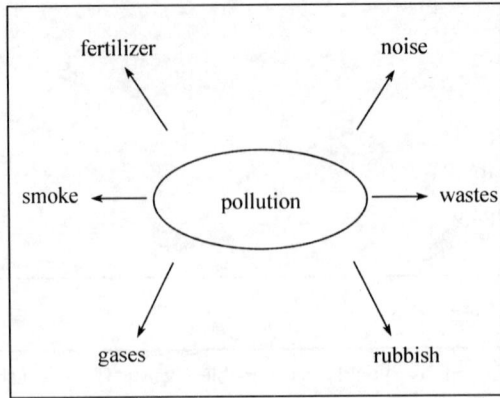

3.1.3 Stick figures

1. Definition of stick figures

Stick figures, a form of effective teaching which students love, is an English teaching and effective teaching method that can not be replaced.

While the development of modern educational technologies, multimedia technology in English teaching and English teaching methods are constantly enriched, and now the English classroom teaching (as compared with traditional classroom teaching) are becoming more and more animated. However, the modern teaching methods are sometimes affected by economic conditions, and other constraints, and the production of multimedia courseware takes some time and effort. For example, in the usual classroom teaching of English, teachers can use stick figures of this simple and effective means to improve the teaching effect. Looking at the Oxford Junior English, use the stick figure quite a lot of places.

2. Advantages of stick figures in English teaching

(1) Visual image

The stick figure composed from simple lines, making them very simple and convenient, easy to understand the content.

(2) Concise

The teaching of new vocabulary, you can present them with stick figures to enable students to perceive and understand new knowledge, arouse the students desire for knowledge. Many English words, such as nouns, adjectives, adverbs, verbs and numerals, etc. can be achieved through stick figures at a glance the effect of teaching.

(3) Moisten things silently

The stick figure teaching also enables teachers and students to play with the materials to form complementary relationship.

Therefore, we must continue to learn, and seriously study the materials, depending on the different teaching content to adopt an appropriate means of teaching.

3.2 Skills and Abilities

Now that students have already learned some strategies of using multimedia, board designing, and stick figures, here are some cases to analyze to improve problem-solving abilities and practice your creative thinking skills. Students may also design their own board by using stick figure skills. At the same time, think about these two questions: Why is multimedia necessary for the class? Can blackboard writing be totally replaced by multimedia?

Cases

Case One

在教授句型"What are they? They're birds. How many birds are there? There are …"时,便可运用这样一幅简笔画:先画出小鸟,再画出湖、小鱼、树,最后树上结出苹果等。让学生在学习时充满期待:我们还将看到什么?在介绍完所有内容后,还可以引导学生自由想象,在这样一个美丽的大自然里还有些什么?学生通过自由发挥,积极讨论,不仅记住了单词和句型,还能熟练地将它们运用到相关情境之中。在教学"What is it? It's a …"句型时,教师可边画边说,并着重复述画中的关键句型:"What is it? Look! It's a rabbit!"然后引导学生看图进行反复跟读、师生对话、生生对话、集体复述、分角色实际操练和对话表演等。不仅使学生理解和掌握课文内容,还提高了学生视听说的能力。

思考问题

1. 多媒体在教学中的作用有哪些?
2. 简笔画教学有哪些特点?

「Case Two」

板书设计

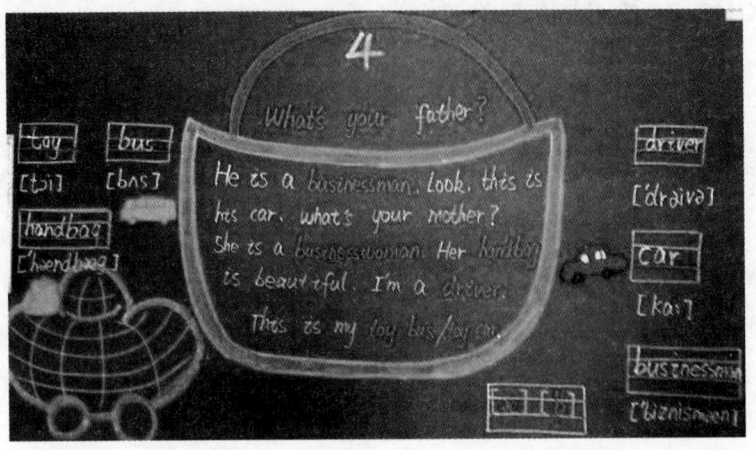

思考问题

1. 如何设计板书?
2. 如何规范板书书写?

✦ 亮考帮

亮闪闪：请总结学习过程中,哪些是自己记忆深刻、受益最大、最欣赏的内容呢？请写出具体内容。

考考你：请把自己弄懂的但觉得别人可能存在困惑的地方,用问题的形式表述出来,来挑战一下其他同学。

帮帮我：请把自己不懂、不会的地方或想要了解的内容,用问题的形式表述出来,并带到课堂上加以讨论。

✦ 参考文献

[1] Chickering, A. W. & Gamson, Z. F. Implementing the Seven Principles: Technology as Lever. The American Association for Higher Education Bulletin, 1987.

[2] Rerraro, J. M. Reflective Practice and Professional Development[J]. ERIC Digest, 2000(15).

Task 4   Assessment and Assignment

Assessment and assignment are the two "must-do" things in the process of teaching and learning. Task 4 offers the knowledge and skills of these two points. Besides, students have opportunities to practice skills after analyzing the cases.

4.1 Knowledge Points

Outline

The following knowledge points discuss the research results of the assessment. After that, students may get information about the assignment in the reading materials.

4.1.1 A brief introduction to English teaching assessment

Teaching assessment is the process of collecting, comprehending and analyzing information and evaluating teaching process and results according to requirements of teaching objectives and principles. According to the purpose of assessment, there are three types in teaching assessment: diagnostic assessment, formative assessment and summative assessment. Teaching assessment is an important element of the teaching activity. How to use it properly and correctly plays an important part in improving our education quality.

4.1.2 Measures to reform English teaching assessment

The traditional teaching assessment is lack of advanced educational concepts to support and evaluate which are often confused with concept of examination and test, so assessment focuses only on students' learning results. Assessment can be reflected in the following aspects:

(1) Summative assessment

Summative assessment is mainly based on testing. It is done mostly at the end of a learning period or the end of a school year.

(2) Formative assessment

Formative assessment is based on information collected in the classroom during the teaching processes for the purposes of improving teaching and learning, therefore, it is sometimes termed as classroom assessment as well.

It is important to pay attention to students' emotional evaluation from neglecting emotional assessment. In the past, teaching assessment only pays attention to the development of students' cognition; some people think that study of theory is irrelevant with emotion. In fact, it is a misunderstanding.

As we all know, interest is the best teacher. More importantly, any subject is not only composed of a knowledge system of concepts and principles, but also by a system of nature and social attitudes. As for English, it cannot be taught without the knowledge of vocabulary and grammar behind which hides natural and social views, attitudes and values about world.

4.1.3 Assessment purposes

Assessment in ELT means to discover what the learners know and can do at a certain stage of the learning process.

A close study on the assessment purposes will make it clear that all the people involved in education have some reasons to consider assessment necessary.

(1) For administrators

They need to know whether the programmes they have planned are working well. The only way to do this is to discover how well the students are doing with their courses.

(2) For teachers

Teachers put the administrators' plans into practice. They need to know what has been done, what needs to be done next, what the students know or can do and what they do not know or cannot do yet.

(3) For parents

They are anxious to know how their children are doing in school. Unable to watch their kids in the class, parents value the feedback about their children's performance from the teachers and the school.

(4) For students

They need to know what they've accomplished, be aware of what they need to work on next, and build up their confidence and satisfaction from what they have achieved.

It should be noted that both positive and negative assessment should be made available to the learner, as honestly as possible.

4.1.4 Ways to gather students learning information

(1) Teacher's observations

Teacher's observations of the learners' overall performance or achievement can be quite accurate and fair.

(2) Continuous assessment

(3) Self-assessment and peer assessment

(4) Project work

Project work requires students to complete a set of tasks designed to explore a certain idea or concept.

(5) Portfolios

A portfolio is a purposeful collection of materials assembled over a period of time by a learner to provide evidence of skills, abilities and attitudes.

4.2 Skills and Abilities

Appropriate assessments mean to be equal and fair to the students. Now that you have already learned the knowledge of assessment and assignment, here is a case to analyze to improve your problem-solving abilities and practice your creative thinking skills.

Case

语言神情手势评价

课堂中，善用多样简洁的评价语。如：OK, Good, Very good, Super, Great, Wonderful, Excellent。学生会根据老师的评语，对自己有个评价。清晰地记得，有次我对一位学生说了一句："Wonderful!"这位学生马上很自豪地对同桌说："Wonderful 比 Good 要好!"有时有必要对学生做出详细的评价。如：在一位学生很有感情且流利地读完一个对话后，微笑地对他说句："You read it very well."能起到很好的作用。在新授完一个单词后让一位学生读单词，当他读得很标准时，用为他自豪的语气，对他说句："Your pronunciation is pretty good."当被老师做出详细评价后，这几位学生会成为部分学生的榜样。课堂中，运用神情手势对学生进行肯定评价。当学生很出色地完成一个任务后（回答问题、表演对话），与他击个掌或带动其他学生为他鼓掌。当内向的学生小声地发言完后，和他击个掌，能带给他信心，促使他下次能响亮地发言。

思考问题

1. 语言对教学的作用有哪些？
2. 体态语的重要性有哪些？

亮考帮

亮闪闪：请总结学习过程中，哪些是自己记忆深刻、受益最大、最欣赏的内容呢？请写出具体内容。

考考你：请把自己弄懂的但觉得别人可能存在困惑的地方，用问题的形式表述出来，来挑战一下其他同学。

帮帮我：请把自己不懂、不会的地方或想要了解的内容，用问题的形式表述出来，并带到课堂上加以讨论。

参考文献

[1] Harmer, J. *How to Teach English* [M]. Beijing: Foreign Language Teaching and Research Press, 2001.

[2] 王蔷.英语教学法教程[M].北京:高等教育出版社,2006.

[3] 教育部.英语课程标准解读[M].北京:北京师范大学出版社,2001.